Stefan Stein

THE
WEST INDIAN ISLANDS

(overleaf) Balandra Bay, Trinidad

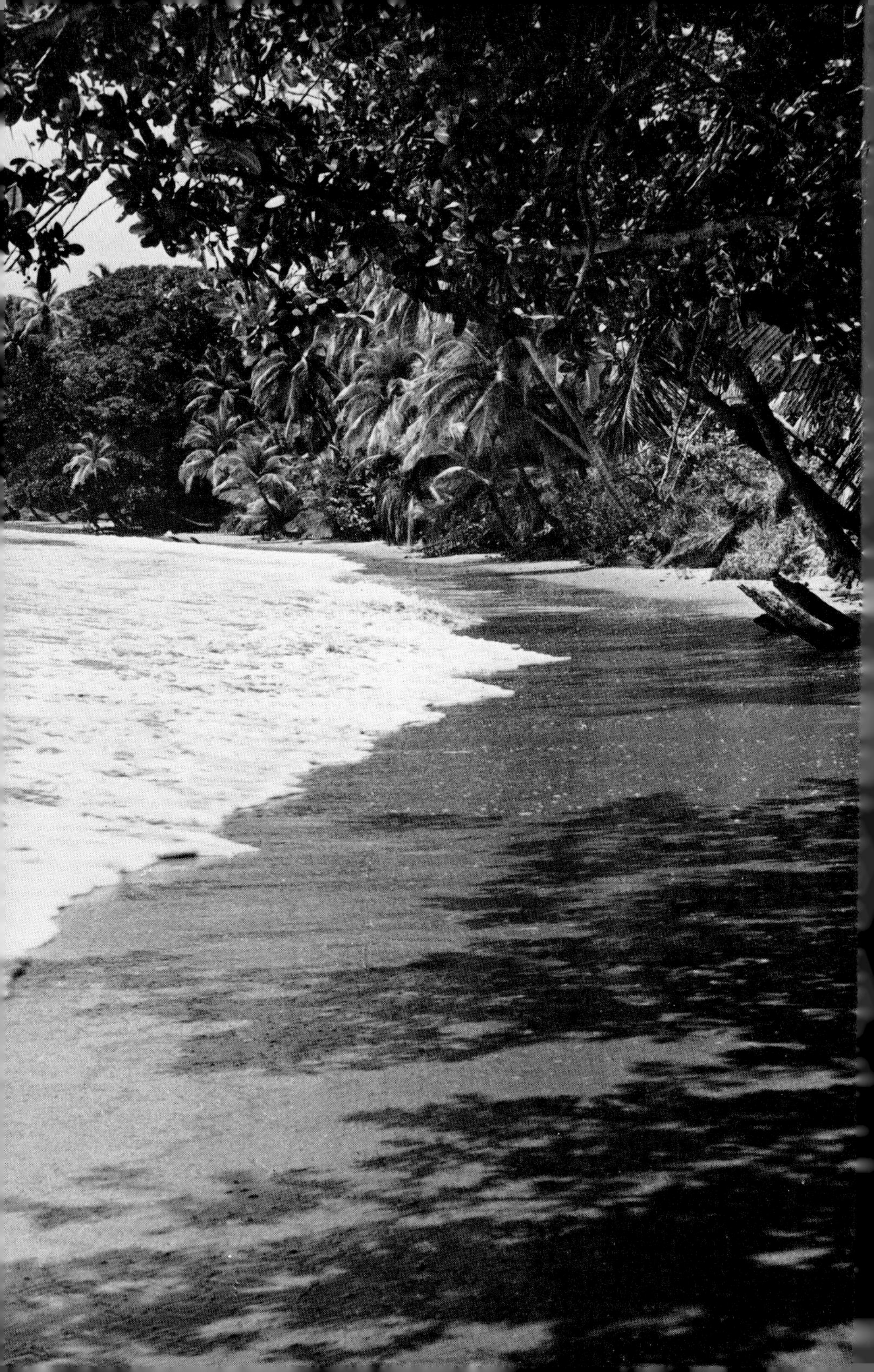

THE
WEST INDIAN
ISLANDS

George Hunte

A Studio Book . The Viking Press . New York

Copyright © 1972 by George Hunte

All rights reserved
Published in 1972 by The Viking Press, Inc.
625 Madison Avenue, New York, N.Y. 10022

SBN 670-75733-0

Library of Congress catalog card number: 70-183931

Text printed in Great Britain by Northumberland Press Ltd., Gateshead.

Plates printed and books bound by Richard Clay (The Chaucer Press) Ltd., Bungay, Suffolk, England.

For
Emma, Rupert, Bernard
and Silvia

Contents

	List of Illustrations	10
	Introduction	11
	I BACKGROUND	
One	Settlement and Mercantilism	15
Two	The People and their Rulers	28
Three	The Islands—Paradises?	44
Four	Arts, Crafts and Folklore	53
Five	Unity and Diversity	67
	II FOREGROUND	
Six	The French Islands	77
Seven	The Dutch Islands	98
Eight	The British Leewards	108
Nine	The British Windwards	135
Ten	The Independent Islands	170
Eleven	The Virgins	202
Twelve	Puerto Rico	216
Thirteen	The Future	229
	Tips for Tourists	234
	Bibliography	237
	Acknowledgments	240
	Index	241

The Maps

1. The West Indies — 8-9
2. The French Islands — 79
3. The Dutch Islands — 101
4. Leeward Islands — 112
5. Windward Islands — 138
6. Trinidad and Tobago — 172
7. Barbados — 180
8. Virgin Islands — 205
9. Puerto Rico — 221

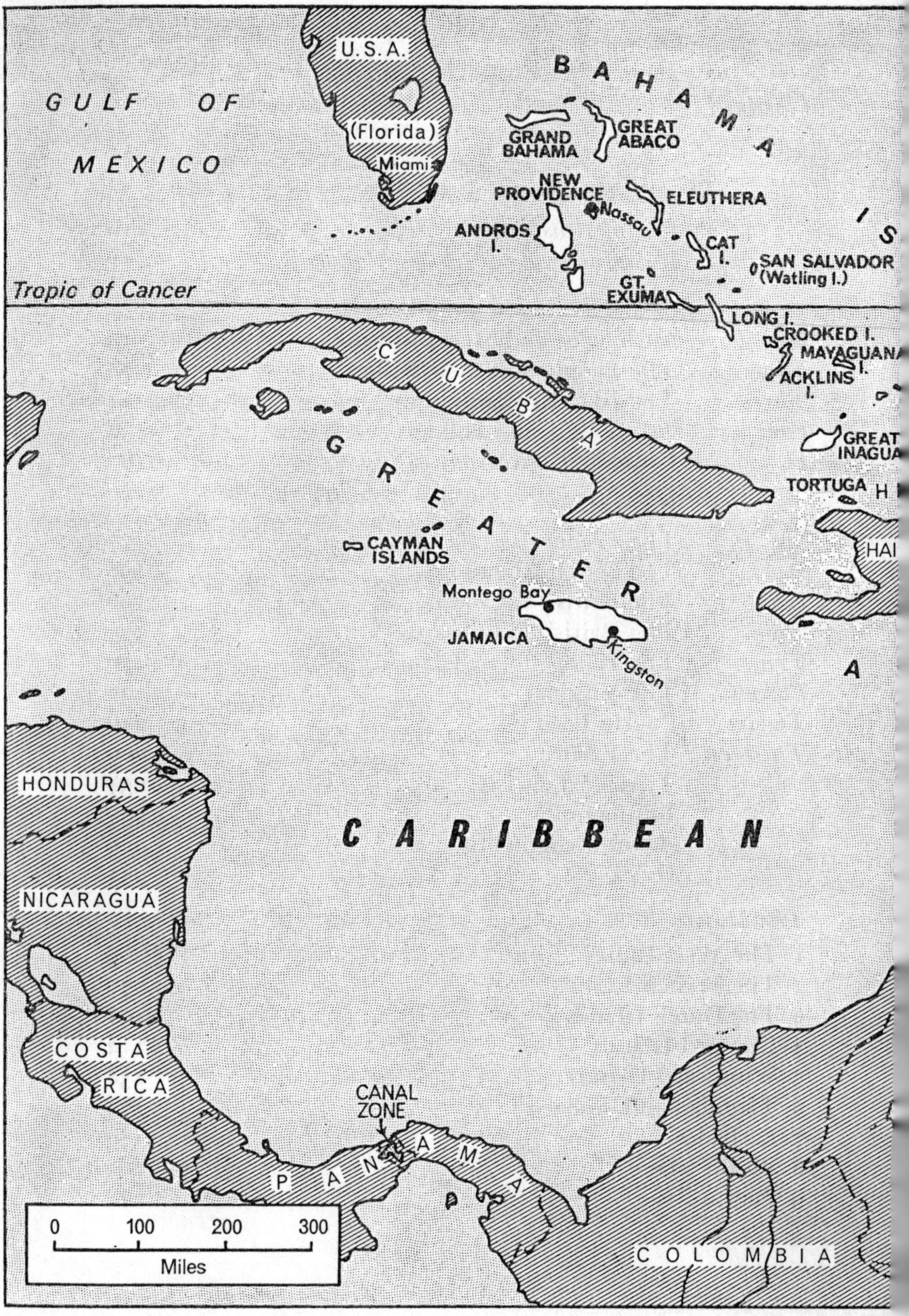

U.S.A.
(Florida)
Miami
GULF OF MEXICO
BAHAMA IS
GRAND BAHAMA
GREAT ABACO
NEW PROVIDENCE
Nassau
ELEUTHERA
ANDROS I.
CAT I.
SAN SALVADOR (Watling I.)
GT. EXUMA
Tropic of Cancer
LONG I.
CROOKED I.
MAYAGUANA I.
ACKLINS I.
CUBA
GREAT INAGUA
TORTUGA
GREATER
CAYMAN ISLANDS
Montego Bay
JAMAICA
Kingston
HONDURAS
CARIBBEAN
NICARAGUA
COSTA RICA
CANAL ZONE
PANAMA
0 100 200 300
Miles
COLOMBIA

DISTANCES BY AIR
NORTH AMERICA
NEW YORK
1096 miles
911 miles
3430 miles
LONDON
EUROPE
BERMUDA
NASSAU
ATLANTIC OCEAN
AFRICA
JAMAICA
ANTIGUA
BARBADOS
TRINIDAD
GEORGETOWN
SOUTH AMERICA
N
CAICOS ISLANDS
TURKS ISLANDS
DOMINICAN REPUBLIC
PUERTO RICO
San Juan
VIRGIN IS.
TORTOLA
ST. THOMAS
ST. CROIX
ANGUILLA
ST. BARTHOLOMEW
ST. MARTIN
BARBUDA
SABA
ST. EUSTACIUS
ST. KITTS
NEVIS
ANTIGUA
MONTSERRAT
GUADELOUPE
MARIE GALANTE
DOMINICA
MARTINIQUE
ST. LUCIA
BARBADOS
ST. VINCENT
GRENADINES
GRENADA
TOBAGO
TRINIDAD
Port of Spain
LEEWARD ISLANDS
WINDWARD ISLANDS
Lesser Antilles
SEA
Lesser Antilles
VENEZUELA
Georgetown
GUYANA

List of Illustrations

1	Balandra Bay, Trinidad	*frontispiece*
2	A typical Dutch building in Willemstadt, Curaçao	17
3	Sands at Road Bay, Anguilla	18
4	Welchman Hall Gully, St Thomas, Barbados	37
5	El Moro Fortress, San Juan harbour, Puerto Rico	38
6	Cathedral and Plaza, Puerto Rico	55
7	Looking across Long Bay, Tortola, British Virgin Islands	56
8	Bacolet Bay, Tobago	73
9	Falling water, Dominica	74
10	The cathedral in Fort-de-France, Martinique	91
11	Beach at Deshaies near the Club Méditerranée, Guadeloupe	92
12	Traditional West Indian balcony, Basse-Terre, St Kitts	109
13 and 14	Two views of Nelson's Dockyard, English Harbour, Antigua	110
15	Coconut grove, St Kitts	127
16	The Old Bath House on Nevis	128
17	Soufrière 'volcano', St Lucia	145
18	The Small Piton rising behind the fishing nets, Soufrière, St Lucia	146
19	The Roman Catholic church, Kingstown, St Vincent	163
20	Open-air market, St George's, Grenada	164
21	The Old Guard Room on Savannah, Barbados	181
22	Bridgetown, capital of Barbados	182
23	The harbour at Charlotte Amalie, St Thomas	199
24	Trunk Bay, St John	200

Introduction

Many geologists and geophysicists believe that some 500 million years ago North America, Europe and South America and Africa were joined together. Studies in the North Atlantic indicate that today's ocean formed there some 200 million years later. No one knows exactly when the islands of the Antilles, which are situated in the North Atlantic, were first considered to be more than mythical, but an imaginary island of Antilia appeared on old sea charts as early as 1424 and from Antilia Peter Martyr d'Anghiera got the name Antilles which he applied to them in 1493, the year after Columbus' memorable landfall at San Salvador in the Bahamas. The name still applies to the French islands which are departments of France and to the whole group of the Netherlands possessions which have become integral parts of the Kingdom of the Netherlands.

The British Antilles, insofar as they still exist, are more commonly called the West Indies, a title which has since their first discovery been applied to all the islands, for Columbus believed that he had reached islands east of India by sailing west.

Years before Alfred set up his dynasty in England, Amerindians who made decorated pottery and cultivated simple food crops were living on the island of Barbados. Archaeologists who make this claim say that these Indians with highly artistic pottery spread from Surinam and eastern Venezuela into Trinidad and up the lesser Antillean arc of islands as far north as Puerto Rico. They say that charcoal from sites in Venezuela, St Lucia, Guadeloupe, Antigua, and Puerto Rico, when submitted to radiocarbon analyses suggest that the first Indian occupation began around the time of Christ and ended about A.D. 750.

Other Indians, who fished, grew manioc and made pottery with quite different ceramic features, are thought to have been in possession of Barbados before William conquered England.

By the time Columbus saw the people whom he mistook for subjects of the Great Khan, the Arawak Indians had spread to the Greater Antilles and the Virgin Islands. The Caribs who in 1492 were conducting raids in the Virgin Islands and eastern Puerto Rico are thought to have set up their headquarters in Barbados after driving out the Arawaks and from that island launched marauding expeditions northwards until their own expansion was stopped by the new and stronger adventurers from Europe. Because no pottery like that left by Caribs in Barbados, Tobago and other islands of the Antilles has so far been discovered in Trinidad, it is reasonable to suppose that the Caribs who had taken possession of the eastern islands by 1492 made their first landing in Barbados from a port near the mouth of the Orinoco river on the South American mainland.

The first Europeans were after bigger gains than the small or lesser Antilles could offer. Some Caribs therefore survived on several of the isles until serious European settlement was started by English, French and Dutch colonisers during the first half of the seventeenth century. Others were taken to work Spanish mines on the mainland.

The French Dominican priest Father Labat has left a vivid picture of Carib society in his *Voyage aux isles de l'Amérique 1693-1705*. He tells us that Caribs were as at home in the sea as on land. The men hunted and fished, and spoke their own 'men's' language. The women were model wives who seldom needed to be told what to do. Their role in life was to keep their men happy. They anointed and painted men's bodies, knitted hammocks for them to sleep in, cooked their food and reared their children. Carib men loved liberty, only did what their spirit moved them to do, and later learnt to despise European men for showing respect and obedience to their superiors.

They were expert marksmen with bows, excelled in guerilla warfare and used camouflage expertly to deceive their enemies. They made fire by rubbing sticks together. Syphilis, for which they had their own methods of treatment, was a major disease amongst them. They had no religion but prayed to the principle of evil, Manitou, in the hope of warding off misfortunes. They saw no point in praying to a principle of good since it seemed a loss of time to beg anything of the source of good fortune and bounty. Father Labat emphatically denies that Caribs, whose name has become synonymous for 'Man-eaters' went to war expressly to eat their enemies, although he confirms their addiction to barbecuing the limbs of opponents they had killed in war.

They would, he said, then take back home the barbecued joints and fat of persons killed in war as trophies and as proof of their prowess and victory. The picture he leaves of the inhabitants of the Carib isles during the early years of European settlement is of a society of men who spoke little, who acted as impulse moved them, killing suddenly for personal motives, who knew no discipline and who were wholly materialistic in their attitudes to life. Their lack of 'culture' was particularly evident in hours of toneless music issuing from flutes, or monotonous whistling. A male society of warriors – 'carib' means 'brave warrior' as well as 'cannibal' – who fought with bows and arrows, stone hatchets and spears, had taken the islands of the Antilles nearest to Africa and Europe away from the vegetarian Arawaks. They could harass and murder, even for a time coexist and cohabit with incoming Europeans and their African slaves, but their period of unchallenged possession was over from the moment that English, Dutch and French challenged Spaniards in the exercise of seeking new wealth from settlement in the islands which Columbus had discovered.

It should surprise no one that Caribs should then have earned the reputation, which Europeans were to give them, of killing, barbecuing and even eating the invaders who had come to deprive them of their sweet liberties and their natural enjoyment of islands so richly endowed with all the good things they sought from sea and land. Never were people less prepared for progress; more certain to disappear from history's pages.

I BACKGROUND

Chapter 1

Settlement and Mercantilism

In the sixteenth century French, Dutch and English privateers kept up constant attacks on Spanish treasure ships. As early as 1538 the Spanish government had to decree that all Spanish merchantmen had to travel in convoy for protection. Spanish sea power was an effective barrier to permanent settlement by other European powers in the newly discovered islands and mainland, but their power did not last for ever and before 1600 dawned Dutch, English and French sailors had joined in a struggle for overseas possessions. The islands of the East Caribbean had often been visited during the sixteenth century by sailors from raiding or contraband ships. Dominica especially was a natural landfall for vessels sailing from the Canary islands. John Hawkins called there and at other island harbours on his way to Hispaniola in 1562. Twenty-three years later Drake called at Liamuiga, the fertile island of the Caribs to which Columbus gave the name of his own St Christopher. Although it was most certainly in the possession of Caribs when Drake visited he found 'no people at all' there.

Roger North, brother of Lord North and a member of Raleigh's disastrous expedition which had failed to discover the mythical El Dorado, tried too soon in 1619 to establish a British tobacco plantation in South America but had to evacuate his settlement in 1620 under Spanish pressure.

The renewed outbreak of hostilities between Holland and Spain in 1621 signalled clear opportunities for the European rivals of Spain. The formation of the Dutch West India company of that year was intended to break Spanish monopoly of Caribbean trade as the Dutch East India company had earlier been a pistol pointed against Portuguese trade in the Far East. For nearly 20 years after 1621, Dutch, English and French were able to settle in the Carib islands which the Spaniards were too weak to defend because they no longer enjoyed a supremacy of sea power.

In 1628 the Dutch Admiral Piet Hein surprised and captured the Spanish silver fleet in Matanzas Bay, Cuba. The booty he took in gold and silver has since been valued at five million American dollars. Six years later the Dutch took possession of Curacao, about 38 miles off the coast of Venezuela, a conquest which formed a threat to the Spanish Main and was a symbol of Spain's decline.

St Eustatius was settled the same year. The English who were experiencing intense Dutch hostility to their own East India company were reluctant to join with the Dutch in the West Indies, but parliamentary proposals for a British West Indian Association as the best means of reducing Spanish power and adding to English wealth came to nothing. Britain's first settlement in the Carib isles was promoted instead by London merchants drawn from the same class which had been actively engaged in the foundation of Virginia and Bermuda.

The merchants who sponsored the settlement of St Kitts and other Caribbean islands were protected by lords proprietors, who were tenants in chief of the King and held their provinces from him as private feudal estates. All titles of land were derived from the proprietors. Troubles arose early when grants of the same islands were made to different lords proprietors. There was a struggle for the ownership of Barbados between Lord Montgomery, later Earl of Pembroke, and the Earl of Carlisle. In 1629 Barbados, which had been settled two years before, finally passed under Carlisle's rule and he became a virtual feudal chieftain of all the Caribbean islands lying between 10 and 20 degrees north latitude.

2 *A typical Dutch building in Willemstadt, Curaçao*

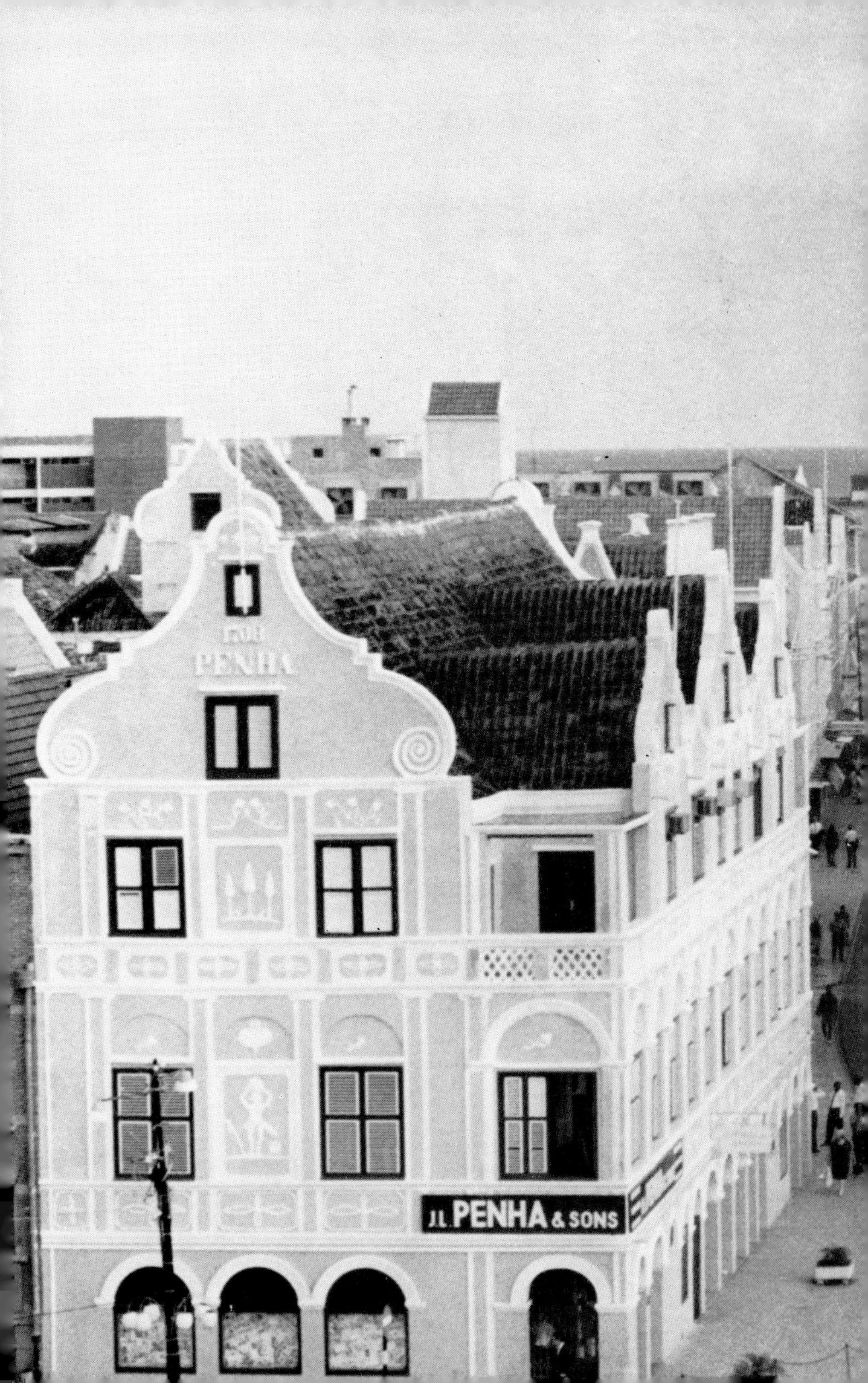
PENHA
J.L. PENHA & SONS

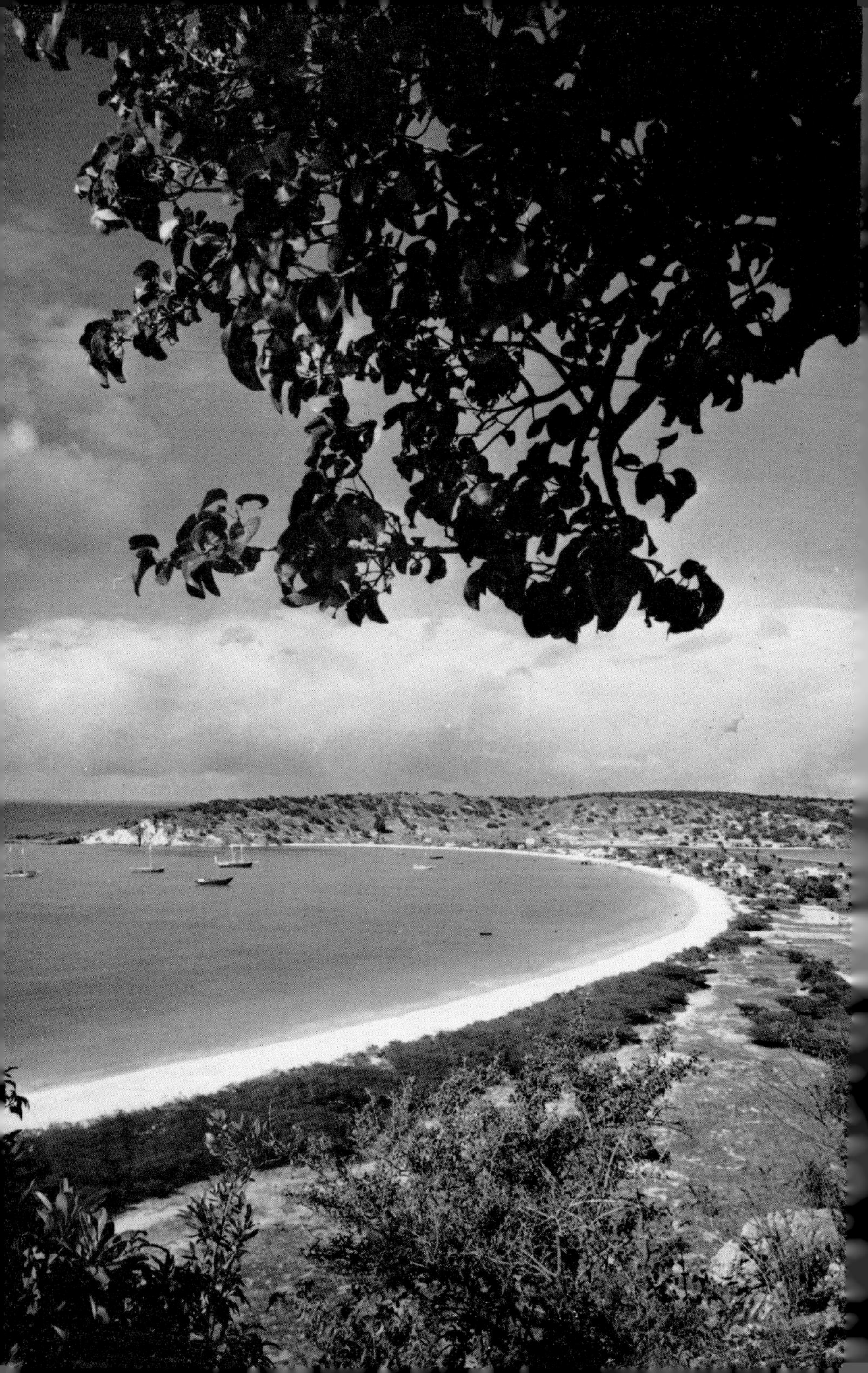

SETTLEMENT AND MERCANTILISM

St Christopher, which had been settled by Thomas Warner as early as 1624, was shared with the French under d'Esnambuc who arrived in 1627. About a hundred Caribs who had survived there were driven out that year; the English took possession of the central part of the island which included the Wingfield river on the leeward side. In 1629 the Spaniards drove both French and English away, leaving St Christopher devastated. After his return from England in 1630 Warner proceeded to build up the property of St Christopher which became a spawning ground for other British and French settlements.

Antigua and Montserrat were planted before 1630 and by 1639 French control had been established over Martinique and Guadeloupe and its dependencies. During the first 40 years of settlement the Dutch controlled the commerce of the English and French Caribbean islands.

English statesmen were too busy trying to sort out problems of foreign policy to interfere with the plantations overseas.

During these years the constitutional struggle between 'king and Parliament' at home meant that only overseas could Englishmen debate their affairs in constitutional assemblies. As early as 1631 English traders were breaking English regulations by shipping produce directly to Holland, while Dutch agents had erected a store on St Christopher at Sandy Point in the French section. St Eustatius, a Dutch settlement, had already become a trading centre for all the East Caribbean islands. The dismal condition of England encouraged an exodus from the Mother Country. By the beginning of the Civil War in 1642 no less than 80,000 English people had crossed the Atlantic. Conditions in England had been made difficult by loss of markets caused by the Thirty Years War (1618-48) and people poured overseas in what has been called the 'great emigration'. So great was the influx into St Christopher and Barbados by 1640 that almost every acre of cultivable land was occupied. Barbados had over one thousand proprietors and a total population of 30,000, while in St Christopher and Nevis there were about 20,000. In so brief

3 Sands at Road Bay, Anguilla

a period were these small islands 'over populated', not surprisingly since the area of St Kitts and Barbados together was only just over 300 square miles. Once the King of England had been beheaded (1649) there was no authority but Parliament to govern the colonies. The Civil War had encouraged Englishmen overseas to think of themselves as equals of home-staying Englishmen. The colonial rebellion of 1649 reflected the constitutional growth of the colonial legislatures of Barbados, Antigua, Bermuda, Virginia and Maryland.

They proclaimed Charles II as King, not only out of loyalty to the Stuarts but because they realised that in London the merchants behind Parliament wanted a monopoly of colonial trade and the exclusion of the Dutch traders and entrepreneurs who had built up Caribbean prosperity in the difficult years when England could give no help. They were perfectly right, as the boycott trade act of 1650 made clear. From that year onwards colonies were considered by the Home authorities as integral parts of the English economic organisation: English and colonial shipping was to be developed at the expense of the Dutch.

English prosperity was the purpose of the overseas plantations. The first Dutch war, the Western Design, the capture of Jamaica in 1655 were all preludes of a new imperialism which was to survive after the Restoration and to be harshly confirmed by the Navigation Act of 1660. By this Act and the Staple Act of 1663 English colonies were forbidden to trade with foreign countries. At the same time it should be noted that by the Book of Rates (1660) colonial produce received a practical monopoly of the English home market. The effect of the new policies was to strengthen the English mercantile marine, which doubled within 30 years. After the Restoration the proprietary patents were abolished and the islands became Crown colonies. In return for genuine title deeds colonists were saddled with a $4\frac{1}{2}\%$ duty on exports which continued to be levied until the nineteenth century.

Dutch Jews from Brazil had introduced sugar growing in the Caribbean islands during the period of the Civil War.

The highly capitalised sugar industry caused an exodus of small farmers who had previously grown tobacco, indigo, cotton and ginger. Workers were gradually replaced by black slaves. In Barbados sugar yielded three times as much per acre as tobacco had previously earned. Barbados by 1650 was already known as 'the brightest jewel in His Majesty's crown'. Its exports to England were much greater in value than those of Virginia and very much greater than those of New England. Public opinion in England began to favour tropical colonies more than temperate ones.

The West Indian lobby was formed early in England as rich sugar planters took up residence there, leaving attorneys to conduct their affairs in the islands. They made their influence felt at court and were able to rule the islands through the oligarchic assemblies which had developed during the Interregnum.

The sugar industry, which mostly benefited rich planters, merchants of London, and the slave trading African companies was built up against a background of European wars and privateering.

Barbados was attacked by De Ruyter in April 1665. He was beaten off there but he captured the English half of St Kitts and raided Antigua and Montserrat. Barbados was on the verge of bankruptcy, Surinam was lost to the Dutch and refugees from that colony resettled Antigua in 1667. Financial losses, the African slaving monopoly, the quartering of British troops on the island, the appointment of English officials to key positions and the perennial resentment against the Navigation Act and the $4\frac{1}{2}\%$ taxes led the Barbadians to seek home rule in 1668.

Charles II's reply on 22 November 1671 was symptomatic of a regime dedicated to tightening control over its empire. 'Distance of place', wrote the King, 'shall shelter none from our justice and power'. Mercantile statesmanship had made the Caribbean the centre of international rivalry and English sea power was now strong enough to keep under subjection the island plantations which could not resist blockades by sea. There was reason for the Barbadian bid for independence. The island had been heavily settled by Royalists; surrender to the Commonwealth forces in 1652 had been made on the understanding that a large measure of internal self-government would be granted: Barbados had supplied 3,500 men for Cromwell's Western Design and had sent settlers to Carolina, Surinam and Jamaica; moreover in 1663 the landowners had gained freedom from the lord proprietors.

The system of commercial rigidity which caused so much resentment in English continental America was designed to benefit the Caribbean trading depots. By 1668 the English thought so highly of the Caribbean islands that one of them wrote: 'without them this nation must long since have totally sunck'.

It was during the reign of Charles II that Jamaica outstripped Barbados in terms of trade because of its more favourable position in relation to the major Spanish settlements. Jamaica had been conquered in 1655 and remained under military rule till 1660. It did not have a legislative assembly until 1664.

English mercantilism was matched by Colbert's reorganisation of the French navy and his sponsorship of the monopolistic Company of the American Isles. Martinique and Guadeloupe outstripped Canada in trade with France and in the eighteenth century became more prosperous than Barbados. The size of the islands, with more virgin soil, was partly responsible; another reason was the decree of the French to permit the refining of sugar on their overseas plantations. Before 1688, when the long battle between France and England for world supremacy started, the English, Dutch and French traders had to suffer the assaults of buccaneers largely drawn from their nationals who operated mainly from the Virgin island of Tortola. Both French and English officials used buccaneers to attack the Spaniards, but before the eighteenth century opened the heyday of the filibusters had ended. Piracy however continued to be a threat to trade and the plantations relied on English naval protection not only from Caribbean filibusters but also from Algerian pirates. Many an Englishman ended his life at sea pulling oars as a galley slave on Algerian ships, while a playmate of the future Empress Josephine, Aimée Dubucq de Rivery, was captured and sent to a Turkish harem where she became mother of a Sultan.

The mercantilist concept of colonies was enshrined in the English committee for Trade and Plantations, formed in 1696. It was later to become the Board of Trade. There was a wholehearted support in England for slavery as an essential part of the colonial system since exports to Africa were paid by the proceeds of slaves sold in the West Indies.

At the same time the Board of Trade recognised as early as 1709 the dependence of the islands on the northern American plantations for bread, drink, fish, flesh of cattle, horses, lumber, slaves and timber. After 1713, the year of the peace of Utrecht, the Northern plantations began to sell timber to the French colonies in exchange for their sugar and molasses, which could be bought cheaper than from the British islands. Even merchants in the British islands, especially in Barbados, took advantage of the cheaper French price to make a profit on French sugar exported illegally into England as Barbados sugar.

The Molasses Act of 1733 was a deliberate attempt on the part of the Government in England to help West Indian sugar growers at the expense of the developing northern plantations. However, wholesale enforcement of this act was impossible and sugar merchants pressed instead for the privilege of exporting sugar directly to the Continent, a privilege they obtained in 1739.

By the middle of the eighteenth century a wind of change began to blow with respect to colonies. Mercantilism, which had been the essence of the West Indian sugar system began to give place to new ideas which came into vogue because of the growth of manufacturing in England. The northern American colonies with their expanding populations (over a million white inhabitants and about 300,000 negroes by 1750) began at last to seem more desirable than the West Indian plantations as markets for English manufactured articles.

A new chapter in colonial relationships opened with the capture of Guadeloupe and Martinique from the French during the Seven Years War. It seemed at first as though the exhausted British islands would be replaced by new fertile fields which would attract sugar growers from the English plantations, while the captured islands would be bastions of defence against the French imperialistic aggression which Choiseul and Vergennes were preparing and which was not to be repulsed finally until Trafalgar in 1805.

The return of Guadeloupe and Martinique to France in 1763 and the later development of San Domingo 'the pearl of the Antilles' heralded instead a golden age for the French West Indies.

The inhabitants of the English sugar plantations in the eighteenth century were never able to follow the daring of the expanding Northern colonies in protests against the Mother Country. They had become completely dependent on English protection for their very existence. Without trade they faced starvation and ruin. Except possibly Jamaica none of the islands were self sufficient. The society of the islands was alien, based upon profit and forced to depend on slave labour for economic function.

Within the framework of a British tradition the islanders were citizens of lower status than the English born and their dearest hopes were to win fortunes and return to the parent society or to emigrate to the thriving northern plantations. Economic conditions fluctuated violently even for the more prosperous families. By 1741 Barbados had become so impoverished that legislation had to be passed to prevent debtors escaping without payment of their obligations. The Caribbean swarmed with privateers and shipping costs rose. The years of peace between 1749-53 gave the islanders a healthy breathing space, the best times that Barbados had experienced since the early days of sugar cultivation a century ago. The French, who had taken advantage of the neutral position of Dominica, St Lucia and St Vincent since 1713 to promote Carib resentment against the English, suffered heavy losses in the Caribbean during the Seven Years War. After the treaty of 1763, the return of the major French islands, and the French settlement at Cayenne, which was designed to carry on illicit trade with the rebellious North American plantations, the English Parliament experimented with certain palliatives to alleviate West Indian depression.

Jamaica and Dominica, for example, were authorised to become free ports and immediately recorded marked increases in trade, although many of their resident planters suffered losses. Yet on Barbados famine threatened in 1776 because of the loss of the island's primary trade with North America. Food prices rose by 150% in less than two years while the price of corn increased by 400%.

American ships which found hearty welcomes in the French ports of Guadeloupe and Martinique operated off the Barbadian coasts where defences were hopelessly inadequate. Some Barbadians fled to St Lucia in hope of better times there. The Dutch in 1771 confiscated Barbadian property in Demerara and in 1780 Barbados and other islands were devastated by a violent hurricane. Bridgetown became a heap of ruins.

It is heartening to record that Dublin subscribed £20,000 for the relief of Barbados' distress, the English Exchequer £80,000,* while Benjamin Franklin, although a rebel against the Empire, asked his fellow Americans to let Dublin relief supplies pass to Barbados unmolested.

In February 1781 Rodney devastated the great trading depot which the Dutch had established at St Eustatius with the help of illicit traders from all over the islands, especially from St Christopher. The value of goods captured on the island and aboard ships was estimated at more than £3 million. Tons of materials from roofs and buildings were

* It is, of course, very difficult to make an accurate comparison of modern US dollars and eighteenth century pounds. However, the ratio of £1 (1780s) to 100 modern US dollars may be allowed to serve as a rough guide.

despatched to Barbados, St Lucia and Antigua to be used as repairs for hurricane damage.

A year later the French had almost driven the English out of the Caribbean. All the English possessions left in February 1782 were Jamaica, Barbados and Antigua. Demerara fell to the French a month later. The French triumph was to be of short duration. On April 11, 1782 Rodney defeated De Grasse near the French islands of the Saints near Guadeloupe, capturing or sinking one quarter of the French fleet.

Jamaica was thereby saved from invasion and the threat of French sea power had passed from the Caribbean. April 11 ought to be remembered always as a red letter day in Caribbean history.

But the islands could not reap the full benefit of English victory over the French because of the loss of trade with the American former colonies. When the English lost the 13 American plantations, the knell sounded for a mercantile system which had been fashioned by the Acts of Trade. Without the American leg to support their economies, the sugar islands were like cripples. They lost the lifeblood of their economic vitality, their cheap supplies and provisions and their chief market. The English parliament was not ready for a situation which had arisen unexpectedly through the loss of the 13 American colonies. Then, as later in the age of declining Empire, the English golden rule was to apply *ad hoc* methods of administration. No thought had been given in advance to the effect on the West Indies of the loss of their North American markets. The West Indian merchants had hoped that trade with America would resume after hostilities had ceased. Through smuggling and illicit trade they attempted to postpone the day of their demise, but their slow economic decay began when they could no longer buy their provisions from North America. The English for their part were unable to continue paying higher prices for the islands' main export, sugar. The American Revolution made possible the dynamic growth of the United States. It marked the death of the West Indian plantation system, even though the final gasps were delayed until the fourth decade of the nineteenth century. There was a temporary period of false revival after the destruction of San Domingo and the damage done to the French plantations by the revolutionaries in the Caribbean. Yet doom was certain and there could be no recovery for a mercantilistic system after the emancipation act of 1833 and the freeing of slaves in 1834.

The apprenticeship system was a slight buffer which took up some of the strain in Barbados, but the act which opened in the seventeenth century when the sugar cane became the major West Indian crop in the Carib isles closed in 1834, with the ruin of the original plantation economy.

New soils in new imperialist outposts could yield better sugar at lower prices than the West Indian sugar planters – who made efforts to survive in the melting pots of new societies – had any reason to expect from their old lands. From having been the gems and pearls of the Empire the sugar plantations had fallen to the level of 'imperial problems'.

They were to sink even lower until in the earlier part of this century they were frankly recognised to be 'slums of empire'.

Chapter 2
The People and their Rulers

By 1666 the life of a prosperous sugar planter living in a great house which resembled a small castle was considered satisfactory, at least to Governor Sir Thomas Modyford. He estimated plate jewels and household stuff in Barbadian homes to be worth £500,000. Long before then, however, the desire to 'suck in some of the sweet ayre in England' had set in. Ligon, who arrived in Barbados in 1647, attributed such a desire to Major Hilliard, who for the reason expressed sold a half share of a 500 acre plantation for £7,000 to Colonel Modyford. The plantation at that time had 200 acres under cane, 120 in forest, 70 growing corn, potatoes, plantains, cassava and bonavist, 20 under tobacco, five under ginger and five yielding cotton. Diversification of agriculture goes back to the seventeenth century. The workers on the plantation were 28 Christians (white), 96 negroes and three Indian women with their children. To help with the labour there were 45 head of cattle, 12 horses and mares and 16 assinigoes (donkeys).

Plantation life offered few amenities. Water had to be caught in ponds or in cisterns located close to dwelling houses, unless the plantation was near a natural spring. Houses, for those who had them, were made of timber and were so low that a man could hardly stand upright with his hat on. In the afternoon sun they became like heated ovens inside. Ligon wrote that on a very hot day (over 90° Fahrenheit in the shade) 'it might raise a doubt whether so much heat without and so much tobacco and kill devil within might not set the house on fire'. Christian servants had worse places to live in. Their 'homes' were cabins which they had to make for themselves from 'sticks and plantain leaves' under shade trees which would only keep light rains from penetrating their improvised roofs. Food was insipid and labour arduous. A Christian servant went to work from 6 till 11 a.m., when one hour was given for a dinner which consisted of 'loblolly made from maize, bonavist beans and potatoes'. In the evening after work ceased at 6 p.m. the same diet was offered as supper with the addition of water and mobbie, a drink fermented from potatoes. In the fields servants were often beaten by cruel overseers. Ligon commented: 'I have seen such cruelty there done to servants, as I did not think one Christian could do to another.' In a society designed for masters, servants and slaves, white bond servants quickly discovered that African slaves who were 'subject to their masters for ever were kept and preserved with greater care'. They attempted to foment a rebellion against their masters but their plot was discovered. The pillory was waiting for those who 'dared to resist authority by word or deed'. A certain Futter was placed in the pillory between noon and one o'clock on a day so parching hot that the sun was said to 'have pierced his head'. Another lover of liberty, John Wiborne, who wrote a 'book' which was called a 'libel' had his ears nailed to the pillory with tenpenny nails.

Such religion as existed (between 1637 six churches and chapels had been built) aimed at giving comfort to the men who enjoyed power. Rev. Thomas Lane in a letter to Archbishop Laud described the Ministers who were chosen by the Governor as 'no better than mercenaries'.

The cruelty inflicted on Christian servants who had to serve five years of bondage in an island which was teeming with mosquitoes, merrywings, cockroaches, centipedes and ants was appalling: the absence of genuine religion and social justice was indicative of the treatment awaiting African slaves who were torn from their tribal communities and shipped like packages in small overcrowded sail boats exposed to disease, bad weather, scurvy and yellow fever. Slavery was hell for those who had to endure its foul treatment during passage.

Thomas Philips, who made a voyage from England to Africa and so 'forward to Barbados' in the year 1693, has left us a vivid account of the methods of transporting slaves. When the ship was in port they were shackled two and two, to prevent attempts at escape or mutiny. Sentinels were posted on the hatchways and a chest of small arms 'ready loaded and primed' was kept on the quarter deck with some Granada shells. Two of the quarter deck guns were kept pointed at the deck, and two more out of the steerage, the door of which was always kept shut and well barred.'

Twice a day the slaves were fed on deck at 10 in the morning and at 4 in the evening, under armed guards. Afterwards they returned to their 'kennels' between decks. Conditions improved after sailing, when the slaves were let out of irons, because there was no longer danger of escape or mutiny. Some slaves of another tribe were however appointed as 'spies' during the voyage and special 'guardians' were equipped with 'cat of nine tails which was exercised with great authority'. Despite attempts by the crew to amuse their human baggage with 'bag pipes, harp and fiddle' two or three slaves died every day. When the ship *Hannibal* of 450 tons reached Barbados on November 14, having left the port of Whidaw on July 27, Commander Philips delivered 372 slaves out of 700 to the African company's factors who sold them at £19 per head. He had lost 14 of his crew by death. In a moment of self pity the captain commented: 'By their mortality our voyages are ruined and we pine and fret ourselves to death, to think that we should undergo so much misery, and take so much pains to so little purpose.' Slavery was hell for the miserable sailors who served the ends of the syndicates in England.

The slaves who survived this dreadful crossing worn out by smallpox and flux came to an island in the grips of plague and recovering from a violent hurricane. They worked the same hours as the Christian servants and lived in small houses which were built from local materials.

Some of their descendants today might think themselves fortunate in not having to wear as many clothes as the white servants who worked beside them in the hot fields: African men wore canvas drawers and women petticoats; the rest was topless. The slaves were valuable possessions of their masters, but they could not call their souls their own, nor was it possible, as it was in the Catholic islands ruled by France, for their 'souls' to be 'saved' through conversion to Christianity. Slaves in colonial possession and serfs in Eastern Europe were accompaniments of the century of enlightenment.

A still small voice of conscience was however slowly beginning to set a spark alight.

Christopher Codrington, the son of a Barbadian smuggler who had amassed the largest West Indian fortune in the Carib isles, on his way to fight in Guadeloupe willed much of his property to the Society for the Propagation of the Gospel which met for the first time in England in 1701. Impressed by Codrington's legacy the great Bishop Fleetwood preached to the annual meeting of the Society in 1711 words which foreshadowed the emancipation of negro slaves. Between the years 1711 and 1785 the Society despatched to Anglican stations in British America 353 missionaries and many schoolteachers, doctors and libraries. It founded not only Codrington's school and college in Barbados but also Columbia University in New York.

An element of religion as a civilising influence began to penetrate the wilderness of materialism. Codrington's school at Lodge was opened in 1745, twelve years after Harrison's Free school in Bridgetown, so some finer influences could be discerned at work, even though the Codrington experiment in black and white relationships seemed to the average merchant and planter sabotage of their establishment. Yet how could islanders, who regarded themselves as Englishmen overseas, behave better than their English brethren at home, where in 1713 there had been torchlight processions in celebration of

England's winning from Spain the Asiento which gave them right to sell slaves in Spanish American colonies?

Codrington had left the Society 800 acres and 300 slaves. The College was not opened until 1830, five years after William Hart Coleridge was appointed as the first bishop of Barbados.

In 1831 it was seriously damaged by hurricane. Codrington's economic miracle of survival was due not only to dedicated workers but to the funds provided by the Society from England during bad years. The records of the Society are valuable historical proofs of the up and down cycles which the Caribbean sugar isles experienced through the centuries. Profits were not constant year by year, losses were often considerable. Planters suffered losses from drought, insect attacks, animal distempers, competition from other sugar producing islands, enemy activity by sea, and shortages of slaves.

The inhabitants of the Carib isles were not the only people to suffer from the ups and downs of agricultural production in the eighteenth century. In Sicily 30,000 people died of famine in 1763-64, while in 1770 those dying of hunger in Saxony were reported at 150,000 and in Bohemia at 80,000. Hunger and famine are killers to this day. There was acute suffering in the West Indies for most of the centuries of European settlement, but this suffering ought to be seen in the perspective of world suffering and not as something peculiar to these islands.

John Augustine Waller, surgeon in the Royal Navy, visited most of the Carib isles in 1807. He noticed the great neglect of religious instruction in the English islands and compared this lack with the different practices in the French islands where 'the French slaves are in some respect incomparably in a better condition than the English, as they are regarded and treated like Brethren and Christians'. The callous attitude of the English is illustrated by an advertisement in a Barbadian newspaper offering for sale 'two mules, three goats, a sow with eight pigs, and a fine healthy young woman with four children'.

Free people of colour were also better treated in the French than in the English lands. John Waller attributed this to the fact that men of property in the French islands often, from religious considerations, married the coloured women by whom they had children. Such marriages permitted the children to inherit their father's property. In an English colony, said Waller, 'such a marriage would be contemplated with a degree of horror'. Despite all the efforts made on the Codrington estates to instil the high-minded principle of Bishop Fleetwood, the Barbadian antipathy to the Christianisation of slaves was so deep-rooted that the Anglican rector of St Lucy's Parish church was imprisoned in the first decade of the nineteenth century for administering Holy Communion to certain slaves. He was later released through a Royal pardon.

It is not surprising that the movement for the abolition of slavery which was largely Christian and humanitarian (although helped by competing vested interests) should have drawn all its strength from the Mother Country.

There was no hope of reform originating in the islands where slavery had, in the words of John Waller, fed 'sloth and pride'. The British government of the day displayed unprecedented wisdom in creating the first governor-general of the West Indies who from his headquarters in Bridgetown could ensure that the act of 1833 was carried out in Barbados, St Vincent, Grenada and Tobago.

Wisdom was also apparent in paying the governor-general and the lieutenant-governors in the three other islands from the imperial exchequer.

It is noteworthy that Antigua, where the Moravians had been active as early as 1754, and where there were few absentee proprietors, because of soil depletion and drought, passed a bill to implement the abolition of slavery before any other West Indian colony.

August 1834 ended Slavery in the British isles. It did not create a West Indian society, which is still in the making.

Slave owners, many resident in England, received less than

ten shillings in the pound compensation, while estates were nearly all short of capital. Henry Lascelles of the house of Harewood, owner of extensive estates in Barbados, had unsuccessfully spent £100,000 in contesting Wilberforce's seat in Yorkshire. No amount of money or influence could reverse the decline of the planter class after 1834. The golden age of mercantilism of the West Indian lobby was ended, never to revive. All that has happened since 1834 has been a slow, gradual, often painful effort to knit together a social fabric from the fragments of a system which had little use for idealists like Christopher Codrington, and which by definition was opposed to equal rights for all men.

The ordinary difficulties of building new societies in the islands were enhanced by other tendencies in Europe. Advocates of free trade wanted to see the abandonment of all colonies, at the same time as humanitarians were exerting political pressures on behalf of subject races. No one seemed to understand that abolition of slavery would intensify the existing depression of the sugar industry which was the only visible and economic means of maintaining even the low standards of living of the subject races whose 'freedom' was ardently championed from a distance.

The years between 1846 and 1874 were a time of acute depression and suffering in the West Indies, while in England statesmen like Disraeli had no other policy than to say that the 'wretched colonies were millstones around England's neck'. Similar sentiments have been expressed in our day by English writers who blame all of England's difficulties on the 'bloody Empire'. Despite the urgings of the Little Englanders, some efforts were made by officials and by the survivors of West Indian 'society' in the islands. One example may be given during the American Civil War, when opportunity was taken to stimulate the planting of cotton in the West Indies, Natal and Queensland. The 'empire' has never been more real to Englishmen than during periods of war.

From 1865, when the Jamaican crisis began, may be dated the beginning of active English intervention to prepare the

West Indian people for responsible government of their own. Crown colony government, which had been the method used for Trinidad after its capture from the Spanish, was decreed for Jamaica in 1866. Britain then used financial pressure to apply this system of administration to ten of the thirteen Caribbean colonies which voted out their legislatures and introduced Crown colony government. Only Bermuda, the Bahamas and Barbados entered the twentieth century with the seventeenth-century constitutions which they had shared with the thirteen American colonies. A change in British thinking, the rebirth of a new imperialism, may be discerned by 1870. New men began to preach the value of Empire and trade for the residents of Britain. Seeley's *Expansion of England*, published in 1883, became a bible of the Imperialists, while a year later the Imperial Federation League was founded by those who believed in a central parliament and administration for the whole Empire.

Interest and pride in the Empire captured the imagination of the British people whose pride in their Empire reached its zenith between 1885 and 1902. Between 1895 and 1903 colonials took heart from the vigour of Joseph Chamberlain. Not since the eclipse of mercantilism had a Secretary of State attempted, as Chamberlain did, to implement a positive programme of imperial development. The West Indies and West African possessions then seemed to have an economic future which would buttress their slow growth towards responsible government. Loans were granted at $3\frac{3}{4}\%$ to construct railways and harbours in the West Indies and West Africa. By the Colonial Stock Act of 1899 bonds of colonial governments were given a status as privileged as that of Consols and trustees began to invest in them. The West Indies Department of Agriculture, which is now an integral part of the University of the West Indies, was established in 1898. A year later Parliament approved a loan of £3 million for the West Indies, and in 1902 bountified sugar which had been undercutting West Indian was prohibited from entering the British market.

Chamberlain saw that imperial preference was the cement of Empire, but not until the Ottawa conference of 1932 was it to become official. The new British policy was too late to save the concept of an Empire which was already under assault from emerging Dominions, whose leaders were chiefly concerned to protect their burgeoning industries from the competition of British manufacturers. Before the First World War exploded these new offshoots of Empire were not thinking imperially but of their own self-interests: they were not likely to be interested in sharing the burden of responsibility for a far-flung Empire of non-white people: their thoughts were all about personal maturity, of being 'equal adult members of a family working in consultation'. The full germs of a loose Commonwealth had been active since 1897 when the Colonial conference rejected Imperial Federation. The only programme available for West Indian leaders to follow after that was a struggle for such political power as could be grasped inside their islands, where support had to be sought first from the middle classes, then from the proletariat. The First World War was the school of the first West Indian political leaders. It fashioned Manley of Jamaica, and Cipriani of Trinidad. When Canada, Australia, South Africa and New Zealand signed the Treaty of Versailles separately in 1919 another chapter of Empire had ended; the era of Commonwealth opened. The West Indian leaders could now translate their hopes into plans for a federated West Indian Dominion. No longer need coloured bourgeois accept white West Indian merchant planters and officials as masters and social superiors. Coloured West Indians had served in their thousands at overseas stations in France, West and East Africa and Palestine. They deserved equal opportunities in their island homes. There were few men of vision like Chamberlain in post-war England, so the islands of the West Indies between the two World Wars became neglected paradises, slums of Empire, unfit for heroes to live in, with only isolated pockets of prosperity to recall more prosperous times, earlier promises.

West Indians emigrated by the thousands before the era

4 Welchman Hall Gully, St Thomas, Barbados

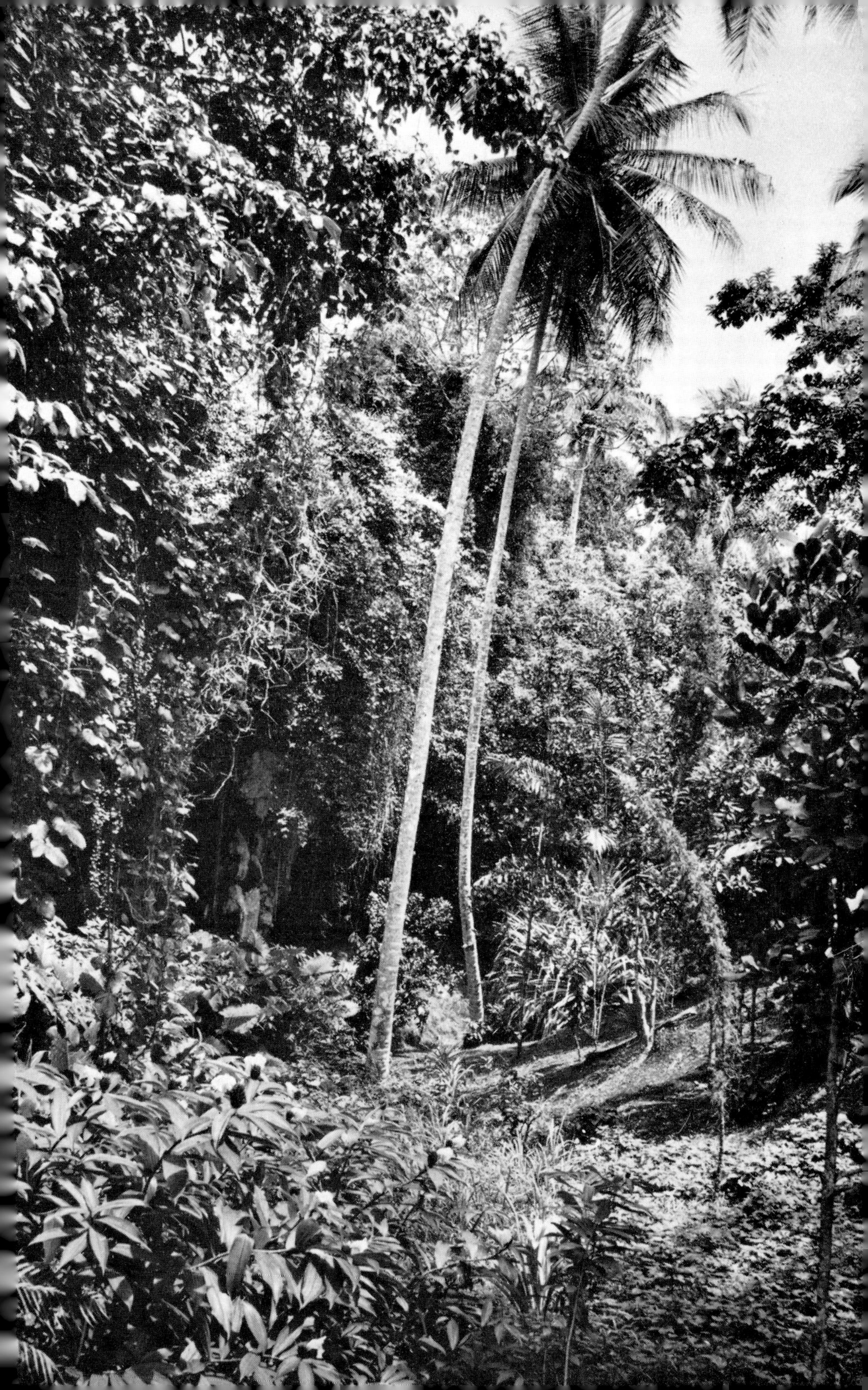

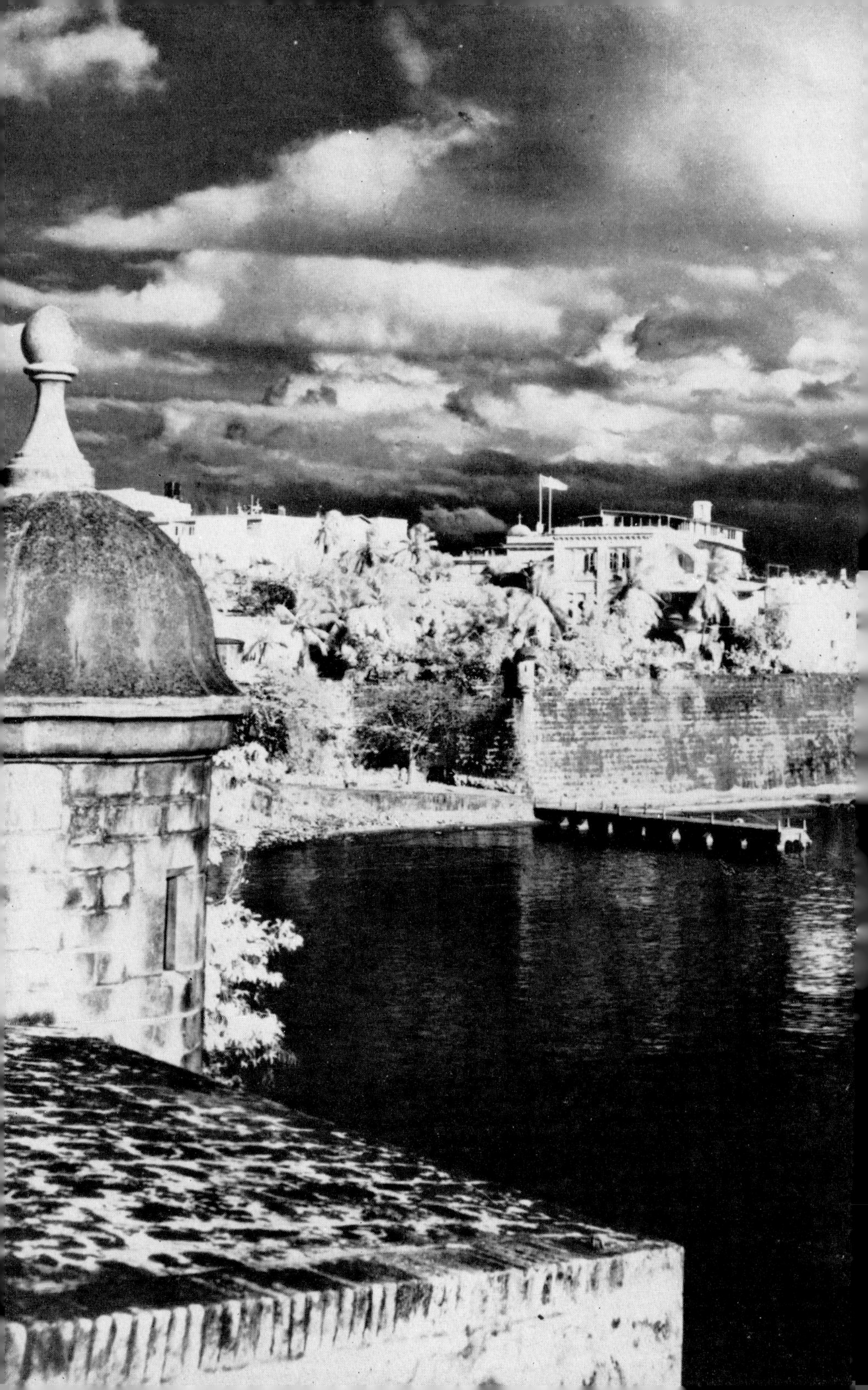

of passports and visas but by the 'thirties those left behind began to feel the effects of the great depression in the United States.

The British had tried with the Empire Marketing Board from 1926 to encourage the idea of mutual benefits from imperial trade, and the West Indians began to breathe again the air of hope when a preferential trading system emerged from the imperial economic conference at Ottawa in 1932. The first Colonial Development Act was passed in 1929.

But things got worse, not better, in the West Indies when the long-pent-up desires of coloured majorities found combustible political fuel in conditions caused by a general world depression. West Indian emigrants returned to find that their economies, except for Trinidad where oil had been worked since 1910, had remained primarily agricultural and depressed by low prices.

The British had warnings enough from the West Indies before the riots of 1937 brought the islands into the news of the world. The Royal Commission on the West Indies reported on conditions which were so stark that no general publication was made during the war years although urgent attention was given to some of its recommendations, and a Comptroller for the Colonial Development and Welfare Organisation was appointed in 1940.

From its headquarters in Barbados this organisation attempted to 'prime the pump' for a revitalisation of West Indian economies. It offered West Indians opportunities to think regionally. Unfortunately it was so divorced from insular society that its members were known throughout the islands as the 'circus'. Despite this expression of parochialism the headquarters at Hastings House offered a meeting place for the discussion of West Indian affairs and the organisation made available an office for the secretariat of the Regional Economic Committee, the West Indian regional organisation, whose secretary was later to become the first Chief Secretary of the West Indies Federation and eventually Deputy Governor-General.

5 *El Moro Fortress, San Juan harbour, Puerto Rico*

Before the formation of the Regional Economic Committee the British Caribbean islands had achieved considerable experience at working together in regional approaches towards the marketing of sugar, citrus and copra. Cricket and British West Indian Airways were other forces working for union which was the professed objective of the Standing Closer Association committee who drew up the blue-print of federation.

The federation of 1958 failed because of intense West Indian opposition to the federal idea. The islanders only understood what their representatives told them at election time and federal elections were conducted in the same way as island elections: there were no federal programmes as such put before the electors.

Hardly one voter in a thousand realised that the Federation was only a glorified Crown Colony and that the powers of Jamaica, Trinidad and Barbados were each superior to those of the federal government. 'One day federation will come', said Sir Alexander Bustamante during the Montego Bay conference of 1947, 'but I cannot see the possibility of walking with a group of creeping and non-creeping persons.' His view finally triumphed and when Jamaica in a referendum was given the opportunity to remain or leave the federation, the experiment of welding together a single nation which could speak to the world with one voice was over. The islands chose to walk alone, as did Trinidad soon after. Efforts were then made by the leaders of the Leewards and Windwards to enter into a political union with Barbados. But in 1966 Barbados became the third of the West Indies Federation to walk alone.

The other islands are still creeping around in a new political association with Britain, which cannot be more than a passing phase until the moment also arrives for them to walk singly or in one or more groupings.

The British are reluctant to admit that their colonial record is not the best the world has ever seen: at the United Nations their spokesmen are never weary of recounting the millions of human beings who have been freed from their raj since India became a republic.

There is no doubt that the British contributed much to the formation of a West Indian society of today. On the whole, however, it seems that in England severance of ties with the West Indies is regarded as relief from a burden which had become heavy and very little profitable since 1834. British treatment of their oldest imperial possessions in the West Indies differs from the treatment offered by France, the Netherlands and the United States to their Caribbean possessions.

The old French islands of Martinique and Guadeloupe have for centuries sent representatives to the French legislature in Paris and on several occasions the islanders have been given the opportunity in a referendum to vote for leaving or remaining with France. Today Martinique and Guadeloupe derive benefits from very high prices paid for their sugar and from large sums of money provided by the European Economic Community. Their rum also enjoys special preference in the markets of the European Economic Community. As departments of France, too, they receive a share of French social expenditure, and as French citizens they have freedom to move into France and Common market countries.

Puerto Rico's economic progress has been the most spectacular of all the islands because of large-scale investment by American manufacturers whose products have free access to the huge continental market of the United States. Tourists from the United States also enjoy special advantages from holidays spent in Puerto Rico and the American Virgin islands, which as American territories have been pace-setters for post-war tourism throughout the Caribbean.

The Dutch islands in the East Caribbean and along the mainland of Venezuela are, together with the mainland territory of Surinam, integrated into the Kingdom of the Netherlands. Britain therefore stands alone in attempting to launch independent islands in the Caribbean in modern times; a policy which could only have become effective through the co-operation of political leaders in the islands. No attempt has ever been made to consult the people directly through a referendum, other than in Jamaica.

Time alone will decide future West Indian alignments. Ideally there can be little doubt of the benefits which the islands would enjoy from freedom of movement, free trade and improved communications. Practically, obstacles to such movements for integration have increased because of British policies of multiplication of independent and semi-independent nations. It will never be easy for those politicians who capture sovereign or near sovereign power in each of the Caribbean states to pursue policies which will lead to the curtailment of their own special privileges and spheres of influence. Yet the movement for co-operation is far from dead in the Caribbean, as the creation of a Free Trade Area and a Regional Development Bank illustrate.

Young people of the future may accept political change because they will grow up in a world unlike that of their parents. In such a world earlier contributions of France, Holland, Britain, Denmark, Sweden, the United States, Africa, India, Spain and Portugal may all be merged into a pattern which could be more economically advantageous and more culturally significant than any one territory is ever likely to achieve through working alone. Towards such a development no country is likely to be opposed. For the survival of mankind everywhere today depends on the capacity of people of differing backgrounds, culture patterns and experiences not merely to live together, but to draw on the greatest human and scientific sources available to them.

In the West Indies the historical backgrounds have more resemblances than differences. The way ahead ought to be easier once the sea is no longer regarded as a barrier but as a natural connecting link between islands.

Hitherto the sea has largely been responsible for the survival of so many conflicting spheres of influence in small Caribbean islands whose rivalries are fanned by competing

THE PEOPLE AND THEIR RULERS 43

vested interests from outside.

The sea has prevented greater movement of people between the islands and has fostered suspicions of neighbours. In Barbados, for example, St Lucians are still called foreigners. The sea water fallacy is at the root of West Indian disunity. Few people have recognised this, although the history of the West Indies is in its most important aspects the history of sea power. When the sea is regarded as the natural highway between the islands there will be no further talk of walking alone. The islanders will have become united in a common Caribbean destiny.

Chapter 3
The Islands – Paradises?

The Carib isles are not places for those who dislike the sea. Islands are like huge anchored ships and the people who live on them are always near to the sea, the great mother whose vast oceans make the whole earth tolerable for men. Islands are relaxing, as Shakespeare wrote in *The Tempest* with 'noises, sounds, and sweet airs that give delight and hurt not'. Islands breed sailors and fishermen who go down to the sea in ships, probe the mysteries of the deep, see new lands and sometimes return to their shores where they can hear the roar of breakers on coral reefs and feel the freshness of the breeze as though they were still at sea breaking the ocean's waves with the prows of their vessels. The Carib isles belong in a special way to those who man the island schooners, now mainly built in Bequia and Carriacou. For hundreds of years schooners have carried the produce of the islands from port to port. The tiny national harbours of the Caribbean are the meeting places of the men of the sea whose schooners, laden almost to the point of overflowing, ride alongside the streets of West Indian towns to discharge their cargoes into hand-drawn or donkey carts and as progress catches them up, into lines of waiting trucks. Already there are signs that motor vessels and steamships will take over from the bellying island schooners just as motors have replaced sails in the local fishing fleets.

The islands have been caught up by modern winds of change but seamen will continue for centuries yet to escape from the onrush of civilisation, trusting themselves to the swelling seas where yachts under canvas make harmony with the strong breezes and the drenching salt sprays, while the pigments of their skin darken as they absorb the health-giving rays of the sun.

Commercial pleasure yachts are already advertising barefoot 'vacations to remote islands' which are only just beginning to advance to the 'nudge of tourism'; while air-conditioned staterooms with private bathrooms are available for those who like to combine the simple life with the comforts of home. The sea is for sailors, its mood changing from placid sun-dimpled calms to white-flecked angry rollers. The surface of the sea changes suddenly, winds veer to gusty and boats roll or bang from trough to trough.

The sea is exhilarating for those who love its capricious nature, punishment for those who cherish dry land. Only if you love the sea should you be tempted to take a small launch through the channel which separates Montserrat from Antigua or dare even to go fishing off the north coast of Barbados. The sea there is alive and seldom like the placid blue ponds which are familiar in so many Caribbean brochures. From out to sea off the north point of Barbados the rollers rush inland in a continuous line of moving spray as if spouted from the mouth of a 'ghost whale', or lurch inwards twisting like a London underground train before it throws into the air great columns of white spume which are converted into light-toed shapes like ballet dancers. Then with a roar and a deafening thud the rollers disappear beneath the cliff surface to surge upwards into a single gigantic spout of 'solid' water shooting 50 feet above ground level. Everywhere on the Atlantic coasts of the islands the breakers ceaselessly dash against coral rocks making the music of the Caribbean seas and exalting the grandeur of nature.

For men the sea, for women the moonlight.

'Its wondrous glory', said the Reverend S. H. Sutton Moxley, Chaplain to the British Forces in Barbados in 1886 'is alone worth the voyage from England to see.' No one has excelled this early booster for West Indian tourism in his descriptions of moonlight nights on a Carib isle. 'Looking out through the tangles of stephanotis, ipomea and many other creepers (to) watch the breakers in lines of silver light chase each other to the shore, the roar of the surf reduced to a murmur by distance, the balmy air breathing the perfume of those old favourites, the English roses from the garden, is enough to make one imagine that he has realised his childhood dream of fairy land, and it is difficult to recognise the fact that he is not among the lotus eaters.' The sea makes harmony with the land, with moonlight, with stars, with blushing dawns and scarlet-splashed sunsets, with fleecy clouds that hover and float above snug tree tops. The sea broods with the rains which ping like pellets on to its watery bosom, grows black as the storm clouds brush the azure sky away, roars to the shriek of air-splitting thunder, gapes wide at the dazzling lightning forks, pounds to the fury of hurricane winds, spills its massive strength on to the coastal roads and erodes defensive stone ramparts. The sea is mighty, for the islands lie in the open ocean, but its energies relax as storm, wind, thunder, earthquake and volcanoes too exhaust their temporary frenzies.

The islanders have many companions, yapping dogs, squealing pigs, restless roosters, stinging ants, winged roaches, whistling frogs, choruses of crickets, bats, flies, merrywings, mosquitoes, lizards, frogs, crabs, wood ants, rats, mice, godhorses and plural mongoose. All these and many more, including snakes in the thick forested islands, clamour for their shares of the Caribbean sun, their rights of survival. In the gardens of well ordered hostelries you are likely to meet socially only the friendly lizards who are adorable fly catchers and the croaking frogs who are beloved by gardeners as insect eaters. On the beaches you may sometimes see land and sea crabs or, if very lucky, young turtles going down in file to the sea. If you are less lucky you may be tormented by sandflies against which hoteliers wage constant war on your behalf, hoping that total victory will soon be theirs.

In the sea where there are reefs or loose stones it is wisdom to avoid putting your foot down on the black spines of sea eggs whose prickles may penetrate your skin and cause painful hours of lost vacationing pleasure. Sneakers should be worn by those who have never learnt how to tread water. Other creatures of the sea you will do well to avoid meeting are Portuguese 'men-of-war' (gay bladders with long tails) or stinging jelly fish. They are fortunately infrequent visitors, the men-of-war hugging the Atlantic coastline, the jelly fish the sheltered Caribbean shores. By and large animal life is friendly in the Caribbean, but visitors take most kindly to birds, especially the yellow-breasted banana quits who share with the finches (called sparrows) a love of sugar bowls at mealtimes. Some visitors have been known to make pets of lizards while others have actually taken pleasure from the loud-mouthed grackles, the blackbirds whose mob instincts when aroused simulate the cries of angry human beings. Everyone in Barbados has a special affection for the brown-coated, red-footed doves who loudly coo that 'Moses spoke God's word', while weather watchers pay close heed to the rainbird who perches on the highest bough so that all may know that bad weather approaches. The siffleur of Dominica, the blackbird of St Lucia and the Barbados thrush are renowned for their glorious songs, while Trinidad and Tobago are only surpassed by Guyana for their colourful bird life. In Trinidad too you may still hunt the deer or eat the hardbacked armadillo.

People from wintry climates flock like the migrant birds to the sunny isles where the seasons are perpetual summer. Even when it rains the temperature is in the high seventies or low eighties and the sea is never really cold. As if to please the visitor who comes in winter, rain then falls mostly by night, although weeks of winter rain sometimes make nonsense of the West Indian claim that the rainy season is officially from June till November. Sometimes in winter it seems more true to say that 'the rain it raineth every day'. From June the islanders stand by for the hurricanes, which are always to be feared, though less frequent than might be expected in a hurricane-forming region.

Rain is hardly mentioned by the image makers who seek to woo the traveller to the 'sunny Caribbean year round', yet without the rain the islands would lack the lush green grass and trees, and their good earth would yield less vegetables, fruits and other agricultural crops needed to feed teeming populations. Without rain, too, water would be scarce as it is in some islands, and trade would come to a standstill. Sugar, bananas, citrus, cotton, mangoes, green vegetables, coconut and breadfruit trees flourish in the rains which also make the grasses green and juicy for cows, goats, sheep and other meat-producing cattle. Rain waters the roots of the gorgeous flowering trees, the immortelles, the frangipani, the pouis, the flamboyants, the Queen of flowers, the Pride of India and hundreds of vines, perennials and shrubs whose splashes of colour bring refreshment to islanders and welcome visitors in thousands of friendly wayside gardens.

Modern tourism began in Miami, took hold of Puerto Rico, dug deeply into Bermuda and the Bahamas, and has a strong hold in Barbados. It is sweeping like a hurricane wind into every Caribbean island which has a beach. Land in the Caymans already has been advertised at £15,000 per acre and has reached $3 US a square foot in some of the tiny Grenadine islets. A holiday for a family of nine over a ten-day period cost $4,000 in Barbados during December of 1969.

Magnificent homes designed by architects have been built on exclusive estates at Mill Reef in Antigua and at Sandy Lane in Barbados, while some ancient mansions and great houses have been renovated by millionaires from overseas. In Martinique and Barbados some seventeenth- and eighteenth-century homes still bear witness to an age of gracious living for those relatively few families who dug deep roots into the social and economic life of the Caribbees.

Martinique and Barbados most truly reflect respectively French and English civilisation in the West Indies. Modern jet planes, airports, deep-water harbours, telecommunications, roads, international hotels, air conditioning, ships and yachts have today made developments possible in islands which until recent years had no other economic hopes than those to be expected from improved agriculture. Development varies from island to island. Tourism provides almost the whole economic life of Bermuda and the Bahamas and will eventually predominate in the Virgins, the Grenadines, Tobago and Antigua and Barbados. In one respect modern tourism has a similarity to developments which followed upon the switch from small farming to highly capitalised sugar production in the mid-eighteenth century. It is financed largely from overseas. Big international hotel operators have introduced techniques and skills which promise visitors at the very least comfortable beds and the appearances of that luxury which the language of tourist brochures and their carefully modelled photos teach them to expect. At the same time sales and market organisations of the big hotel chains have been able to entice Caribbean travellers who would otherwise not have sought the islands. The budgets of island tourist boards and of small hoteliers are much too small to influence greatly the competitive world of travel advertising.

International hoteliers, airlines and ship companies now pool resources with hotel associations, travel agents and tourist boards to promote Caribbean holidays all the year round. Success can almost be charted.

Barbados for example in 1968 received more than 50% of its visitors during the so called 'off' or summer season months between April 15 and November 15. The paradox of modern tourist development of the Carib isles lies in a lack of balance between the claims of the image makers who advertise unspoiled islands, perfect for relaxation 'away from it all' and the fixed determination of island governments to get the maximum economic benefit from the new money which tourism injects into their economies. Visitors are welcome, but less welcome for being visitors than for spending money. The fact that Jamaica advertises 'friendly, smartly uniformed members of a courtesy corps who are at your service with a smile in the city, tourist resorts and beauty spots' is a sign not only of advanced techniques in servicing tourists but also recognition of the need of tourists to receive warmer welcomes than they could normally expect from the average Jamaican whom they might meet in the streets. Visitors to Barbados still proclaim that the friendliness of the people is the island's greatest single attraction, yet some people who have been visiting the island over long periods have noted a falling off in courtesy. Other Carib isles have earned an unenviable reputation for the surliness of their population, while language difficulties debar some English-speaking visitors from visiting Guadeloupe, a French-speaking island which has much to offer. The growing popularity of St Martin in the North may be partly due to the use of English which is spoken in all the small northern islands. Despite efforts made by BWIA, LIAT, CARIBAIR, the French line, Yacht centres and other inter-island agencies of transport, getting around the islands is less easy than flying or sailing to the countries of Europe or North America. However, people are moving more frequently.

The political and international fragmentation of the West Indies, island jealousies, and the prices of most West Indian hotels, which are beyond the reach of most West Indians, are further deterrents to inter-island travel. The islands however are being drawn closer together by the international chain operators. Hilton hotels, Holiday Inns, Pegasus hotels, Trust House hotels already advertise holidays which can be spent in three, four, five or six islands at no extra cost to the traveller for board or transportation.

Tourism is being welcomed and encouraged for the money it brings, and governments are directly investing in hotels and resort developments, but some West Indian natives deplore certain effects. Sex exploitation is perhaps no more entrenched in the Caribbean than in the homelands of the visitors who seek fun in the Caribbean. Yet young West Indian men rightly resent the suggestion that their womenfolk are plentiful and for sale. A photostat of an article urging

Americans to visit Barbados because its women were long legged and 'cost only five dollars' was posted on the notice board of the Cave Hill campus of the University of the West Indies in a worthy protest against this debasement of tourism.

Sex perversion, and sex exploitation arouse less resentment however than is generated by nationalist West Indians who dislike the tourist industry as something mostly foreign, which deprives them of their beaches, and makes them if not 'hewers of wood and drawers of water' at least modern servants of the almighty dollar. The resentment is intellectual rather than physical. The revolt is against outside values and an imported concept of living.

The West Indies today have much to offer visitors who seek sun, sea and relaxation, because tourism is only in the early stages of development and in some islands just beginning. The market for mass travel has already been exploited and Miami, San Juan, the Bahamas, Bermuda and parts of Jamaica are highly developed tourist playgrounds. Their beaches are as crowded as West Indian market places and their advertisements are beginning to stress the 'comforts' of air-conditioned hotel boxes 15 or more storeys up overlooking the Caribbean sea. You have to go further south or into 'out' islands to find miles of open sandy beach.

More hoteliers in the big islands are seeking to attract medium-sized conventions to hotels which can seat up to 600 people in a single hall. A few, notably San Juan, Puerto Rico and Curacao, attract visitors through casinos, but several islands are chary of gambling because of its attractions for undesirables and criminals. The dominant slogan in the West Indies today is 'don't stop the carnival', for tourism alone promises rapid release from the centuries of heritage of poverty and primitive living.

Tourist dollars may and often do corrupt but stark poverty corrodes the spirit. So long as people want to share in the Caribbean sun so long will hoteliers, travel agents, and transportation companies persuade them to come. Only if visitors decide that the image makers are taking them for a ride may there be a diversion to some other 'unspoilt' destinations, which may satisfy their eternal search for island paradises.

Chapter 4
Arts, Crafts and Folklore

Islands are more open to cultural changes than mainlands. Sea lanes are the roads which connect them to mainlands and even in small islands there can be greater awareness of the larger world than is possible for the inhabitants of inland villages or towns. Ships do not call at villages or at landlocked towns. Yet cultural patterns can be imposed on islanders as firmly as on those who have never seen the sea. The dominant cultural patterns of the islands are, as might be expected, those laid by the parent countries. Neither India, Africa, Portugal, Spain, America nor China infiltrated cultural systems as deep rooted as those nurtured by Holland, France and England in the non-Spanish Caribbean.

Armistice Day celebrations in Fort de France, Martinique, are as recognisably French in inspiration as they obviously are in the towns of any department of mainland France; in Trafalgar Square, Bridgetown, on the same day there is a mini-performance of the impressive ceremonial at the Cenotaph in Whitehall, London. The British English and the British Barbadians honour their dead in the same ways. The uproarious welcomes which all the islanders gave to Princess Margaret, Prince Philip and Queen Elizabeth II were born of centuries of loyalty to the British throne. Barbadian children by their thousands in 1955 sang a song of welcome which spoke of tradition and honour going hand in hand and made promise as 'patriots' to cherish them more and more.

They roared lustily the words:

*So hail to our Princess Margaret,
welcome to our sunny isle
Evermore we'll be true to the Red, White and Blue.*

Devotion to blessed Royalty was as real as subsequent devotion to nation could be. Today the Barbadian schoolgirls are taught to salute another flag and to sing on independence day, November 30

*the blue and golden flag we hoist as symbol
we are free, just goes to show we have
the choice to chart our destiny.*

Somehow the words are less inspiring.

English schools, English history books, English novels, the English language, the English Bible, English religion, English law, English tradition of individual freedom, representative parliamentary government and the right to public expression of opinion are all as deeply engraved on West Indian minds as on English. Cricket, a sense of fairplay, love of animals, the ideals of public service, tolerance and the Anglican establishment are some of the legacies which England gave to the West Indies.

Despite changes which have followed independence and a search for new national identities there is no sign that these essentially English gifts are held in lower esteem today by the majority of islanders. The English imprint is naturally most evident in Barbados where there has been unbroken English influence since settlement, but it is also visible in St Kitts, St Vincent, Antigua, St Lucia and Grenada. French influences have left their impresses on St Kitts, Dominica and Grenada throughout the centuries and are marked in St Lucia, where French culture is fostered by French-speaking families and kept alive by frequent contacts with Martinique and sometimes with France. St Lucia issued a set of stamps to commemorate Napoleon's birthday.

Colonial societies are productive of élites. The concept of

6 Cathedral and Plaza, Puerto Rico

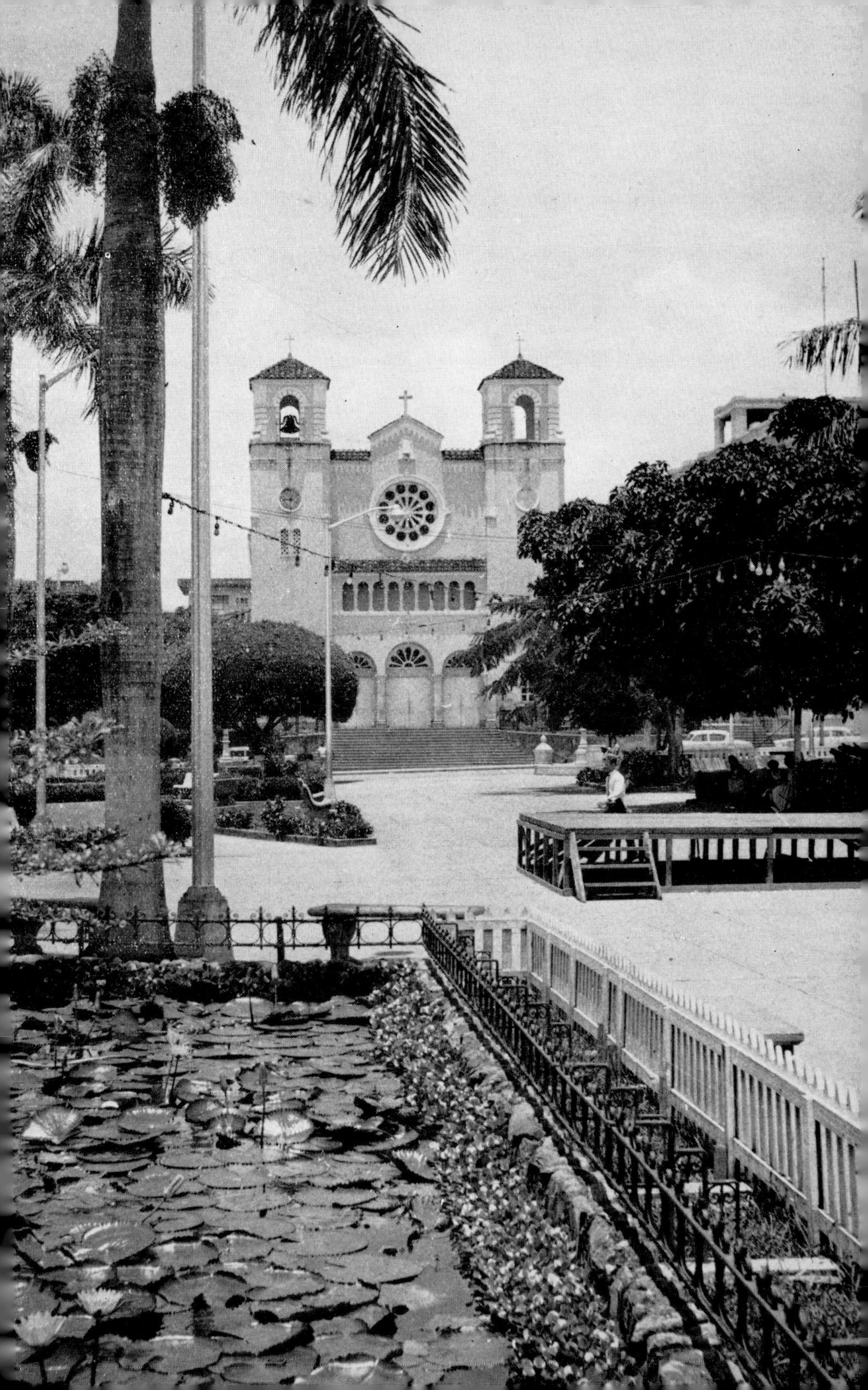

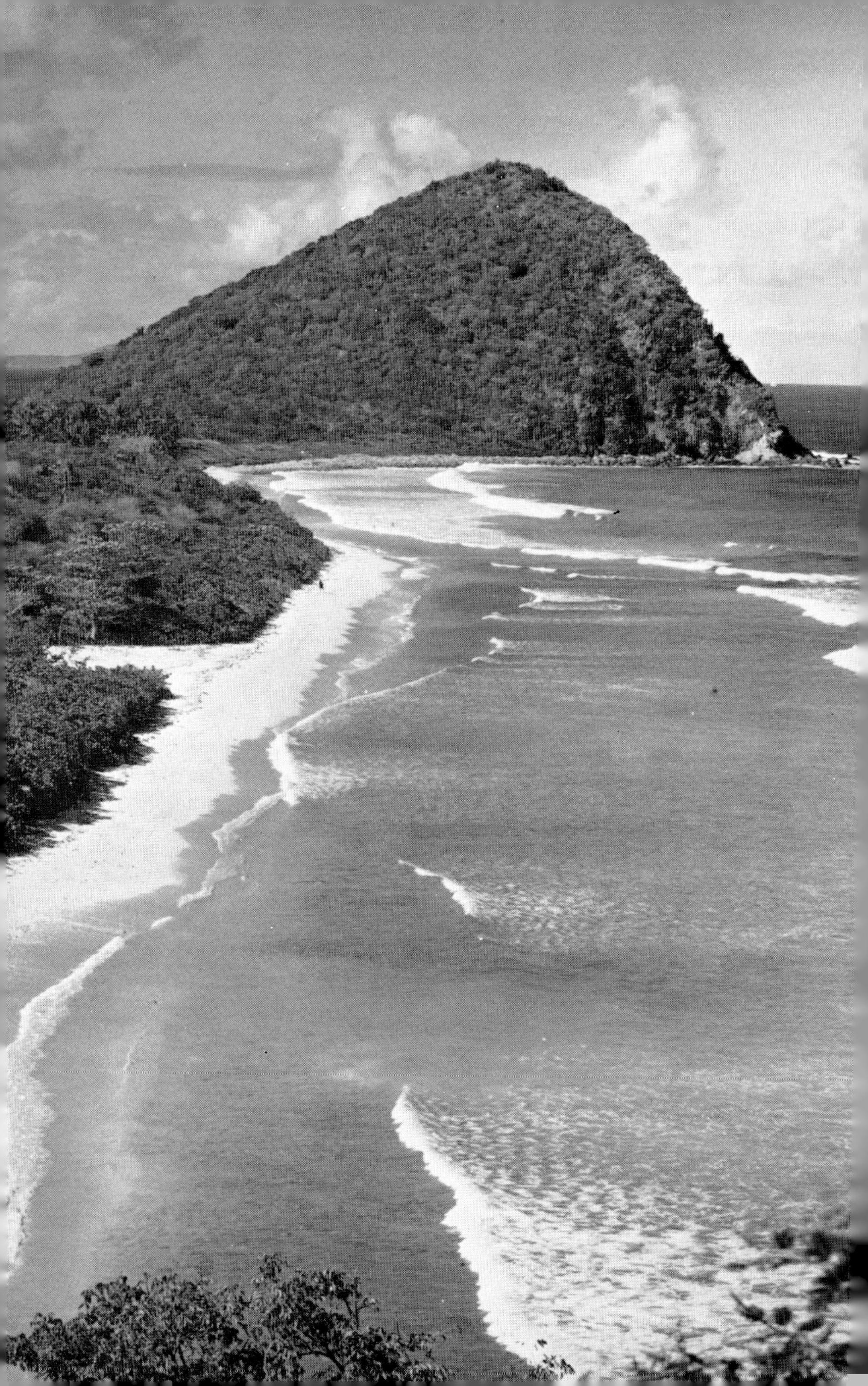

training people for self-government implies that élites have first to be created.

West Indian writing is therefore the creation of persons who have been educated within the cultural and language patterns of the dominant mother countries. West Indian writers began their literary activities under colonialist régimes. Their works had to be published in the capitals of Empires and to undergo the scrutiny of readers and critics who were accustomed to the reading habits of cosmopolitan cities.

Like the great West Indian athletes, and cricketers, the successful singers and actors, West Indian authors and poets had to appeal to citizens of countries who were familiar with the literature of the most highly developed cultures. West Indian writers, who are nearly always major critics of their societies, cannot live by selling their books in the West Indies because the islands are too small to produce adequate markets for the publishers of creative books. The same is true of entertainment. West Indian dancers and musicians have made good in cities as far apart as Stockholm and New York, while some operate night clubs or amusement places in European capitals.

Despite the handicaps and difficulties of transplanting themselves overseas, the achievement of West Indian writers in this century has been almost as sensational as that of their great cricketers. St John Perse, who spent his childhood in Guadeloupe, Aimé Césaire of Martinique, Derek Walcott of St Lucia, Edward Brathwaite of Barbados are poets who deserve their eminence in West Indian literature, while the excellence of their work has received acclaim from critics throughout the French- and English-speaking world. V. S. Naipaul, author of *The House of Mr. Biswas* and *The Middle Passage* is a writer who belongs to all mankind. Another Trinidadian novelist, Sam Selvon, writes of his fellow countrymen with a Runyonesque touch. He has the great gift of laughter. Michael Anthony of Trinidad and Geoffrey Drayton of Barbados both excel in the creation of adolescents. Their

7 *Looking across Long Bay, British Virgin Islands*

worlds are poles apart, but both have produced authentic representations of West Indian life which help the readers to understand the fundamental simplicity of people who live close to the soil. George Lamming of Barbados is capable of fine poetry, and uses the raw dialects of Barbados to great advantage in *The Emigrants* and *In the Castle of My Skin*. He draws from a rich vein of Barbadian common speech and strikes ore as quickly as does his fellow countryman Austin Clarke, who lives in Canada.

St Lucia is the island of Garth St Omer, whose novels faithfully reflect the frustrations of those who seek to discover meaning from social life on small islands after contact has been made with other countries. Outlets for creative writing exist in BIM, a literary quarterly edited by Frank Collymore of Barbados and regarded by many as the seedbed of West Indian writing in the English language; *The Bajan*, a monthly magazine circulating in the East Caribbean; the *Journal* of the Barbados Museum and Historical Society; and *Caribbean Quarterly* published by the Extra-Mural Department of the University of the West Indies. The historical Society of St Lucia has done much to encourage research and discussions of historical interest and is deeply indebted to the Rev. Father Jesse and Mr B. H. Easter for their contribution.

The Barbados Museum, housed in a former military prison, is an outstanding cultural centre relatively rich in furniture, glass, stuffed fish and other items originating in the West Indies and overseas. The rapid progress of the Museum since 1948 has been due to the untiring energy and knowledge of its director, Neville Connell, who built on the solid foundations laid by the late Eustace Maxwell Shilstone, a Barbadian solicitor who was awarded an honorary master's degree by Durham University for his contribution to historical studies of Barbados.

In all the islands there is interest in archaeology which is receiving greater attention since the formation of the Congress for Study of Pre-Columbia cultures of the lesser Antilles which brings together experts from the Caribbean and beyond every two years.

The architecture of the islands reflects many levels of social achievement of the past and present. Forts and military fortifications are impressive. Fort Richepanse south of Basse Terre in Guadeloupe, Fort St Louis at Fort de France and Fort Napoleon at Bourg follow the style of the great seventeenth century fortresses in France. Brimstone Hill in St Kitts was completed in 1690 and has ever since been known as the Gibraltar of the West Indies. The ruins at Shirley Heights, Antigua, speak eloquently of an age when empires were won or lost with the whiffs of cannon shot, while Nelson's Dockyard below recalls the days when supremacy at sea was earned by men who sailed and fought in ships. In Barbados there are many buildings which survive from the centuries of war and help to explain why Major George Washington described the island on a visit in 1751 as an 'intire fortification'.

Conspicuous among them are the military prison, the old Guard Room with Clock Tower and the red brick living quarters which surround the Savannah.

In St Lucia there is a remarkable cast-iron building, formerly a barracks, dating back to 1833, while the old Fort and Army Post on the Morne overlooking Castries has been converted into a complex of monuments, technical and academic schools, research laboratory and Museum. El Morro in old San Juan, Puerto Rico dates back to 1539 and San Cristobal to 1634. There is also a Naval and Military Museum at San Jeronimo.

The French built many churches, some equipped with elaborately carved altars. Interiors frequently have barrel-vaulted naves. In the early cathedral of St Marie de Guadeloupe in Basse Terre and in the Church at Marin in Martinique the classical façades resemble French eighteenth-century styles; in Barbados the Church of St John is a replica of many an English country church.

The Catholic Cathedral in Castries St Lucia offers an

example of the use of cast-iron for peaceful purposes. In Kingstown, the capital of St Vincent, there is a cluster of fine churches – the Anglican cathedral, the eighteenth-century Methodist church and a Catholic presbytery which is known locally as the wedding cake and offers samples of Norman, Saxon, Saracen and Moorish styles with cloisters, turrets and perambulatories. Impressive Anglican churches have survived in St George's, Grenada and St John's, Antigua, while the Catholic churches of Basseterre St Kitts, Roseau, Dominica and Marie Galante symbolise the deep religious and cultural influences of the Roman faith.

The Regency Government House overlooking St George's Grenada has one of the finest locations in the West Indies, looking on to the sea on one side and on the other facing the mountainous, tree-clad interior.

Barbados is still relatively rich in architectural heritages, of which Codrington College with its Palladian façade is the most remarkable. Farley Hill, where Royalty and other famous personages were sometimes entertained, was temporarily restored to its former glory and embellished by carpenters and gardeners of 20th Century Fox as the Fleury home in *Island in the Sun*.

One of its permanent features is the provision of slits in the outer walls upstairs from which rifles might be trained upon rebellious servants or slaves. St Nicholas Abbey, still used as a comfortable country house, is unique in the West Indies and closely resembles a small English manor house. Drax Hall, another of the earliest great houses, contains a staircase built of a local hard wood which has been extinct for centuries. It has been acclaimed as one of the finest colonial stairways surviving in the hemisphere.

The original castle built by the Lord family on the southeast coast is similar in design to other mansions in France, and is noteworthy for the battlements on the roof, a feature which early writers specially recorded about Barbadian great houses. Bridgetown has some attractive warehouses near the sea front, many of which are being converted into modern offices.

Several of the homes which have been constructed or renovated in Barbados by settlers since 1939 are of exceptional architectural interest. Heron Bay, Heronetta, Bachelor Hall, Glitter Bay, Holders, Crystal Springs, Maddox and Welches are outstanding, but many others on beachlands or hills are tributes to the architects who designed them. Like the houses at Mill Reef, Antigua, these new homes have challenged older styles of buildings and in consequence some West Indians are gradually being weaned from the wiles of jerry builders to an appreciation of architecture.

Unfortunately many of the attractive features of nineteenth-century houses, such as jalousies, window bars, sash windows, fretwork decorations, wooden porches, verandahs, welcoming steps and shingled roofs have become expensive items of luxury today and craftsmen skilled in such work are disappearing along with joiners and other manual makers of chairs, tables and other household furniture. Efforts are being made to stimulate architectural studies at the University of the West Indies and to train workers for the building boom. It is to be hoped that, as a consequence, mass production and new techniques will not entirely replace the skilled worker whose contribution to West Indian culture through the ages has been considerable.

Allied to furniture making as an art is the craftsmanship of those who make mats, baskets, wooden trays, fish nets, hammocks, pottery, turtle and other shell work and a wide assortment of articles which are produced in cottages for sale to residents or tourists. Most of the island skills have been introduced from outside the Caribbean. As a result of teaching by foreign nuns Dominican straw hats have acquired a vogue throughout the Caribbean and have been exported to North America.

The skills of West Indian women are exploited by some American manufacturers who employ workers in the islands to do smocking or piece work for dresses.

Wrought-iron gates and wrought-iron furniture have become popular in the islands in private homes and hotels. They are in great demand for burglar proof windows, patio tables and chairs, and as gates.

Sculptors and painters are to be found in all the islands and some painters in the larger islands have discovered how to live from the sale of their work. Small canvases in Barbados have been sold for as much as $2,000 United States to visitors.

Average successful painters charge somewhere between $200 and $600 West Indian for paintings which remind buyers of beautiful scenes of native life.

The West Indies have not produced folk or religious artists comparable with Hector Hippolite, the Voodoo priest of Haiti. African influences are rare. Styles are largely representational of beauty spots with occasional excursions into caricature. More sophisticated painters who have studied art in North America or Europe show influences which are derived from these countries. American visitors prefer to buy what they call 'primitives'. Art is popular on the islands and is encouraged and taught in most schools. Children's exhibitions are held frequently and sidewalk and gallery art shows are put on regularly for tourists in Barbados and other islands.

Music, singing and dancing are essential ingredients of West Indian popular culture, especially in islands with French and Spanish association.

Children respond to the beat of music almost from the moment they can walk. From infancy Africans beat out their rhythms on drums, rattles and percussion instruments. Singing, dancing and music have always had religious as well as social significance and in days of slavery offered the only spiritual or 'soul' exaltation possible for those whose bodies were traded and regarded as commodities. Cuba is the island pre-eminent for the blending of African and Spanish dances. It has given the world the rhumba, the conga, the guaracha, the bolero and the mambo. Puerto Rico is the mother country of the plena, and San Domingo of the merengue. Martinique claims the beguine as its own, while Trinidad is, above all islands, the land of the calypso, a folksong hurriedly composed as a commentary on topical events and not unlike a Greek chorus in its audacious references to people in high places. In more recent years Trinidadians complain of a tendency for calypso to degenerate into crude obscenities. Other islands have borrowed calypso as a medium of flattery for politicians or patrons and for purposes of political propaganda.

Calypso dancing is closely allied to 'bop' or 'bebop' which originated in the United States amongst the negroes of Harlem. It comes into its own at Carnival time in Trinidad where jump-up, calenda, limbo, Bongo, Bel Air, Beguine, Shango and the Road March shatter bourgeois respectability and release the ecstasies of the descendants of Africa and of those who share some of their blood, or who are simply caught up by the infectious gaiety and abandon of the Carnival spirit. All the islands which are or have been French celebrate Carnival.

Closely allied to the calypso is the music of the steel-drums, which in recent years have replaced stolen garbage cans on which makers of music used to beat out their soul music, when drumming was prohibited by law. Before the era of the garbage can, in the bad old days of slavery, bongo drums used to be the accompaniment of calypso commentaries. When these could not be obtained bamboos were knocked together, or beaten with sticks or rammed. Bamboo music, the forerunner of the modern steel band, was known as 'Bamboo-tamboo'. Today the Trinidadian is still adept at accompanying calypso by beating any two objects together. In a public restaurant these can take the form of a knife and a glass or a coffee cup and a spoon. Making music is a part of Trinidadian life.

Today the steel drums are eminently respectable and recognised as distinctive West Indian instruments of music. Beethoven, Mozart, hymn tunes and church music are reproduced on steel drums as impressively as on more conventional instruments.

Europe also influenced West Indian dancing and folklore.

The minuet, the rigodon, the contradanza, the Spanish danza, the Austrian waltz and the Polish mazurka and the French quadrille were introduced by Europeans, but they were seen and copied by the African population of the islands. St Croix has preserved a dance jig with recitation, Irish jigs and fiddle playing were very popular among the white poor of Barbados, while minstrel singers with guitars still play for gain in some parts of the islands.

The guitar is a natural accompaniment of the Barbadian folk song with their 'bumpety' lilts, so well illustrated in 'The Buggy'.

> *Bought a buggy for two and sixpence,*
> *two and sixpence, two and sixpence*
> *Bought a buggy for two and sixpence*
> *Me and my wife drive out.*
> *When the buggy get old and rusty*
> *old and rusty, old and rusty*
> *when the buggy get old and rusty*
> *Me and my wife fall out.*

Repetition is the main feature of West Indian folk songs and sometimes is responsible for an almost supernatural note of reverence as in the refrain of 'murder in the market' where voices chant:

> *Payne dead, Payne dead, cold dead;*
> *Payne dead, Payne dead, cold dead*
> *Payne dead, Payne dead, cold dead*
> *Bessie Thomas she kill Payne stone dead.*

The religious forms of dance are strongest in Haiti, but Shango in Trinidad still has its ceremonies and dances derived from the worship of the Yoruba god whose characteristic is to 'strike violently and bewilder'. The Shakers and other emotional religious sects, although nominally Protestant Christians, do, in their rituals of possession and trance, stimulate dancing which will probably be regarded by most non-members of the sect as uninhibited, if not orgiastic.

Several wayside chapels rely on the music of tambourines to attract their worshippers, while 'religious picknickers' in buses praise God with enthusiastic banging of tambourines and singing of hymns as they roll merrily along 'Barber green' highways or cavort around very narrow country lanes.

West Indians are superstitious. In Barbados in recent years a priest had to complain to the postal authorities because someone had used the postal services regularly to send his cook dead chickens to 'work obeah' on her. White rum is rubbed on the hair with garlic to prevent 'snakes' from 'entering the brain', white cocks and goats are sacrificed, frogs are made 'to eat' summonses so that the case will go in favour of the 'victim' and not of the courts.

The Cannon ball and silk cotton trees are the natural 'spirit' trees of the obeah man. It only takes a bundle of coloured rags, a vial of dirty water, a few strands of human hair, a dead frog on a doorstep to put shivers in the heart of credulous West Indians or to send them scurrying to an obeah man to break or send back the spell.

In St Lucia taxi-drivers claim to have regular clients who come from all over the Caribbean each year to consult 'practising doctors' who specialise in love philtres and are said to treat only those who can afford to pay well. *Kembois* or *Chembois* is the French version of Obeah and is known by these or similar names in St Lucia and Martinique. The *chemboiseur* has a collection of working materials almost as fantastic as those of Granpa Munster in the television programme. Among them are parrots' beaks, cats' skulls, bones from a rattle snake's tail, dogs' teeth, grave dirt, pins and miniature coffins, holy oil and books on the magic art. The most dangerous of all the tools of the magic workers are 'art books'. More than one murder in the islands during the past two decades is attributed by barristers to ideas learnt from magic art books which have been imported from the United States.

For purposes of *chembois* in St Lucia human bones and human flesh are taken from graves. Mourners throughout the islands remain at the graveside until the coffin has been well and truly buried under six feet of earth and so is relatively free from tampering by obeah practitioners.

Superstition in the West Indies originated in other countries besides Africa.

The 'witch pots' of Dorset and Devon have been likened to the obeah bottle of the islands, while the Irish took their superstitions as well as their faith with them when they were deported by Cromwell. *Loups-garou* and succubi, spirits who turn into vampires by night, were almost certainly 'introduced' into the French islands by criminals and other undesirables who were deported from France in the early years of settlement.

Sir Hesketh Bell, who wrote a book on witchcraft in the West Indies in 1889, describes a book, which was published in New York in 1878 and regularly imported into the islands for purposes of witchcraft, as a 'dangerous' publication. West Indians, like human beings anywhere, are superstitious, some more than others. Under the influence of religion, education and higher living standards it would be strange if the hold of obeah, and fear of duppies and zombies does not weaken where it has not already been relaxed. But the hold of superstition is great. Like ghost or horror stories, tales of obeah men, vampires, diablesses and other weird creatures will survive in West Indian history for as long as men and women are human, and delight in hearing tales, strange, wonderful and horrible. When West Indian dramatists and players find audiences large enough to sustain their art in the islands, they will have much rich material with which to plot their plays.

The dance theatres of Jamaica, Trinidad and Barbados and the dramas of Derek Walcott already indicate the evolution of dramatic art which may some day be as identifiable with the West Indies as cricket, calypso or literature. So far the drama has been largely confined to amateur performances, in schools and by dramatic societies like the Barbados Green Room Theatre, of classic or popular drama from overseas.

Chapter 5
Unity and Diversity

What unites the islands, the sea, also separates them. The islanders when they travel are always 'foreigners', and to be 'foreign' in the West Indies is to be undesirable. To be a St Lucian, a Trinidadian, a Barbadian is to be a person, to be a 'foreigner' is to be an outcast, a pariah. The extensive dislike of St Lucian 'foreigners' in Barbados can be illustrated by the exchange of obscenities which may be heard in the inner careenage of Bridgetown when a motor vessel leaves for Castries. The instinctive dislike of the Barbadian man in the street for the St Lucian 'foreigner' is deep-rooted and personal; it has nothing to do with the political or religious differences which are also conspicuous at other levels of intercourse.

To be a Trinidadian is to be a person, to be a 'coolie man' or an East Indian is to be undesirable. To be a 'West Indian' is to aspire to something which has not yet happened in the islands. Too many influences keep tugging apart the slim cords of unity which men of vision have groped to find throughout centuries of exploitation, slavery, imperialism and fragmentation.

The ex-British West Indian people are all survivors of trading settlements, inheritors of divided societies, individuals struggling to achieve identities. In Martinique and Guadeloupe and its dependencies islanders are full citizens of France, and in no way legally inferior to Frenchmen born in the home country. They are French citizens sharing in the benefits and responsibilities of French citizenship. They are not Frenchmen living abroad: they inhabit departments of France. Administratively such an arrangement is difficult: distances are real, local problems or difficulties tend to become 'national' in France, and the presence of France in the West Indies adds to the divisive force which hampers the growth of regional West Indian co-operation.

It should be realised, on the other hand, that the power of France in the Caribbean can prevent revolutions such as those which have followed independence in Haiti, San Domingo and Cuba. The fact remains that Port of Spain or Willemstadt has to deal eventually with Paris about Martinique: no final answer can be given by Fort de France to proposals affecting French sovereignty over the islands.

The presence of the Netherlands is very real too in the West Indies, since the Dutch colonies were integrated into the Kingdom by the Union of 1954. Dutch 'integration' does not prevent the expression of discontent in the Antilles when decisions which are unpopular are made in Holland. Riots in Willemstadt in 1969 and diversities of interests between Dutch-born and Antillean Netherlanders illustrate how difficult it is to reconcile West Indian and European influences.

The people of Puerto Rico have been given several opportunities to become independent from the United States, but the advantages of full economic union and American citizenship have so far triumphed over the wishes of a minority who seek separate Puerto Rican nationhood. Since 1952 the island has enjoyed internal self-government, while defence and the handling of international affairs in Puerto Rico remain the responsibility of the United States. Entry into Puerto Rico is equivalent to entering the United States for the traveller, as the posters at the airport proclaim.

The American Virgin Islands, though technically colonies of the United States are so close to the mainland that they can be considered as small outposts of the American way of life and are favourite retirement centres for well-to-do Americans.

Over a five-year period from 1964 to 1968 the number of tourists, mostly American, going to St Thomas, St Croix and St John were 923,025, the second largest number in the Caribbean after Puerto Rico with 1,030,840. By comparison Jamaica, the third leading tourist resort of the region had no more than 396,447.

The United Kingdom never offered the inhabitants of its Caribbean colonies the opportunity to choose between integration and independence. Political leaders of the islands had no alternatives to independence, except the preservation of colonial status or the unsatisfactory associated statehood which was devised for some of the Leeward and all of the Windward group.

The goal of 'dominion' status which was the West Indian objective immediately after the war, foundered on the shoals of a dissolving empire, a movement largely spearheaded by Canada – and made possible through the lack of policies which could create effective regional, economic, financial, administrative and inter-connecting structures.

A stop-go attitude was adopted in London and reflected in the island capitals.

Political federation of the entire British Caribbean was encouraged at the same time as doses of increasing political power were ladled out to the 'big' islands. The larger federation of the West Indies, which required sacrifices of provincial power in favour of centralisation, was doomed to seem less important to local leaders, who were enjoying their very first experiences of power and who were extremely suspicious that Big Brother in the big island wanted to keep him down to size!

The isles which the Caribs inhabited during the early days of European 'take-over' differ physically, economically, politically and socially. All have evolved from European absolutist and imperialist systems whose gods were racial superiority, mercantilism and oligarchy, and whose altars were lit to the adoration of mammon. Other influences filtered into these non-communities and non-societies: religion, education, humanitarianism, sport, dancing, travel, metropolitan habits, sexual intercourse between master and slaves with consequent fusion of races, common endurance of catastrophes like earthquakes, volcanic eruptions, hurricanes, plagues, floods, droughts, and constant wars. Some islanders who accumulated money could maintain exclusive attitudes to 'the negroes' and if also of light pigment could easily emigrate to their respective 'mother' countries. Others found outlets for emigration by signing on as workers on ships, or sought new opportunities in the great cities of the United States: more found temporary occupation in Panama, Cuba, San Domingo or Brazil.

The majority remained in the crucible which was painfully transforming men and women of toil into aspirants for better living. They had some compensations.

All the islands have easy access to the sea, and enough trees, from which simple boats and rafts could be built. Fishing and hunting developed habits of self-confidence and self-reliance. Rain forests, mountains, lakes and rivers in some islands added variety to a life nourished and sustained by the sea and sun. Availability of land for peasant owners, freedmen and slaves bred habits of industry and established traditions about suitability of crops, seasons and times of planting. The introduction of European trees, flowers and fruits created oases of gardens and sometimes parks. Pigeons, birds, dogs and horses were kept as pets. West Indians adore animals, despite instances of cruelty.

The rainbow of human relationships had many hues. Avenues were open to the professions. Universities in Europe and North America welcomed young men who would return to their islands as doctors, dentists, lawyers and teachers after graduation. The civil services, the schools, the Churches, agriculture and commerce offered executive posts to some islanders. Persons of colour in the islands and in Guyana reached posts of great distinction in the overseas service of France and England. A black man, Mr Eboue, became governor of a French West African colony, some men of colour became governors in British colonies and others reached high rank in the Home and Indian Civil Services and a few were elected to parliaments in Westminster and Paris. One of these told me that his father was a priest in Grenada.

Before the nineteenth century closed there was throughout the islands a recognisable meritocracy of coloured families whose loyalties were sincerely European but whose way of life was essentially West Indian. Their pride of achievement, their bourgeois standards of respectability, their unwillingness to be regarded as 'fourth class' or anything less than 'first class' citizens, provided the yeast which gave rise to the public opinion which was expressed or shouted at street corners, reflected by locally owned newspapers or outlined in speeches made in legislative assemblies. While they achieved influence and made social and economic progress, the coloured West Indian middle class lacked adequate political support until they left the ivory towers of their personal achievements and went into the market place and cane fields where the vast majority of West Indian workers had been waiting without much hope.

The West Indian social revolution, as distinct from the occasional social explosions of rioting and violence, began when leaders of the coloured West Indian middle class made actual contact with the barefoot proletariat through the formation of political cells and trade unions. Groping beginnings were made during the interval of peace between 1918 and 1939, but the workers' movement gathered impetus during the Second World War and dominated West Indian thought and life in the latter half of the 'forties. In the late 'fifties and early 'sixties the experiment of the West Indies federation failed, largely because of its anaemic central government, a creature of Jamaica and Trinidad. It had no powers of taxation and no money to spend other than the contributions given grudgingly and these mainly by Jamaica and Trinidad. Only massive sums of money could have transformed islands, where the accumulated poverty and neglect of centuries had bred slum cities and insanitary hovels, into the miniature Edens which tourists find today in nearly all the islands. The federation had little more than a cap and an extended hand to offer potential donors. The great majority of the islanders were slum dwellers and no statesman, particularly one without any real basis for his temporary power, could ask slum dwellers to tighten their belts. Slum dwellers don't wear belts!

In marked contrast with the failure of political federation has been the expansion of tourism. Rocky, unkempt, infertile areas of land close to beaches have become playgrounds for the rich. Flowering trees and ornamental plants have replaced tangled shrubs and vines; roads have been made from dirt tracks; desirable resort homes are to be found on every island landscaped against backgrounds of beaches, islands, mountains and blue seas. The rich and the famous early began to seek their own society at Mill Reef Antigua where the American architect Happy Ward designed tropical homes for those who sought their sunshine holidays in elegant surroundings. One Mill Reef resident is reputed to have spent over one million dollars on her home. Mill Reef Club wisely opened its doors to some of Antigua's politicians and prominent citizens but is still primarily an exclusive resort where the former Jacqueline Kennedy, Paul Mellon, Dean Acheson, Archibald McLeish and other world-famous men and women could have nature and themselves for companions. The Mill Reef type resort has been copied or adapted to suit other income groups in several islands. It remains an original design for gracious living and harbinger of a different tourist wave which offers new employment opportunities, larger contributions to island revenues, and free publicising by internationally famous people of the islands which history forgot until American soldiers rediscovered Antigua in the late war years. The American naval bases in Antigua, St Lucia and Trinidad gave the British islands a foretaste of the American tourist invasion which began in the mid-forties and which has been coming in a jet stream ever since.

Rum was to meet a new partner in coca cola. The marriage is still celebrated in the most nostalgic of West Indian

8 Bacolet Bay, Tobago

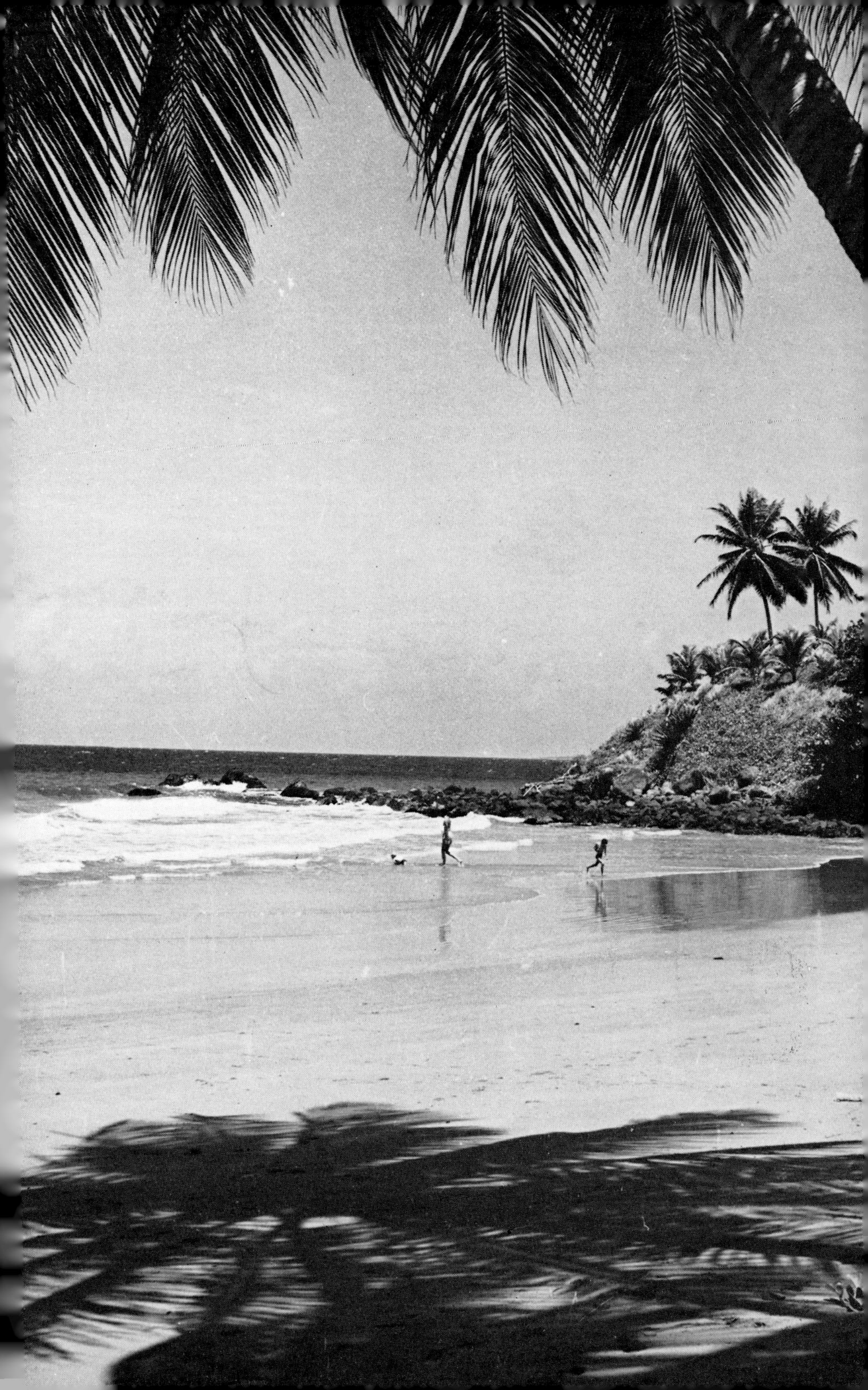

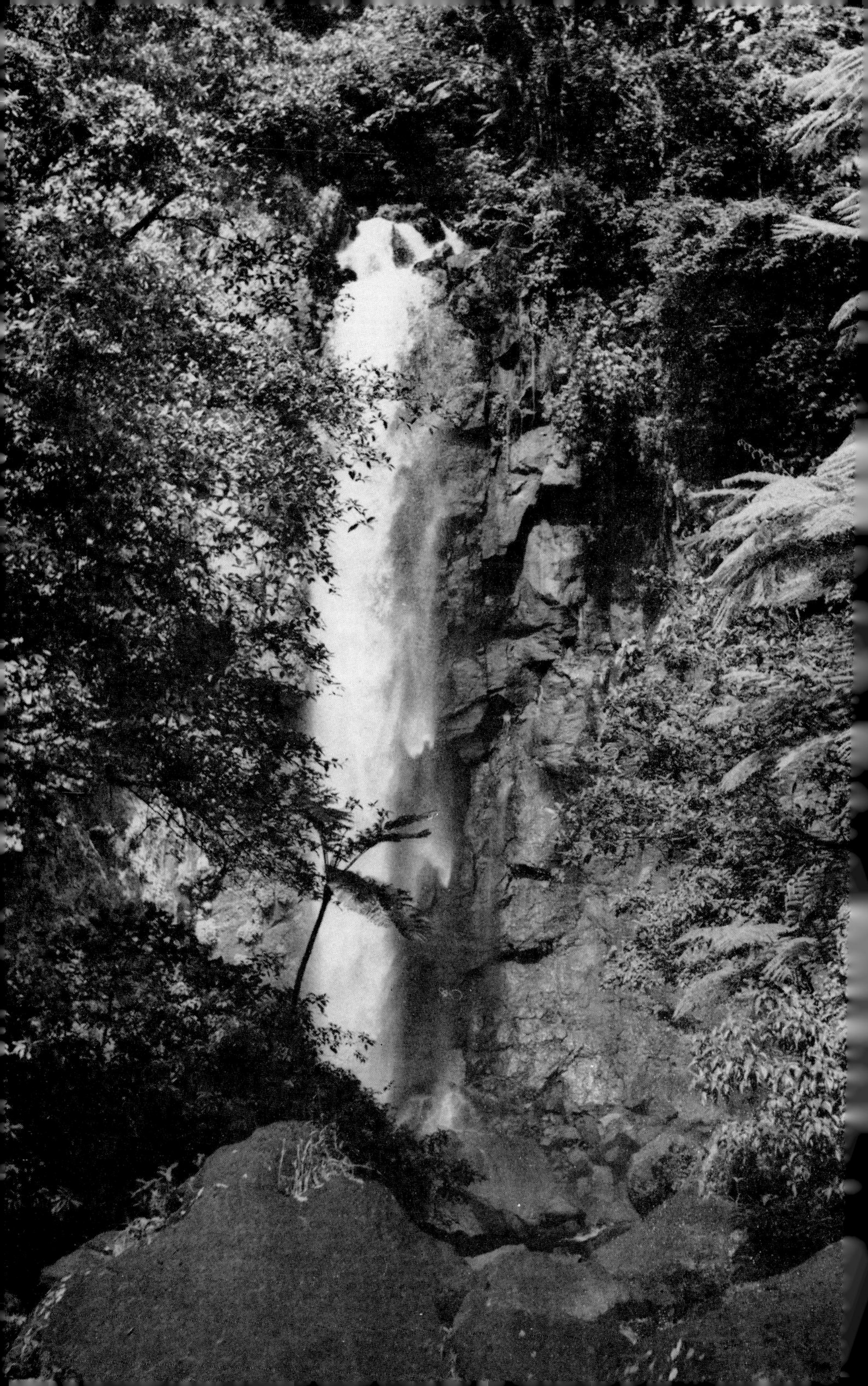

calypsos, unless we give precedence to Brown Skin Gal, which lamented the plight of ravaged West Indian maidenhood as poignantly as Puccini's arias reproached Pinkerton for abandonment of his loving Butterfly.

The barefoot islanders found that tourism brought to their backyards people who had money to spend and who were willing to pay prices beyond the reach or inclination of their own West Indian employers and much higher than their trade unions were prepared to ask for them. Personal contacts with visitors also offered opportunities for emigration and travel. West Indians moved from island to island in the British group, found employment in the American Virgins, or went to work in the United States. Tourism offered quick opportunities for lifting the young West Indian up by his own boot straps, up from a life of toil, hardship, or unemployment in an island hovel to the bright lights and 'honky-tonks' which even in a small West Indian island spelt excitement and adventure, for those on whom darkness normally fell, like tons of coal, at 6 p.m. in the winter and at 7 p.m. on summer evenings.

Conservative elements in the islands rightly saw in tourism a challenge to their own established hierarchies, but the lure of greater profits made their resistance little more than verbal. Tourism meant gain in economies which had become stagnant. It offered chances to West Indians who were emigrating in their thousands to seek, as one young Barbadian schoolgirl leaving for England put it, *her* place in the sun. It created new job opportunities in airports, harbours, hotels, restaurants, night clubs and with real estate and tour operators as well as in building, banking, shops and boutiques. It demanded new skills from electricians, plumbers, carpenters, joiners, sanitary engineers. It provided new livelihoods from sea sports, fishing, cruising, market and flower gardening, handicrafts, painting, sculpture, dancing, singing and music making. And above all it offered hope to those who had almost given up hope of better living.

9 Falling water, Dominica

II FOREGROUND

Chapter 6
The French Islands

The Caribs called Guadeloupe Karukera which means 'l'île aux belles eaux' (The Isle of Beautiful Waters). From the air it resembles a giant butterfly with wings spread out. Guadeloupe is in reality *two* islands separated by a thin channel of the sea, the Rivière Salée. The two islands have an area of 583 square miles, more than three times that of Barbados and nearly half the size of Trinidad. Grande-Terre is a low lying island and has the capital city Pointe-à-Pitre with a population of over 60,000. It has excellent roads, rolling hills and sugar plantations. Most of the modern hotels are situated along its coastline and beaches. The inhabitants of Pointe-à-Pitre are called Pointus. The town was founded by the English whose redcoats took over the island in 1759. It was named after a Dutch Jew 'Peter' who fled from Brazil in 1654 and settled in Guadeloupe where he was a pioneer in sugar cane culture. Pointe-à-Pitre has a sugar factory which throws ash over the town during the grinding season. Close to the city a sign near a sugar mill is inscribed 'danger of slipping' because of slivers of cane syrup in the road. The Careenage at Pointe-à-Pitre, like that of most islands, is picturesque. Double-masted schooners come alongside the streets, as in Bridgetown, while cattle are taken aboard alive with other goods. Opposite the careenage a park commemorates the guillotine which lopped off the heads of Royalists during the Republican revolution led by Victor Hugues. Pointe-à-Pitre, the commercial centre of Guadeloupe, has none of the charm of Christiansted, the Danish-built town of St Croix in the American Virgin Islands, but its shops are filled with French perfumes and other luxury goods imported from France. The town is higgledy-piggledy when compared with Fort de France with its imposing savannah and its charming French homes.

By contrast its airport at Raizet is attractive and was earmarked to be the first West Indian airport to receive the 'Jumbo-jets' the large Boeing 747s.

Gosier is the site of a club-restaurant 'Au Grand Corsaire' and a pergola-type resort which may be considered as a pioneer of Guadeloupe's tourist development. Three miles south-east of Pointe-à-Pitre it was founded by a member of the Petrelluzzi family, an Italian name as famous in Guadeloupe among travellers as Parravicino has been in Barbados for over 50 years.

About four miles further east from Gosier is the splendid coconut-fringed, white, sandy beach of St Anne, as 'dreamy' a beach as any to be found in 'tropical paradises', lapped by seas which God created for water skiing, sailing and underwater swimming. Immediately overlooking this beach the luxury 100-roomed hotel 'La Caravelle' designed by the French architect M. Bruyère seems anchored like a sinuous pleasure liner and was the first international hotel to be built in the French Antilles. Other first-class hotels, inclusive of a Holiday Inn, are planned for St Anne, which offers cockfights as a subsidiary tourist attraction. The season opens in mid-November. Point St François at the extreme eastern tip of Grande-Terre, the Pointe de Châteaux is reminiscent of Brittany; there huge waves dash against the rocks and send up high columns of spray into the air. The 'castles' have been formed over the centuries by the action of the waves upon the rocks. From the Pointe de Châteaux there is a clear view of Désirade, which got its name because it was the first land to be seen by Columbus on his second voyage to the West Indies from Spain. Désirade, which is a mountain with a table land on its summit, is easily reached by air and sea. It is un-

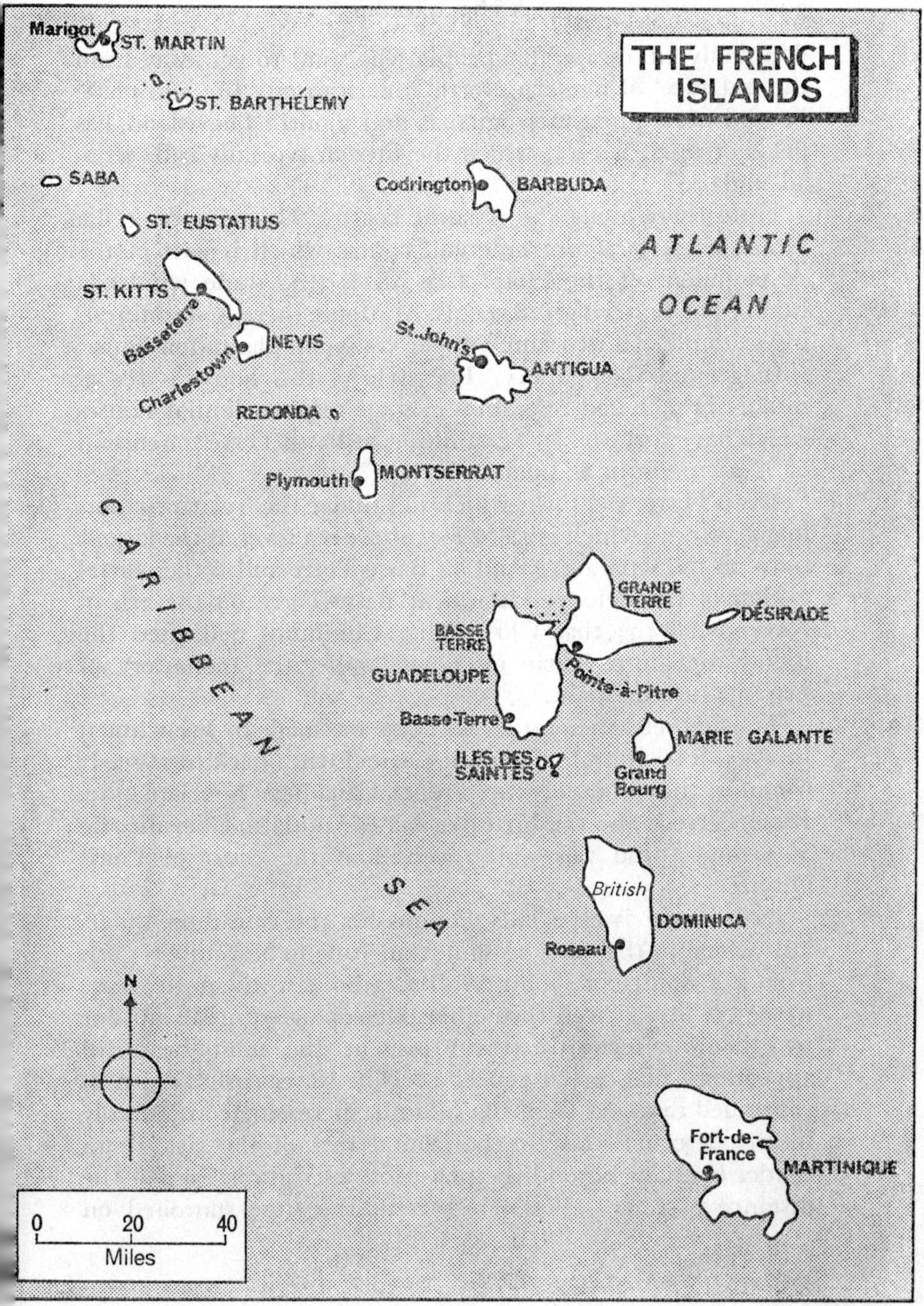
THE FRENCH ISLANDS
Marigot
ST. MARTIN
ST. BARTHÉLEMY
SABA
ST. EUSTATIUS
ST. KITTS
Basseterre
NEVIS
Charlestown
REDONDA
Codrington
BARBUDA
ATLANTIC
OCEAN
St. John's
ANTIGUA
Plymouth
MONTSERRAT
CARIBBEAN
SEA
GRANDE TERRE
DÉSIRADE
BASSE TERRE
GUADELOUPE
Pointe-à-Pitre
Basse-Terre
MARIE GALANTE
ILES DES SAINTES
Grand Bourg
British
DOMINICA
Roseau
N
Fort-de-France
MARTINIQUE
0
20
40
Miles

doubtedly an 'escape' for people who want to get away from the 'rat race' of modern North American city life and chase instead after pheasants, iguanas and ajouti. The island has fields of upright cacti which the French typically call 'têtes-à-l'anglaise'.

From there along the Atlantic coast of Guadeloupe at La Moule there is a nine-hole golf course which is part of the development of the Hotel Les Alizés (the trade winds), a luxury hotel offering 128 rooms. At Moule there is an interesting example of a two-storey upper verandah plantation house, with ground-floor gallery. The style of this house is recognisably French and resembles in some respects similar houses which have survived on Martinique, at Basse-Terre the capital of St Kitts and in St Lucia.

Basse-Terre, the town which lies under the 'relatively dormant' volcano which is 4,802 feet above sea level, is the largest town on the separate 'island' of Basse-Terre and is the official capital of Guadeloupe. It was at Basse-Terre on the 4th of November 1493 that Christopher Columbus dedicated the island to Sainte Marie de Guadeloupe, the monastery at Estremadura in Spain.

The first settlement at Basse-Terre was made by Frenchmen in 1635. The church of Mount Carmel dates back to 1683. It contains the tomb of the French-Canadian Bourlamaque. Basse-Terre is also the birthplace of the mulatto Chevalier de St Georges who was well received at the court of Louis Quinze.

Basse-Terre is especially famous for the cascading waterfalls which in the rainy season, from June to November, gush from La Soufrière. John Waller, who saw them in 1807, wrote: 'when viewed through a telescope at sunrise, and for two hours afterwards (they) present the most beautiful appearance that can be conceived. The water rushes down in continued cataracts from the summit, increasing considerably in the descent: this the horizontal rays of the rising sun render brilliant beyond the power of description, even at the distance of forty miles.' He was at the time stationed on

Guadeloupe's dependency of Marie Galante then under British control. The ascent to La Soufrière is made from St Claude, where the Prefect of Basse-Terre has his official residence. The way is very narrow but is negotiable by car for at least one thousand metres. From there an hour's walk will bring you to the summit where bloom the famous tiger orchids, which are also called orchids of the volcano. A Mackintosh is needed, as rains are frequent and the air is cold.

The south-east side of Basse-Terre is especially scenic, with rivers running down to the sea and in some places waterfalls. At Trois Rivières where there is the Grotto Caraibe with rock paintings done by the Indians boats leave for the Saintes, a cluster of islands named by Columbus on All Saints Day. There are four major islands and six smaller in the group. Off these islands, Rodney, with 50 shops, defeated the armada of Admiral de Grasse and prevented the French attack on Jamaica.

Between these islands and the western side of Guadeloupe sailing ships are wary of the Guadeloupe calm, where it is possible to lie for days without moving. The view has been expressed that it was due to the Guadeloupe calm that the British fleet was able to catch up with de Grasse and engage him off the Saintes. The fishermen who live on the islands of Terre-de-Haut and Terre-de-Bas are of Breton descent. One of the delicacies of the Saintes is roast iguana. The islands can also be reached from Basse-Terre by sea and from Raizet by air. Yachtsmen of experience say that the harbour at Bourg des Saintes is the best to be found in the East Caribbean.

On top of the Ilet à Cabrit is a restaurant operated by Mario Petrelluzzi the owner of Au Grand Corsaire at Gosier. Fort Napoleon on the crest of the mountain on Terre d'en Haut was used during the Second World War as a prison for Frenchmen who protested against the Vichy administration which was established in Guadeloupe and Martinique.

Most of the inhabitants of the Saintes and Marie Galante are white. It takes only 20 minutes to fly to Marie Galante, an island with beautiful beaches which reminded John Waller of Barbados. He was particularly enthusiastic about a lagoon near the bay of St Louis.

'A more beautiful sheet of water,' he wrote, 'was never seen than this, winding round the basin of the hills, as beheld from their summits....'

From Marie Galante the lofty mountains of Dominica are visible, and Martinique can be seen on a clear day, as well as Guadeloupe, the Saintes and Désirade. To Waller a great part of Marie Galante recalled the 'idea of an English gentleman's park' and he concluded that because of its 'internal and external prospects, there are few places perhaps on the globe that can vie with it'. Today the island still offers rustic charm and the coastal road which passes through Capesterre, Grand Bourg and St Louis is as scenic as any to be found in the West Indies. The island named by Christopher Columbus after his vessel, may yet justify the praise lavished on it by the Royal Navy surgeon who spent more than six weeks there when the island was under British occupation during the Napoleonic wars.

The Saintes, Marie Galante and Désirade are neighbouring dependencies of Guadeloupe. Saint Martin, which is shared between the French and the Dutch, and St Barthelemy also depend on Guadeloupe, but lie north of the British Leeward group and are scattered among the Netherlands Antilles of which Saint Maarten, the Dutch part of St Martin, St Eustatius and Saba are the northern half and the ABC islands of Aruba, Bonaire and Curacao are the southern.

Two stories are current as to how the French got the larger portion of St Martin. Both begin with a Frenchman and a Dutchman standing back to back at Cupecoy Bay and walking along the coastline in opposite directions, the Frenchman towards the north, the Dutchman going south. The Frenchman according to one version of the story drank wine and travelled faster, the Dutchman was slowed down by too great an intake of beer. The second version says that both men started out with flasks of fresh water, but whereas the Frenchman refreshed himself only with the pure liquid, the Dutchman laced his with old Dutch gin which made him so drowsy that he fell asleep under a tree, while the Frenchman plodded on till the two met at Oyster Pond. Whatever the truth of the story the island has been shared between the French and the Dutch since 1648. Marigot is the principal town of the French part and is the seat of the sub-prefect and municipal council. The island is mountainous and has beautiful beaches. Both the Dutch and the French parts are being developed for tourists and frequent air and sea communications make St Martin a good jumping off ground for exploration of the neighbouring Dutch and British islands. Its beaches are chalk-white and its water crystal clear.

The journey by sea from St Martin to St Barthélemy (better known as St Barts) is a prospect of high islands. Saba on the starboard is visible seventy miles distant on a clear day. Straight ahead tower St Eustatius and St Kitts, while on the port side lie a cluster of small islands and rocks like signposts leading to St Barts. La Fourche has a genuine pirate's cove lying between two cliffs with deep smooth water. The island, a paradise for goats, is thickly covered with cacti. St Barts is only ten minutes by air from St Martin and one hour's flying distance from Guadeloupe. It is the modern successor to St Eustatius as the freeport of the West Indies.

The motto of Gustavia, the beautiful capital and port of St Barthélemy may be summed up in the words of the song which was very popular in the islands during the late 'forties: 'Enjoy yourself'. Yachtsmen love the island because they can get supplies there duty free and they escape the tiresome small island formalities normally connected with entry and clearance. St Barthélemy, like St Martin, had been French since 1648 but the island was given to Sweden in 1784 in exchange for the use by the French of Gothenburg as a free port for their goods entering Sweden. At least two natives of St Barts in 1969 had been born there during the Swedish regime which lasted until 1887.

Since Scandinavian Airlines System began operations in

the East Caribbean Swedish journalists and broadcasters have given much publicity to the island which Sweden administered for 93 years before selling it back to France. The majority of today's population of 2,200 persons on St Barts are descendants of French men and women who went to St Barthélemy in the seventeenth century from Normandy, Brittany and Poitou.

Quite unlike any other Caribbean island, Saint Barthélemy is a quiet pastoral unspoilt place. It has some beautiful white sandy beaches, but its greatest appeal is for sailors and yachtsmen who can stock up with six months' supplies of the cheapest liquor to be had in the Caribbean.

The Caribs who exterminated the peaceful Arawaks on Martinique sometime during the eleventh or twelfth centuries called the island Matinino, or Madinina, which in French means 'L'île aux fleurs'. A Norman squire Belain d'Esnambuc took possession of Martinique on September 15, 1635 in the name of the French King. His settlement at St Pierre was made from St Kitts.

Peaceful coexistence with the Caribs did not last longer than 1660 when the French drove them out.

Martinique has always been the heart of France, as Barbados has always been the heart of England, in the Antilles. The French made their own corner of France in Martinique as the English made their Little England, their Oxford, Cambridge, Hastings, Land's End, Cheltenham, Bath and little Bristol and Trafalgar Square in Barbados.

The best known Martiniquan of all was to become Empress of the French. She was Marie-Joseph-Rose-Tascher de la Pagerie who was born at Trois Ilets in the significant year 1763, the year in which the British restored Martinique and Guadeloupe to the French, making them into strongholds of resistance, defences and trading stations for the Americans who were soon to strike the blow which would shatter the first British Empire into pieces. From Martinique, which became the principal French naval station in the Caribbean, the Marquis de Bouillé, governor-general of the French

Windward Islands, won several of the British islands during the American revolutionary war against England. The boot was on the other foot during the French Revolution. French Royalists co-operated with the English forces and Rochambeau, nephew of Lafayette, was obliged to hand over Martinique to the English in 1794. The English held it until it was restored to France by the Treaty of Amiens in 1802. They were to hold it again between 1809 and 1814 and for a short period of Napoleon's return to Europe from Elba. It has been wholly French since 1815. Slavery, which had been abolished in 1794 by the Convention, was restored by Bonaparte in 1802 and was not finally abolished until 1848.

Fort Royal, which was renamed Fort de France in 1802, had been the seat of government since 1681, but St Pierre which was totally destroyed by an eruption of the volcano at Mt Pelée in 1902 excelled in social, cultural and commercial life and was regarded as the Paris of the West Indies. The ruins of the Théâtre Royale at St Pierre suggest the extent of French cultural penetration in pleasure-loving St Pierre where on 8th May 1902 30,000 inhabitants were engulfed in the fiery inferno which had been threatening for days but whose signs were ignored by many in authority.

North of St Pierre at the fishing village of Precheur, Françoise d'Aubigné who, as Madame de Maintenon, became the mistress and later wife of Louis XIV spent her childhood. Over on the peninsula of Caravelle on the Atlantic side of Martinique the ruins of the castle which belonged to the family of Dubucq de Rivery can still be seen. A daughter of this family, Aimée, after a convent education in France was captured by pirates off the North African coast and was presented to the Sultan of Turkey Abd-ul-Hahmid by the Bey of Algiers. She became the favourite in his harem and the mother of Mahmud II whom she was able to influence in later years and to persuade of *la mission civilisatrice* of France. The girl from Caravelle gave birth to a sultan; her playmate from Trois Ilets gave Italy a Viceroy, Eugène de Beauharnais, Holland a Queen, Hortense, France an Empress, herself, while her grandson was to rule the Empire as Napoleon III. No one can explain why the island of flowers should have produced so high a proportion of crowned heads; no more than they can explain how a diminutive island like Barbados can have propagated so many famous cricketers. Perhaps the power who fashions human affairs likes continuously to remind men that great things can be done, even in sleepy villages like Nazareth. Napoleon from Corsica, Alexander Hamilton from Nevis are further examples of the role which small island birthplaces have played in human destiny.

The Savannah where in the twilight the belles of Martinique take their walks was reclaimed from the sea. There at the beginning of Lent 50,000 Martiniquans prepare for the burning of King Vaval, who is the Creole embodiment of European Carnival. On Ash Wednesday, the day of the 'diablesses', the carnival reaches its apotheosis, when the whole population of the city, wearing white and black, passes through the streets groaning and howling as the music throbs from the bands. At nightfall on Ash Wednesday Vaval is burned while the crowd parades around his pyre carrying torches. The carnival period can begin as early as January.

The Savannah of Fort de France has been a battlefield four times, once against De Ruyter's forces in 1674 and three times against English troops in the following century. The power of the French Navy in the Caribbean is still symbolised by the naval headquarters at Fort St Louis.

A magnificent view of Fort de France can be had from Fort Desaix or the Chapelle du Calvaire.

The Martiniquans know how to cook fish as excitingly as their names. In the *restaurants typiques* you can enjoy balaous, carangues, bonites, coulirous, dorades, orphies, or stuffed crabs. Fort de France boasts of the Caribbean's only four-star restaurant, The Foyal. The classification is approved by the Tourist office which also grades hotels. The most beautiful of the simple bridges in the West Indies is in Fort de France. It is the Pont de la Rivière Madame, but it is used by fishermen and well deserves the French witticism that 'Les mesdames sont toujours très parfumées'.

Other perfumes of far more delicate and widely sought aromas are obtainable at Roger Albert's, the most popular shopping centre in Town and the 'largest dealer in perfumes' in the Caribbean.

The luxury four-starred Bakoua hotel (bakoua is the Carib word for straw-hat) is only ten minutes boat trip across the water to Anse Mitan. Not far from the hotel at Trois Ilets is the church with a silver virgin where Josephine was baptised in 1763. At La Pagerie, Doctor and Madame Rose Rosette have created a museum which is dedicated to the memory of the Martiniquan girl who became Empress.

The Martinique Hilton, five minutes drive from Fort de France, has 154 air-conditioned rooms with balconies facing the sea and lies in a 12-acre park on a bluff overlooking the Caribbean sea. It has an elegant casino and a nightclub.

Marin, which has a baroque church, is worth a visit on Saturday when the gommiers, Carib type boats hollowed and rounded out of the gommier trees, spread their strange sails for the races. Nearby at St Anne are white sandy beaches fringed with sea grape and coconut trees. (The sands at Carbet, where Columbus first landed are black.)

The St Lucia channel divides Martinique at Pointe des Salines from the northern tip of St Lucia. At the extreme left of this channel, less than two miles from the shore at Diamant lies the famous 'HMS *Diamond Rock*'. On this rock Admiral Hood in 1804 supervised the offloading of five cannons which were hauled up to the summit 574 feet above sea level. The rock, manned by one officer and 120 men and boys, was a thorn in the flesh of the French, who after a bloody battle commanded by Villeneuve in early June 1805 recaptured it. Later in the year he was to lose the most famous sea battle of all times off Trafalgar.

Macouba, the most northern point of Martinique, is the Carib word for fish. The drive between Macouba and Grand Riviere offers a sudden view of Dominica across the channel which is named for that island.

French is spoken and understood by everyone, but the patois creole is the language of everyday use. The patois of Martinique is very close to that of Guadeloupe, French Guyana, Haiti, Reunion, Mauritius, St Lucia and Grenada. The syntax of Creole is influenced by African languages, but the form of words originates with French and has some borrowings from English.

A number of Carib words survive in place names such as Macouba, Carbet, Ajoup-a-Bouillon, in flora such as manioc, ananas (pineapple) and guava, in fauna such as colibri (humming bird), ajouti, anoli, lambi, balaou and in articles of use such as coni, hamac (hammock) and canari.

While the béguine is typical of the French Antilles, African dances survive in the interior of Martinique. Among them are the calenda, haute-taille, lelaghia and bel-air. Among the Hindus a ritual dance of the sabre is performed to the accompaniment of tambourines. Worthy of a visit are the Hindu temples at Fonds Saint Denis and Basse Pointe.

The people of Martinique are descended from white creoles or 'békés', Africans, orientals from India, China and Annam, and Europeans known as 'békés-France'. The population exceeds over 325,000.

Guadeloupe and Martinique are both departments of France and each sends to Paris three members of the National Assembly and two Senators. Guadeloupe has a prefect at Basse-Terre and sub-prefects at Pointe-à-Pitre and St Martin. In Martinique there is a prefect at Fort de France and a sub-prefect at Trinité. Both departments have a general council of 36 whose main function is to vote on the budget. Both departments are divided into 34 communes administered by a mayor, deputy assistant and a municipal council. All representatives to Parliament, Senators, Council and Communes are elected under universal suffrage.

The main products of Guadeloupe and Martinique are sugar, bananas, and rum. Martinique also exports fresh and tinned pineapples. Crayfish are exported from St Martin.

THE FRENCH ISLANDS

The French Caribbean represents a market of over 600,000 with a *per capita* income of $600 US. As in most of the islands the income is far from evenly distributed, the majority living at subsistence level.

As departments of France Martinique and Guadeloupe are full members of the European Common Market. All the products of the islands can be exported to Europe free of quantitative restrictions or customs duties.

Investors in the two departments not only have access to a market of some 200 million consumers but can buy semi-finished goods as raw materials in the Common Market countries and sell them on their local markets or in North or South America.

Only Puerto Rico, which has access to the North American market, offers as great an economic potential in the Caribbean, as that available to the French and Dutch territories.

The road network of Martinique and Guadeloupe covers a total of more than 2,000 miles. A dual highway links Fort de France in Martinique with the airport and industrial area, and absorbs the traffic from the South and East of the island.

In Guadeloupe a scenic throughway links the Caribbean to the Atlantic coast.

GENERAL INFORMATION

Guadeloupe

Churches The bulk of the population are Roman Catholic. In every township there is a church.
Climate Mild and humid, tempered by trade winds. Temperature ranges from 68° in winter to a high of 88° in summer. (Quite cool in the mountains the year round.) There are three seasons, the rainy season being from July to November – torrential rains punctuated by bright sun; the coolest weather from December to March, with warm dry weather from April to July. The island of Grande-Terre has no rainy season and is dry all year, with infrequent showery rains.

Clothing Light washable summer clothes may be worn the year round, though a light wrap (it may be only a sweater) is advisable. Men don't have to wear ties and coats at dinner, though most do.

Communications Telephone, telegraph, and telex. Communications facilities throughout the islands are good.

*Currency** French franc=5.51 (46 N.P.) to American dollar; 5.50=1 Canadian dollars and 3.06=1 E.C.$. Canadian and US dollars, as well as travellers' cheques are accepted.

Documents required No passport is necessary for a stay of up to 10 days. Only a certificate of smallpox vaccination not more than three years old and a return trip ticket are needed. Documentary proof of citizenship (with photograph) is required if you have no passport.

Electrical current The supply to hotels and domestic consumers is at 220 volts A.C. The plugs comply with the Common Market standards: different from the American ones.

Food and Drink Creole dishes and French cuisine, with emphasis on seafood, may be had as well as tropical fruits. Sea turtle is prepared in various ways, stuffed crab with rice, stewed conches and octopus, curry dishes, kid with saffron, roast wild goat, jugged rabbit, fricassee of racoon, ragout of water-fowl, river fish, and such delicacies as broiled dove or skewered larks!

Native drink is rum, excellent and cheap, fixed in many ways but perhaps best in the famous Antilles rum punch. French wines, champagne and liqueurs are in great supply and cheaper than elsewhere.

Holidays and Festivals All Catholic holidays are celebrated, also Bastille Day (July 14) and Armistice Day (November 11). Mardi Gras or Carnival is extremely gay and colourful, reaching a climax on Ash Wednesday though celebrated from New Year's on with singing, dancing, parades and masquerades.

Language The official language is French; however Creole is common and in general use. English and other languages

*All currency equivalents are approximate only.

10 The cathedral in Fort-de-France, Martinique

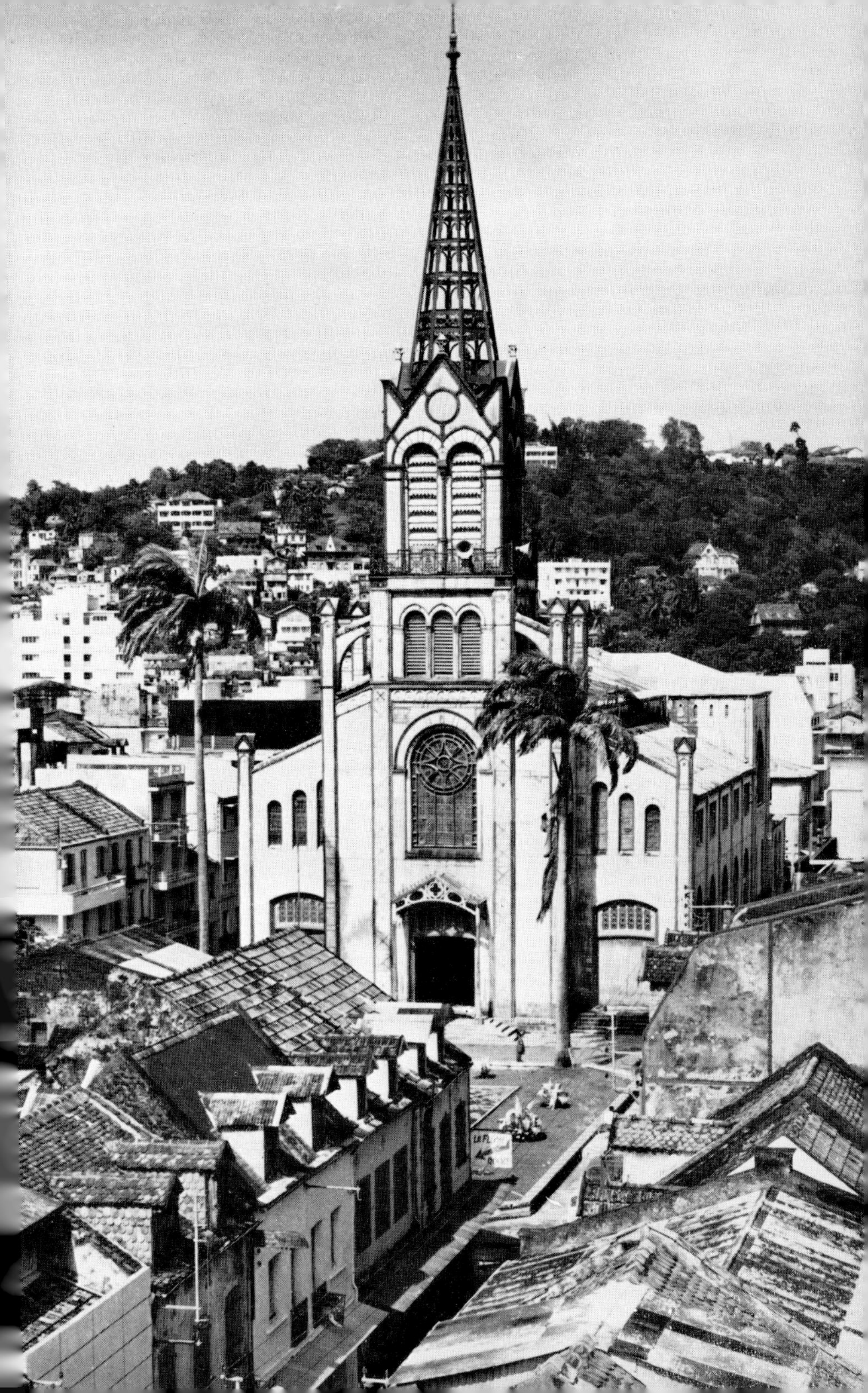

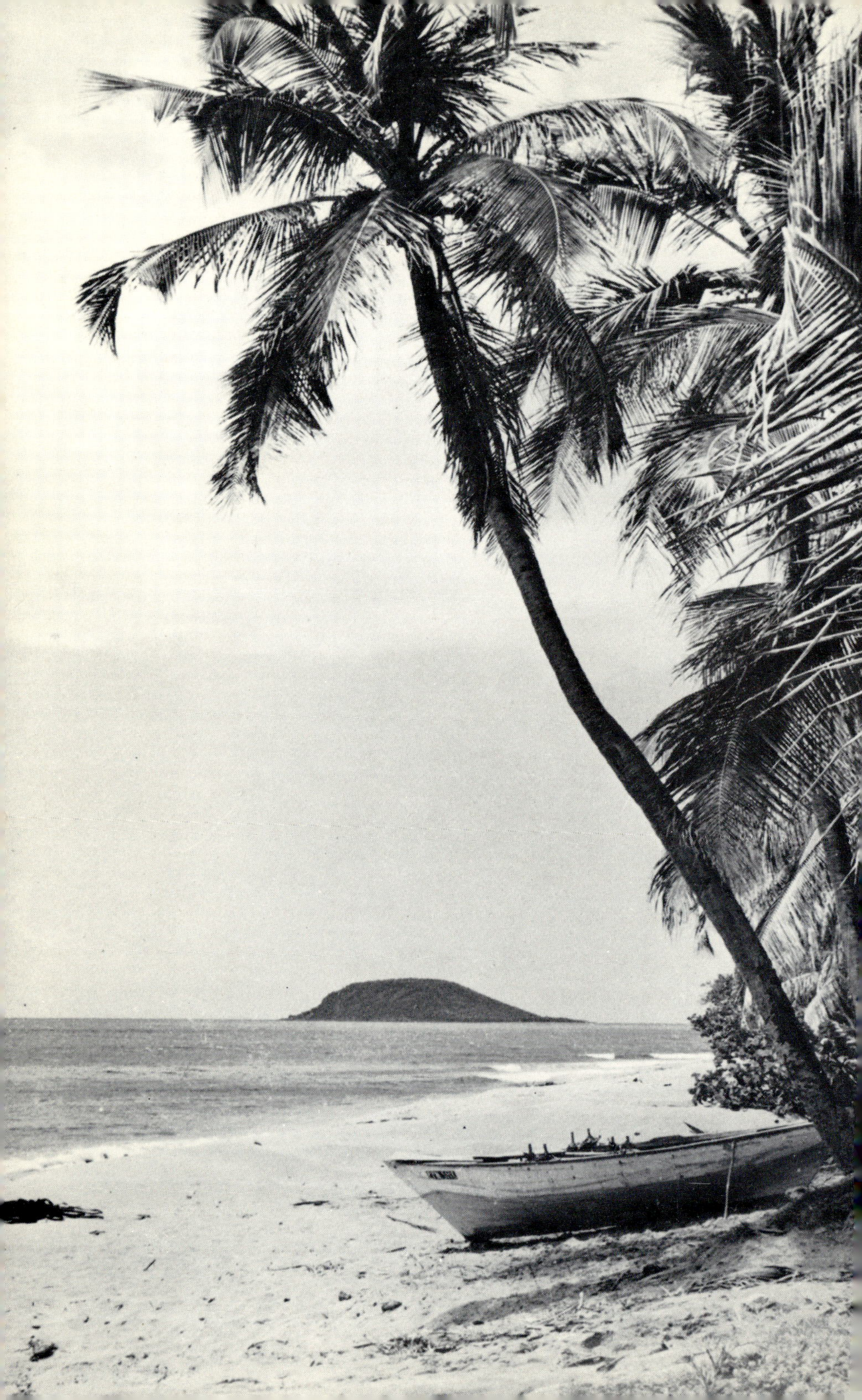

are spoken by personnel at hotels, restaurants and tourist facilities.

Laundry and Dry Cleaning 48-hour laundry service available. Pressing done by maids at hotel – two-hour service. Dry cleaning in town.

Local Courtesies and Customs Hand shaking is customary when greeting or leaving people. Women wear slacks, shorts or mini-skirts in city. Men not obliged to wear a coat or tie in restaurants.

Medical Facilities Modern medical facilities are available throughout the major islands.

Night Life During Carnival, dances held every Saturday and Sunday evenings. Dancing at Maripeim, Boukarour, Cocoterais and discothèque La Pillule on Saturday night all year long.

Other Tourist Facilities Movies (French and American films). Bridge at private clubs.

Pets and Animals A certificate against rabies not older than one month, and good health certificate not older than three days are requested.

Food and Restaurants French cuisine and delicious Creole dishes are offered at low price French wines are available as well as local island rums.

Sports Mountain trips, swimming, power and sail boating, hiking, tennis, bicycling, fishing, spear fishing are among the chief participant sports. Soccer games and cockfighting are considered the more popular spectator sports. Golf at Alizés Hotel.

Time One hour later than Eastern Standard Time.

Tipping 10% to 15% for service rendered by waiters and other persons who perform special services. Hotel adds service to the bill.

Transportation Taxis, buses and rental cars available on major islands. Power boats and sailboats may be rented. American and Canadian drivers' licences are honoured for rental cars. Rental cars, as well as cars with guides, are also available.

11 Beach at Deshaies near the Club Mediterranée, Gaudeloupe

Water Drinking of local water is now safe since installation of purification and chlorination plant. The French prefer their water out of bottles.

What to See POINTE-À-PITRE – BASSE-TERRE TOUR An extremely picturesque road between the sea and mountains passes through Petit Bourg, Goyave, Capesterre, Trois Rivières, Dole and Gourbeyre. The tropical vegetation is magnificent. Beautiful viewpoint overlooking the Saintes islands and the British island of Dominica. At Sainte Marie, visitors may see the spot where Christopher Columbus landed. For the return trip, drive through the charming mountain villages of Saint Claude and Gallard.

LA SOUFRIÈRE EXCURSION The dormant volcano is an impressive sight with its emission of steam, sulphurous gases and boiling water. Starting points for this unforgettable trip are Basse-Terre and Saint Claude. After driving through the magnificent Bains Jaunes forest, a good road takes one to the summit of the volcano, from which a view of the entire island may be had.

BASSE-TERRE – POINTE-À-PITRE via the Côte-sous-le-vent: The road follows the coast very closely, skirting a number of delightful small coves and passing through the picturesque villages of Vieux Habitants, Bouillante and Pointe-Noire. In some parts it passes through areas of dense vegetation. As one approaches Deshaies the country opens up, giving way to a number of wide beaches from which the island of Montserrat may be seen. The road then traverses large sugar plantations, passing through Sainte-Rose Lamentin and Baie-Mahault. The bay of Grand Cul de Sac Marin is the underwater fisherman's paradise.

CIRCULAR TOUR OF GRAND TERRE, with its rolling hills and sugar plantations, possesses all the charm typical of the Antilles. The road passes by Fort Fleur D'Epée, an eighteenth-century fortress, and the scene of desperate fighting between the English and the French; then, following a sea bright with many colours it makes its way through Gosier, Sainte Anne, Saint François, the wild and rocky

Pointe des Châteaux, Moule and Morne-à-l'eau. It is also possible to make the return trip via the 'Grand Central' road, which passes through Anse Bertrand, Port Louis and Petit Canal. Grande-Terre has excellent beaches of fine sand and viewpoints overlooking the Saintes islands, Dominica, Marie Galante and Désirade.

BASSE-TERRE, the seat of the prefecture and the headquarters of the principal public services, is the historic capital of Guadeloupe. The town has a population of 15,000 and is a banana port of some importance. It is also the apostolic seat of Guadeloupe. Adjoining the town is the delightful residential district of Saint-Claude, the starting point of the Soufrière trip.

POINTE-À-PITRE, the commercial centre of the island and the seat of the sub-prefecture of Grande-Terre, has a population of 50,000. Its port, situated behind a magnificent roadstead, is a port of call for ocean liners and many cruise ships. It is also a centre for rum and sugar exporting. The town has a large number of schools, hospitals, consulates, banks, transportation companies and travel bureaux. It is also a lively shopping centre with picturesque markets. The island is also serviced by its international jet airport.

What to Buy French perfumes, cheaper than in France; Doudou dolls; French wines, champagne and liqueurs; native rum; fishermen's hats from Les Saintes; baskets; wooden objects (especially of aromatic vetivert wood); French luxury goods such as lingerie, scarves, gloves, silks; figures of shells and beads skilfully made. Recordings of Creole songs.

Rue Frébault in Pointe-à-Pitre is the shopping centre with many small simple shops in a concentrated area. Hours are 8 am to 12 am and 2.30 pm to 5 pm daily except Sundays, closed Saturday afternoons, though they stay open for cruise ships.

Information from:
The Tourist Office,
Place de la Victoire, Pointe-à-Pitre, Guadeloupe F.W.I.

Cable: OFTOGUA Pointe-à-Pitre
French Government Tourist Office,
610, Fifth Avenue, New York, N.Y. 10020
323 Geare Street, San Francisco, California 94102
1170 Drummond Street, Montreal, Canada

Commissariat Général au Tourisme,
8 Avenue de l'Opera, 75 Paris (1er) France

Also Travel Agents

Bibliography:
La Guadeloupe
Guy Lasserre
Faculté des Lettres, 26 Cour Pasteur
33 Bordeaux.

Martinique

General Most of the general information provided for Guadeloupe will apply to Martinique, which has more hotels, restaurants, clubs and cabarets.
Besides Soroptomists, Rotary and Lions, Martinique has riding clubs, tennis, yacht and sailing clubs and air and bridge clubs.
What to see FORT DE FRANCE The Fort St Louis began in 1640 contains a small historical museum and a zoo.
The Cathedral St Louis, built by Henri Pick in 1895, romanesque in style with byzantine decorations. Fine stained glass windows.
Bibliothèque Schoelcher: rococo style by Henri Pick.
The Sacré Coeur de Balata, built in 1929 in imitation of the famous church of Montmartre. Splendid view of Fort de France and Trois Ilets.
Visit the Fontaine Didier, mineral water spring.
ST PIERRE Approach by the coastal road which passes through picturesque fishing villages and Carbet where Columbus landed.

Visit the museum and return to Fort de France by the route called La Trace which passes through magnificent hill and country scenery.

LA PAGERIE can be visited by boat across the harbour, or by road which passes typical 'Habitations' or plantations of sugar cane.

Visit the museum which commemorates Josephine.

DIAMOND BEACH is attractive, but high seas sometimes make bathing inadvisable. Offers a splendid view of HMS *Diamond Rock*.

GRAND-RIVIÈRE bordered by high cliffs hanging over the sea offers the scenic grandeur of the Atlantic ocean and coastline. It is approached through the hill station of Morne Rouge, which lies under Mt Pelée, and on the coast through Masse Pointe and Macouba. Grand-Rivière is famous for the local dish of 'blaff', and gives a clear view of Dominica. Return by the coastal road through Lorrain, Marigot, Fond St Jacques (where monks of the Order of Preachers made Martinique's first rum), Sainte Marie and Trinité with its magnificent bay. The road overland between Trule and Fort de France passes through Gros Morne where the Courvilli rum distillery invites visitors to taste their product.

THE MARTINIQUE RIVIERA is the description of the pure white sandy beach at St Anne on the southern part of the island. The most southerly Pointe des Salines encloses the Savane des pétrifications where specimens of wood converted into stone may be picked up. From St Anne there is a good view of Diamond Rock and of St Lucia in the distance.

At Marin the seventeenth-century church has a marble altar.

MT PELÉE AND THE PASSES When climatic conditions are right and under supervision of a guide a climb can be arranged to the top of Mt Pelée. From the base of the mountain very hardy explorers can go through a dense tropical forest and cross the passes to the Rivière Falaise where the journey is continued by swimming.

Chapter 7
The Dutch Islands

Sombrero is the northern tip of a group of islands which include Anguilla, St Martin, St Barthélemy, Saba, St Eustatius, St Kitts, Nevis, Montserrat, Antigua and Barbuda. A low flat rock, 25 feet above sea level and about one mile in length, Sombrero is barren and has no landing place. Access is by means of a rope ladder. The island functions as a British Board of Trade lighthouse at the northern corner of the Anegada passage in which Prince Maurice was drowned.

Wrecks galore have been recorded along the reefs which sweep down the Atlantic as far as Barbuda. Anegada and Wickham's Cay are both being developed by a 37-year-old Englishman from Lancashire who has been given very favourable concessions by the British government. Anegada is the most easterly of the British Virgin Islands of which the best known are Virgin Gorda, Fallen Jerusalem, Round Island, Ginger, Cooper, Salt Island, Dead Man's Chest, Peter, Norman, the Dog Islands, Scrub, Great Camanoe, Little Camanoe, Marina Cay, Beef Island, Guana, Tortola, Frenchman's Cay, Little Thatch, Great Thatch, Jost Van Dyke, Green Cay, Sandy Cay, Little Jost Van Dyke, Tobago and Little Tobago. Most of some 8,000 British Virgin Islanders live on Tortola, where Road Town is the seat of government.

The American Virgin Islands of St Johns, St Thomas and St Croix were bought from the Danes in 1917. Two-thirds of St Johns which lies alongside Tortola is preserved as a national park. The islands are beautiful, expensive and

Americanised. The American influence spreads right into the British Virgins from San Juan from where hydrofoil trips to Tortola 80 miles away can be had for $10 US (in 1970). So Americanised is Tortola that East Caribbean currency in sterling is unwanted although technically the official currency is sterling. The dollar dominates, although house prices are quoted in sterling, rising as high as £20,000 for relatively small places.

Anguilla is a long flat island with fine white sandy beaches. Its highest point is 213 feet. It is so low that a yachtsman approaching from the Virgin Islands will not see Anguilla until he is ten miles off, whereas St Martin is visible 30 miles distant.

The people of Anguilla live by emigration, seafaring and salt. The largest salt pond is behind the village of Sandy Ground at Road Bay, the best harbour in the middle of the island. The Anguillans keep close contact with St Martin although the island is legally part of the British Associated States of St Kitts, Nevis and Anguilla. The island's declaration of 'independence' from St Kitts led to an invasion of British paratroopers in 1969. The future of Anguilla was still to be settled at the time of writing; a commission had been appointed by the British and St Kitts governments under the Chairmanship of Sir Hugh Wooding, a former Chief Justice of Trinidad, to make recommendations which should lead to satisfactory solutions of the 'unconstitutional dilemma' provoked by secession.

Geographical location is not the least of Anguilla's difficulties, since it is further away from St Kitts than it is from St Martin, St Barthélemy, Saba or St Eustatius. Whatever its political future may be, Anguilla, the eel-shaped island, 'Malliouhana' of the Caribs, will always be physically closer to St Martin and the Virgins than to St Kitts.

Four islands and over 60 miles of sea separate Anguilla from its 'parent' state of St Kitts, but some 550 miles of Caribbean sea separate the three miniscule islands of St Martin,

* In 1971 Anguilla became, at the request of the inhabitants, a colony of the United Kingdom.

St Eustatius and Saba from their fellow islands of Aruba, Curaçao, and Bonaire which lie to the north of Venezuela. Together the six islands comprise the Netherlands Antilles which is an integral part of the Kingdom of the Netherlands. The northern islands together elect one member to the Staten in Curaçao which has 22 members, of whom 12 are from Curaçao, eight from Aruba and one from Bonaire. A Lieutenant Governor or 'Gezaghebber' is appointed by the Dutch Queen for the Windward islands. He presides over the 15 member Windward Island Council which is comprised of five elected persons from each of the three islands. This council prepares the budget which is sent to Curaçao for approval.

Although located among the British Leeward islands, the three islands of St Martin, St Eustatius and Saba are described by the Dutch as 'Windward Islands' in contrast to the ABC islands which are far to the 'leeward' in the Caribbean sea. The Dutch include in 'the windwards', logically from their point of view, all the islands in the lesser Antillean arc between Puerto Rico in the North and Trinidad in the South. The Dutch followed the French and the Spanish in calling islands leeward and windward, according to the direction of the north-east trade winds as observed from the South American mainland. The British instead used their description to correspond to the strength of the trade winds. Accordingly the British divide the lesser Antillean arc into 'leeward islands' north of Dominica and 'windward islands' to the South.

St Martin, Saba and St Eustatius form a right-angle triangle with Saba in the centre. St Martin is 28 miles north east of Saba and St Eustatius is 19 miles south-east. Under favourable sea conditions journeys between the islands take from three to five hours. Saba may have been named after St Sabas, but other suggestions are Regina Saba (Queen of Sheba), 'Sabot' (the island is clog-shaped when seen from the north) or after the Spanish Sabado (Saturday), the day of its discovery.

Traditionally St Martin was named by Columbus on November 11, the day of St Martin de Tours. However some

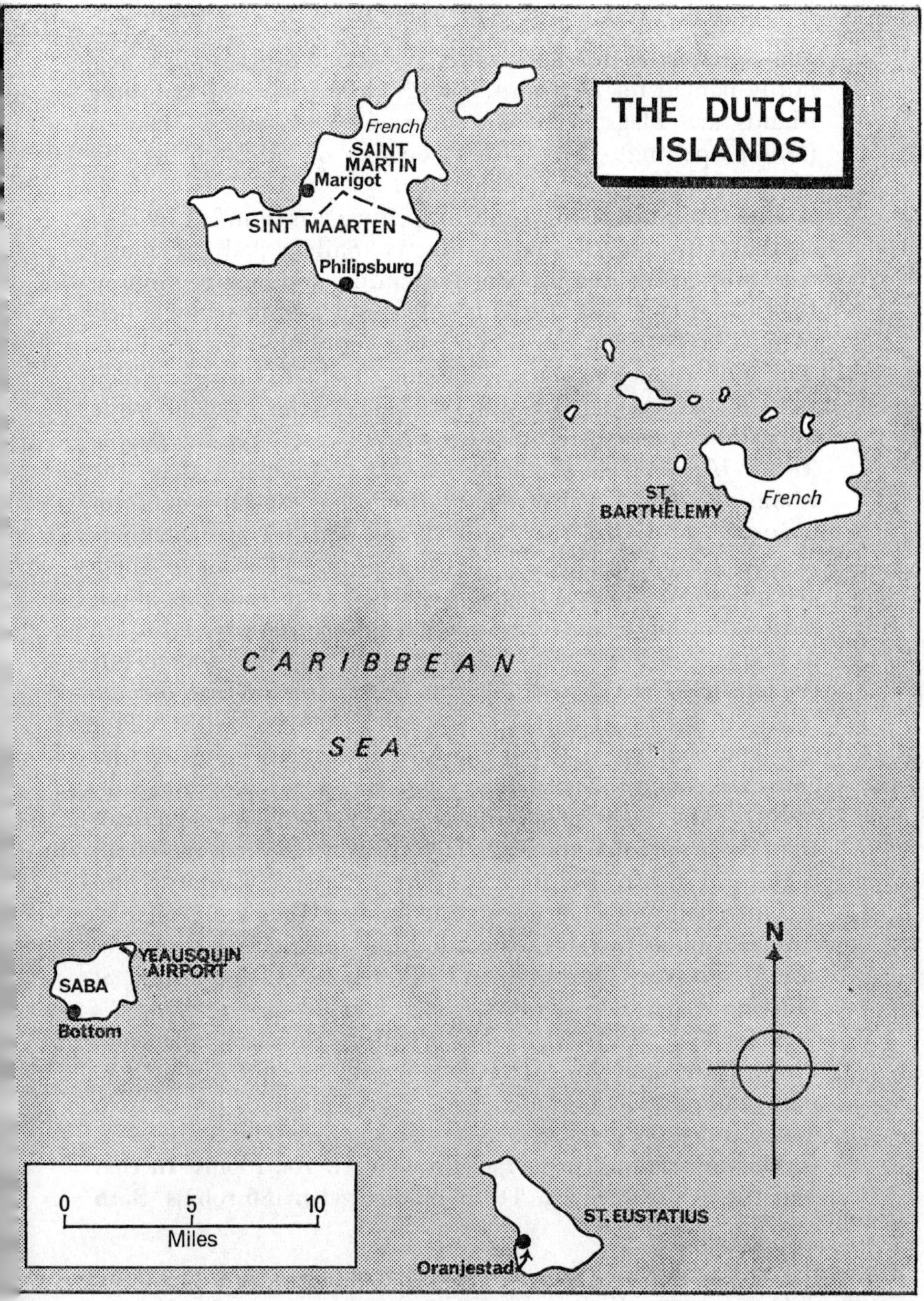
THE DUTCH ISLANDS
French
SAINT MARTIN
Marigot
SINT MAARTEN
Philipsburg
ST. BARTHÉLEMY
French
CARIBBEAN SEA
SABA
YEAUSQUIN AIRPORT
Bottom
N
0 5 10
Miles
ST. EUSTATIUS
Oranjestad

scholars reserve this honour for Nevis. St Eustatius was certainly named for the Saint. The highest points in the three islands are Flagstaff Mountain 1,266 feet on St Maarten (Dutch spelling), the Quill, 1,200 feet on St Eustatius and Mount Scenery, 2,890 feet on Saba.

The capital of St Martin, Philipsburg was founded in 1734 as the centre of the 'salt' industry. Sailors had previously used Simson Bay and Kay Bay for landing and loading. Simson Bay is a village almost exclusively comprised of white fishermen. The hotel on the beach has a reputation for sea food. The total area of St Martin is about 37 square miles of which the northern 20 square miles belong to the French, while four-and-a-half square miles are under water. Yet the people 'think big' and semi-official brochures proclaim that 'the island is fantastically suited for the establishment of industry', and that the Netherlands Antilles are members of the European Economic Community. To make these attractions more beguiling it is stressed that 'thoughts about nationalisation or any other alienation of property rights are unknown' on St Martin. The 'English' may be strange but the meaning is clear, as clear as the assurance that income taxes are low, that there is no capital levy, no withholding tax, and that profits from the sale of securities and capital gains are exempt from tax.

In St Martin as in all the Dutch, French and American islands, cars are driven on the right side of the road. St Martin is an ideal starting point for sea trips to Saba, St Eustatius and St Barthélemy. Yachts, sloops and fishing boats are available. Information as to rates, schedules and reservations is obtainable from the Harbour and Transport Corporation, St Martin.

A 60 foot ketch with 280 hp diesel engines sails from Philipsburg daily for St Barts at 9 a.m. and returns at 5.30 p.m. The fare (last quoted at $20 US) includes lunch with wines and 'unrestricted' bar. Until 1969 the largest hotel in St Martin was the Little Bay Beach with 105 rooms. In that year the St Maarten Isle Hotel opened with 186 rooms. Both these hotels have casinos.

Sentry Hill in the fertile Cul de Sac Valley, when seen from the east resembles the reclining face of an Indian, and is for this reason called the Reclining Face. St Martin is ideal for those who love to be in and on the sea. Its bays on the southern and western sides are popular with water-skiers, snorkelers, swimmers and fishermen. There is a nine hole golf course on the slope of Little Bay Hill.

Inhabitants of other islands call Saba 'Napoleon's cocked hat'. It rises steeply from the sea to a height of 2,890 feet, and is only accessible at three small bays where the beaches are hardly more than six feet in length. These beaches are at Spring Bay, Ladder Bay and Fort Bay. The capital village of Saba, the Bottom, is 700 feet above sea level and occupies a relatively flat area of 200 acres. The village is completely surrounded by mountain tops. An old 'road' leads up by 800 steps to the settlement of Crispin, but a taxi can travel by the picturesque winding new road which climbs first to St Johns (1,000 feet), passes the village of Windward Side which lies 1,400 feet above sea level, and ends at Hell's Gate (1,700 feet).

From Hell's Gate there is an uninterrupted view of St Barts, St Martin, Anguilla and two of the Virgin islands. The summit of Mount Scenery is reached through a forest of tree ferns. Mountain begonias and bananas also thrive there. Looking eastward from the summit, St Eustatius, St Kitts, Nevis, Redonda and Montserrat are visible.

Below Hell's Gate a small airstrip has been built at Flat Point. Some Sabans regret this concession to the modern age, but the facility will be appreciated by anyone who does not like the rough sea which almost habitually surrounds the island. During the hurricane season Saba can be isolated by sea for a week at a time. Red brick chimneys, green and red doors and red roofs make the well-kept houses of Saba very attractive, especially when they are surrounded by flowering roses, hollyhocks, marigolds and zinnias. Saba was once famous for its shoes (the French priest Labat wanted to call the island St Crispin), but the main occupation of its womenfolk today is drawn-thread work. Most of the men live by seafaring and the island has produced several captains of ocean-going liners and many inter-island schooner captains. Limited agriculture is possible on an island which has a maximum of 540 acres suitable for crops, yet the Sabans love their land on which tomatoes, cauliflowers, beans, peas, melons and similar crops can be grown.

Because of the topography of Saba, settlements had to be widely separated and are perhaps for this reason also 'racially' separated. The population of the Bottom for example is nearly all white, while Upper Hell's Gate is mostly white and Lower Hell's Gate largely coloured. Saba is a unique island and it is difficult to imagine it ever supporting more than a few thousand people.

St Eustatius, which is almost rectangular, has a total area of 8.2 square miles. The coasts are less steep than those of Saba and there are small beaches on its bays. At Orange Bay there is a black sand beach. On the bluff above in the town of Oranjestad most of the island's thousand inhabitants live.

The remains of a synagogue, a roofless Dutch Reformed Church, and ruins of forts and warehouses recall the days before the third of February 1781 when Rodney reduced the 'Golden Rock' from splendid prosperity to almost 'nothingness'. St Eustatius knew its greatest prosperity during the war of the American Revolution, its proudest moment when on 16 November 1776 a salute to the United States Flag was fired from Fort Orange in reply to a gun salute from the brig of war *Andrew Doria*. The occasion was officially acknowledged by Franklin Delano Roosevelt when a tablet was unveiled on December 12, 1939 on St Eustatius recording that: 'Here the sovereignty of the United States of America was first formally acknowledged to a national vessel by a foreign official'. The foreign official was Johannes de Graaaff, Governor of St Eustatius. On November 16, 1961 the Postmaster-General of the Netherlands Antilles issued a special stamp to commemorate the first salute to the Union flag.

The American attachment to the action of the Dutch commander in 1776 may better be appreciated when one reflects on the statement made in 1781 by an English peer: 'If St Eustatius had disappeared under the sea three years ago, the American war of Independence would now be finished.'

St Eustatius' prospects depended on the existence of mercantilism. Today its future and the future of the islands in this group depends on the degree of co-operation in the region which will make the words 'West Indian' more than a geographical expression. The future of the three Dutch Windward islands is for historical reasons geared to the future of the three Dutch Leeward islands. The traditions of the mercantile past have no use for logic, even through the international' impact of tourist development is gradually washing away old concepts.

GENERAL INFORMATION

Dutch Windward Islands

Location 150 miles east of Puerto Rico; 550 miles NE of Curaçao. St Maarten is Dutch portion of 37 square mile island shared with French. Saba is five square miles. St Eustatius eight square miles.
Population St Maarten 5,077, Saba 1,136, St Eustatius 1,326.
Language English, Dutch, French, Spanish.
Seaport Philipsburg, Great Bay, St Maarten, can accommodate ships over 700 feet, with 30-33 feet draught.
Documents required A passport or other means of identification (usually not required), US air passengers need vaccination certificate, proof of citizenship and onward destination ticket.
Customs No duties. Port is completely free.
Health No formalities.
Currency Netherlands Antilles florin, equivalent to 53 US cents.
Electricity 110 volts AC 60 cycles or 208/220 volt, 60 cycles.

Water Most hotels serve purified water.
Postage Airletters to all destinations. 0.20 florins. Postcards (maximum five words) 10.10 florins.
Climate Between 80° and 84° Fahrenheit by day.
Time One hour ahead of Eastern Standard Time, five hours behind GMT.
Churches Anglican, Roman Catholic, Methodist, other denominations.
Pets and Animals No restrictions.
Clothing Summer sportswear; light wrap for winter evenings: jacket and tie for men in hotels.
Tipping Service charge in some hotels; ask local advice.
Banks Banco Popular Antilliano NV. Windward Islands Bank Limited (Cable Bank, St Maarten).
Laundry There is one laundry and dry cleaning shop in Philipsburg, the capital of St Maarten.
Extra charges In addition to the ten per cent service charge there is a five per cent room tax on all hotel rates. A discount of 10 per cent is offered on stays of eight days or longer.
Casino At Little Bay Beach and St Maarten Isle Hotels.
Travel Agents Representative of American Express and Thos. Cook, S.E.L. Maduro & Sons, St Maarten.
Transportation Tours through Taxi Association and car rentals agencies. Prices controlled by government.
Sports Swimming, boating, sailing, deep sea and spear fishing, scuba and skin diving, glass-bottom boat, water skiing, bicycling and horse riding.
Eating Dutch, French, Indonesian and Creole cuisine.
Shopping Hours Monday to Saturday 8 a.m. to noon, 2 p.m. to 6 p.m. Extensions on cruise ship days.
What to Buy Sleiff animals, beaded and leather bags, Dutch pewter and Delft ware, gloves, perfumes, watches, crystal sterling silver, Bone and Copenhagen china, cameras, cashmere, Thai silk, Madeira embroidery.
Holidays January 1, Good Friday, Easter Monday, April 30 (Queen's Birthday), May 1 (Labour Day), May 23 (Ascension Day), June 3 (Whit Monday), December 15 (Kingdom Day),

December 25 (Christmas) December 26. Tourist shops open for cruise ships on Sundays and holidays (except December 15 and 25).
What to See MOUNT PARADISE Half an hour's drive from Philipsburg, through the Dutch valleys of Lower Prince's Quarter and Bethlehem and the French valleys of Belleplaine and Quartier d'Orléans leads to the foot of Mt Paradise, where an hour's climb on foot will bring you to the peak.
MARIGOT, capital of French St Martin is seven miles from Philipsburg and takes 20 minutes by car. The town should be seen from Mt Valois.

Saba

Electricity 24 hour service available since 1970.
Harbour Deep-water pier at Fort Bay for landing from launches.
Air Communications From December to May daily flights to St Maarten by Windward Islands Airways. From June to October flights on Mondays, Tuesdays, Thursdays and Saturdays between Saba, St Maarten and St Kitts.
Where to Stay Windwardside Guest House 1,300 feet above sea level has swimming pool and tennis court.
Roads Seven miles of paved roads. Trip around the island $10 US.
Population In 1970 there were 1,017 residents of Saba.
Windward Islands Airways has regular flights from St Maarten to Saba, St Eustatius, Anguilla, St Barts and Guadeloupe. Day sails and charters to Saba, St Eustatius and other neighbouring islands.

Chapter 8
The British Leewards

Antigua owes its foreign-sounding name to Christopher Columbus, who in 1493 named it for a church in Seville, Santa Maria de la Antigua. The spelling has survived but the island today is popularly known as 'Anteega'. English planters from St Christopher settled in Antigua in 1632. Lord Willoughby, who received a formal grant of the island from Charles II in 1663 sent out a large number of colonists in that year. For a short period the French occupied Antigua but it was formally declared a British possession by the Treaty of Breda in 1666.

In 1671 St Christopher, Nevis, Montserrat, Antigua, Barbuda, Anguilla and 'all the other Leeward islands' were separated from Barbados and became the 'Leeward Caribbee Islands Government'. The chief seat of government was then Nevis but was later transferred to Antigua. In 1689 Colonel Christopher Codrington was appointed Governor in Chief and was authorised by William III to call assemblies of freeholders and planters within any of the islands, 'jointly and severally to make laws'. Codrington's commission thus provides the first instance of a 'federal' type of legislature in the West Indies.

In 1806 the Leeward Caribbee islands were joined into two distinct governments, the first comprising Antigua, Montserrat and Barbuda, the second St Christopher, Nevis, Anguilla and the Virgin Islands. In 1832 the general government was restored and Dominica was added to the Leewards. St Christopher, Nevis and Anguilla were placed under one

12 Traditional West Indian balcony, Basse-Terre, St Kitts

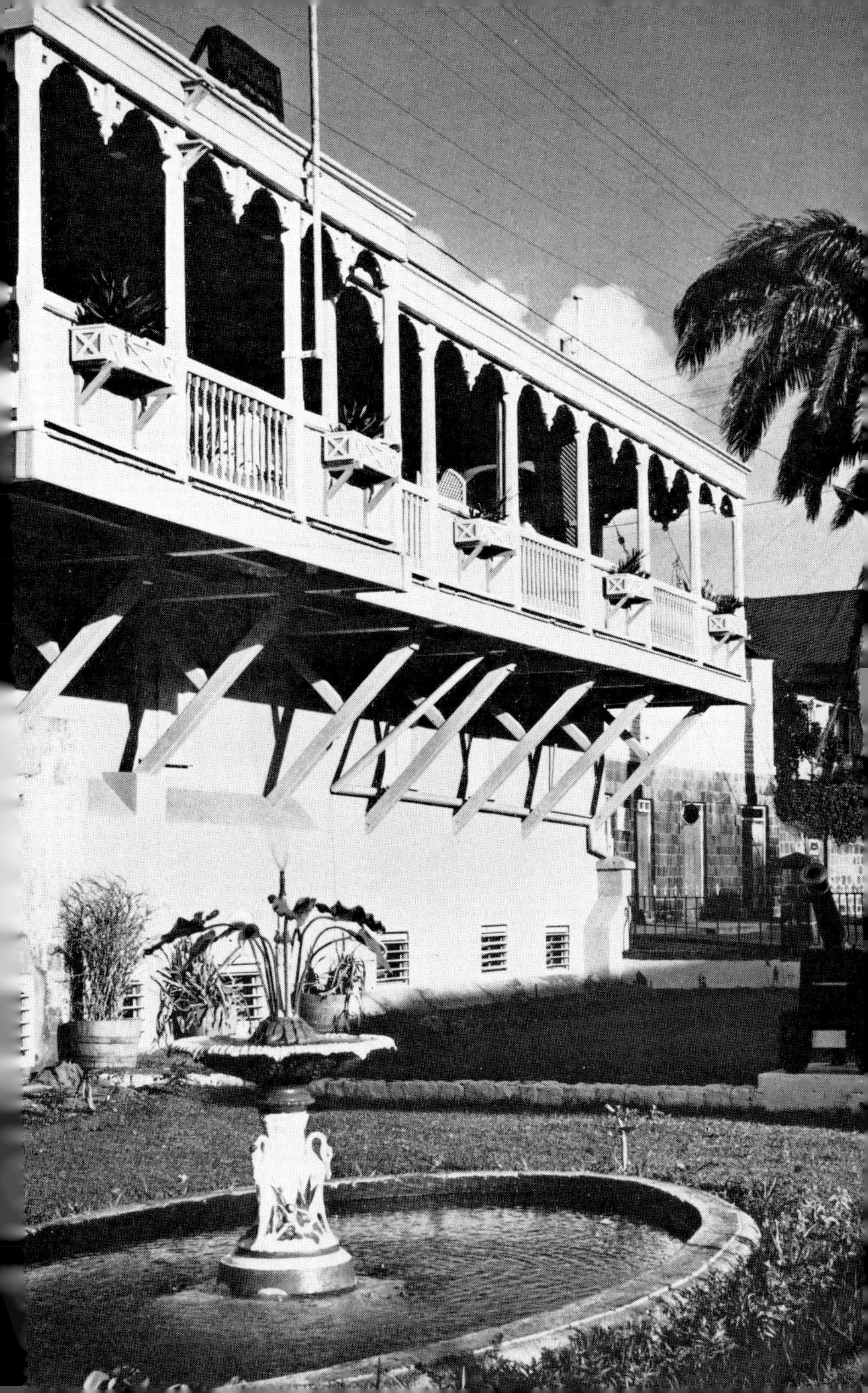

13 and 14 Two views of Nelson's Dockyard, English Harbour, Antigua

Lieutenant Governor, and Dominica under another. The Governor and Commander-in-Chief was resident in Antigua. Each island had its own Legislative Council and House of Assembly.

In 1871, largely due to Sir Benjamin Pine, a single Leeward island colony, consisting of Dominica, the Virgin islands, Montserrat, St Christopher-Nevis-Anguilla, and Antigua with Barbuda and Redonda was created. In 1882 the presidency of St Kitts–Nevis–Anguilla was formally created by an act of the Leeward Islands' federal legislature. Dominica was separated from the federation in 1940, but the Leewards remained united under a federal government until shortly before St Kitts, Nevis, Anguilla, Antigua and Montserrat joined the West Indies Federation as separate governments.

The legislative councils in the Leeward islands for some years included representatives elected under limited franchise, but in 1878 St Kitts-Nevis became a Crown Colony and in 1898 the Legislative Council of Antigua abrogated itself and substituted the Crown Colony system under which all 16 members were nominated by the Governor under Royal Letters Patent.

Barbuda, which lies 25 miles due north of Antigua and 53 miles east-by-south from St Barts, is surrounded by reefs which are known to have caused no less than 73 wrecks since 1773 when a count was started. It has a special appeal therefore for underwater explorers and treasure seekers. All of its 62 square miles are very flat and it resembles a cay of the Bahamas. The Highlands on the eastern side of the island rise to about 200 feet above sea level. On the South side, where the only safe anchorage for yachts is to be found, between Spanish Well Point and Cocoa Point there is a sandy beach approximately six miles long.

Barbuda was the private property of the Codrington family for over 200 years and was called 'the Codrington stud farm' because slaves bred on the island enjoyed a high reputation for physical fitness and tall stature. Deer were introduced into Barbuda by the Codrington family and descendants of

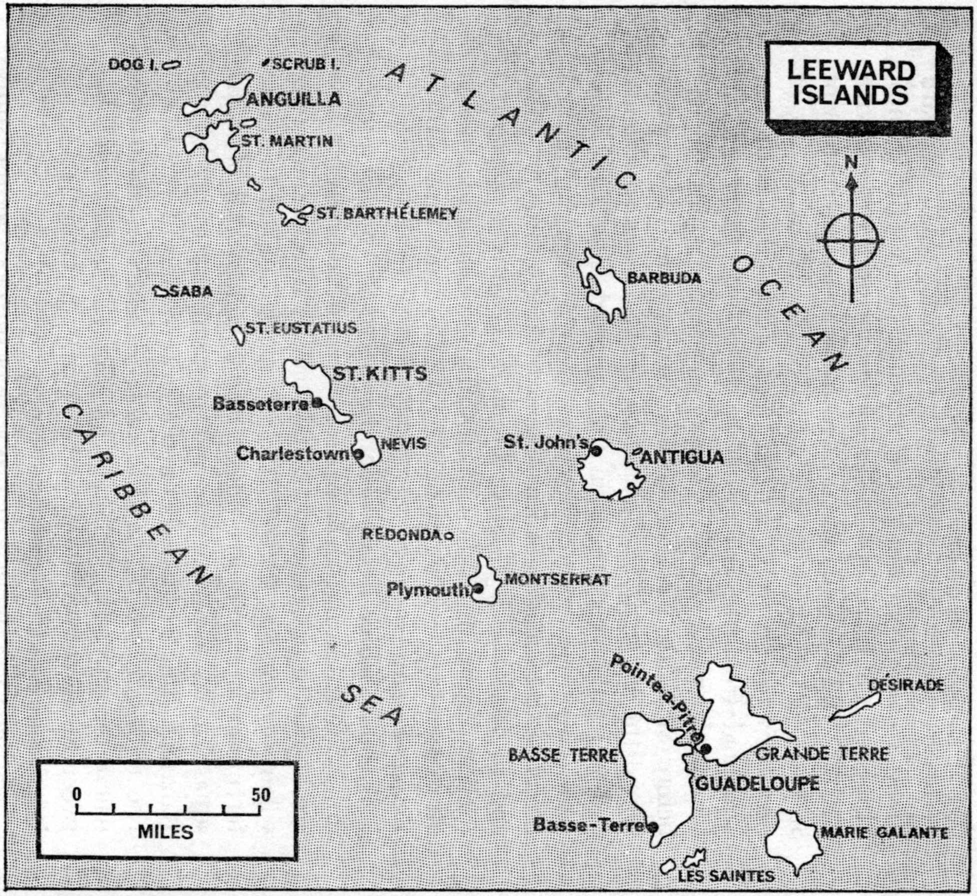
LEEWARD ISLANDS
N
ATLANTIC OCEAN
CARIBBEAN SEA
DOG I.
SCRUB I.
ANGUILLA
ST. MARTIN
ST. BARTHÉLEMEY
SABA
ST. EUSTATIUS
ST. KITTS
Basseterre
NEVIS
Charlestown
BARBUDA
St. John's
ANTIGUA
REDONDA
MONTSERRAT
Plymouth
Pointe-a-Pitre
DÉSIRADE
BASSE TERRE
GRANDE TERRE
GUADELOUPE
Basse-Terre
MARIE GALANTE
LES SAINTES
0
50
MILES

these animals are still hunted today under licence. Wild pigs are also hunted and there is a variety of bird life. Bone fish, tarpon, and snook provide excitement for deep-sea fishermen and lobster catching is one of the island's 'industries'. Salt, sea island cotton and charcoal are also produced, while cattle grazing and horse rearing offer limited opportunities for development. Most of the 1,200 Barbudans live in Codrington, the only village on the island. The Barbuda Lodge has 14 rooms and its rates include 'all meals, liquor, cigarettes, use of small fishing boat, water skiing, aqua-lung and snorkeling equipment, guide fees, hunting and fishing licences and ammunitions. No 10% added.'

At Coco Point Lodge, where there is a hotel near to an airstrip, rates also include air transport to and from Antigua, as well as food, liquor, the use of boats, guides and licences. Seagreen Air Transport of Antigua operates charter flights to Barbuda and LIAT the efficient air service based on Antigua has regular flights to the island.

Antigua is a centre for sea going in the West Indies and trips are easily arranged to Barbuda by sailboat, yacht or motor vessel.

Antigua's other dependency, Redonda, lies 25 miles to the south west between Montserrat and Nevis. It is one mile by one third of a mile in extent and rises to 1,000 feet above sea level. Uninhabited today, Redonda at one time had its own 'King' and from 1865 until well into the twentieth century was valuable for phosphate and alumina mines, exporting as much as 7,000 tons yearly to the United States.

Redonda's King was an Irishman, Mathew Shiel, who claimed to be descended from an Irish Royal family. He spent one day on the island, but passed his kingdom to his son whom he addressed as King Felipe the First. The son, M. P. Shiel, grew up in London and achieved distinction in literary circles. On his death in 1947 the kingdom passed to the poet John Gawsworth. Several famous writers have been created literary dukes of the uninhabited Kingdom of Redonda.

Antigua, with an area of 108 square miles is about half the

size of Middlesex, England. The San Juan islands, which are part of the State of Washington and lie in the Georgia Strait, are much larger having a total area of 265 square miles. Antigua's highest point, Boggy Peak, rises to a height of 1,360 feet. In the eighteenth century Antigua became a bastion of the British Empire after the Admiralty had reported to the King that English Harbour was 'the only place fit for careening and refitting your Majesty's ships employed in the West Indies to the Windward of Jamaica'.

The harbour is on the south coast, 12 miles from the capital city of St John's. It is well withdrawn from the open sea and safe; for these reasons it is still preferred by yachtsmen as a centre from which to operate cruises to neighbouring islands. The dockyard named for Nelson, who was stationed in English Harbour between 1786 and 1788, was abandoned in 1889, but was restored in the 'fifties largely due to the efforts of Sir Kenneth Blackburne, who succeeded Earl Baldwin as Governor of the Leeward islands.

A visit to the restored dockyard is a journey back into the eighteenth century. The tourist potential of Nelson's Dockyard has been further exploited by periodic *son et lumière* productions in recent years. It is one of the ironies of history that Nelson, who has been greatly honoured in the islands as 'the preserver of the West Indies', and husband of a West Indian girl from Nevis loathed all the islanders. He called Barbados a 'barbarous island', referred to the dockyard as an 'infernal hole' and especially hated the sight of the Leeward islanders whom he described as 'Americans by connexion and by interest' and as 'inimical to Great Britain'.

Another 'Nelson', Henry Nelson Coleridge who visited the West Indies in 1825, was very much enamoured of Antigua as he gazed 'on the gentle wooded hills and green meadow vales which decorate the interior'. It must have rained heavily that year! He found the 'numerous houses of the planters embosomed in trees having more of the appearance of country mansions in England than almost any others in the West Indies'. The country mansions have long since disappeared with the decline of Antigua's sugar industry, but it is still as true today, as when Coleridge wrote, that the shores of Antigua 'are indented in every direction with creeks and bays and coves, some of them running into the centre of the plantations like canals, some swelling into estuaries, and others forming spacious harbours. Beyond these an infinite variety of islands and islets stud the bosom of the blue sea, and stand out like so many advanced posts of defence against the invading waves. They are of all shapes and sizes'. Coleridge was the kind of traveller whom all the islanders still adore. He loved superlatives: he called the view of Antigua from the rocks near the parsonage of St Philip's parish 'one of the finest panoramic views of the world'; he enjoyed 'Floating Island', a dish of guava jelly made to 'swim in guise of an islet upon a stagnant lake of cream and wine and sugar and citron'. He danced till four in the morning. But with all his appreciation of things Antiguan, Coleridge could not resist giving advice to his readers: 'not to drink too much; restrain yourself till twelve o'clock or so, and then eat some cold meat and also a pint of porter cup, which is perfectly innoxious to the system, and more restorative to the animal spirits than punch, wine or sangaree. Above all do not be persuaded to swallow any washy tea: it gives neither strength nor vivacity, but rather impairs both, and makes you excessively uncomfortable.' On dress Coleridge was ahead of his day and gave advice which will be welcomed in the gay, men's boutiques now springing up throughout the islands. 'It is important,' he wrote in 1825, 'to remark that your shirt collars should be loose round the neck, and the gills low, a mere white stock of thick holland well starched with arrow root is the best cravate.' Ignoring the advice about the cravate and tea, which can be quite refreshing at 4 p.m., modern tourists in Antigua will wear open-necked shirts and should be greatly delighted to buy liquors there at prices which are among the lowest in the region. Coleridge's Antigua is no more. America is writ large over the hotels which dominate the beautiful sandy bays, over the large United States base, and over Mill Reef's exclusive resort. England still survives as a memory at English Harbour, at the Anglican Cathedral in St John's, and in isolated private homes. The ruins of Empire may be seen at Fort St James near St John and at the massive old fortifications and barracks which survive at Shirley Heights.

In all the islands modern tourism has developed apart from the community of islanders. In Antigua there is physical separation between luxury hotels which are landscaped on or around magnificent natural bays and sandy beaches, but which are isolated from village town or country life. The real Antigua is a sprawl of isolated, badly connected villages where life moves literally at asses' pace, since asses are still regular beasts of burden there, as they are on St Vincent. A great deal of an Antiguan villager's time seems to be passed lying outstretched on stone steps outside small wooden houses around which conch shells do duty for flowering gardens. More children seem to have their heads 'picked' by their mothers in Antiguan villages than elsewhere in the islands. The countryside has a run-down look, with telephone wires sagging from telephone poles beside parched fields. Drought is the enemy in Antigua, but when it rains there is too much water everywhere. Scanty rainfall, however, is welcomed by short-stay, sun-soaking tourists, who also appreciate the lower humidity normally to be found in dry Antigua. Truly, sea, land and sandy beaches combine, as the Tourist Board claims, to make beauty in an island of headlands, beaches, bluffs and bays. Yet there is an air of depression about the islanders. Despite their willingness to earn tourist dollars, carnivals in August, and the persistence of folk traditions like stick fighters, dancing clowns and John Bulls (who lie fully clothed in trash* suits to stop vehicles and beg from passing tourists), Antiguans appear to have interpreted 'freedom' too literally, as though the state of being free is to put in minimum effort to obtain a maximum state of inertia. No one gets the impres-

---

* Trash suits are made from the dried leaves or blades of the sugar cane. Trash is used throughout the islands to describe dry cane grass.

sion in Antigua of a dynamic country bustling with activity. One thinks instead of a clock with a broken mainspring, of an eighteenth-century island suddenly jerked into the late twentieth century by American fun- and sun-seekers, without having requisite resources to meet the demands of a high powered tourist industry, although quite adequately geared for the problems of a small seaport town which is still dependent on ships and motor vessels for supplies.

From the sea St Christopher, which lies 40 miles north-east of Saba, appears as a single mountain mass with Mount Misery rising up to 3,711 feet. The island is beautiful, with ridges separated by ghauts or valleys, that climb up from sea level to the summit. The vale of Basse-Terre was likened by Coleridge to 'green velvet' because of the 'exquisite verdancy' of the cane fields. The fertility of St Kitts, which is the common abbreviation of the Saint's name, was promised in the Carib name of Liamuiga, 'the fertile isle'. For reasons of fertility, and because there was no strong Carib occupation, Warner probably chose the island to be the 'mother colony' of the Caribbees, landing at Old Road on January 28, 1623. St Kitts is an oval island 23 miles long by six miles wide, with a total area of 68 square miles. Until 1713 when it became wholly a British possession it was shared with the French, who occupied the two ends. The salt ponds on the south-eastern peninsula were held in common. The English got Wingfield river, a permanent stream on the leeward side.

The mountains of St Kitts are clothed in dense tropical forest and the summit of Mt Misery has to be approached on hands and knees. Orchids are common at heights above 2,000 feet. The interior of the forest is completely covered by a canopy of trees which hides the sunlight.

Mountain chickens and iguana were once delicacies on the island, but have long since disappeared. Many of the mammals and birds of the Carib islands have succumbed to attacks from rats, aided by the mongoose and the green monkey which were introduced by Europeans.

The European settlers brought as much of their 'homeland'

as they could pack on the small ships of the seventeenth century, but they had to build their houses of local wood. Before the end of the seventeenth century planters were complaining of shortage of wood for building. Today forests are valued on St Kitts and other islands as essential for soil conservation and as aids to rainfall.

Through planned massacres the French and English settlers put an end to Carib occupation of Liamuiga by 1627. From the Caribs they learnt how to prepare manioc, sweet potatoes, peanuts, arrowroot, pineapples, plantains, maize, prickly pears and peppers for eating. The English settlers, who were young men in their twenties or spinsters, were carefully selected by trades. They included blacksmiths, sailmakers, shoemakers, feltmakers, weavers, ostlers and tailors. For the most part they were recruited from Southern England. French settlers came from Normandy and Brittany. Mortality rates were high. Of 500 persons who set sail for St Kitts from France with d'Esnambuc in 1627, no less than 200 died at sea while 100 succumbed after landing on the island.

St Kitts, like other Caribbean islands, was at first a plantation for growing the export crops of tobacco, cotton, indigo and ginger. By 1658 at least six mills were producing muscovado, an unfinished raw sugar made from cane. Labour was originally obtained from indentured servants who were paid £1. 17s. 6d. for four years service and then released. Later malefactors, political prisoners and slaves were forced to work. After the establishment of the Royal Africa Company in 1670 Charlestown in Nevis became the slave market for the Leeward islands. Slaves, first washed and oiled, paraded to the music of drums and were auctioned to the highest bidders. Between 1674 and 1686 the Royal Africa Company brought 8,000 slaves into the Leewards. Runaway slaves of the French on St Christopher became the first 'Maroons' in 1639.

The Leeward islands were recruiting centres for the filibusters who are more commonly called buccaneers. Hilton, an ex-governor of Nevis, took recruits from that island and from St Kitts as early as 1630 to set up a nest of buccaneers on Tortue or Tortuga off the north coast of Haiti. Ten years later Levasseur and French Huguenots from St Kitts took over Tortue and used it as a base for the French capture of St Domingue.

From St Kitts the English settled Barbuda in 1629 and Antigua and Montserrat in 1632, while a French expedition from St Kitts settled Martinique in 1635.

It was no easy task to settle the islands. The first settlers lived in rude Indian or Carib type huts and were forced to grow their own food for survival. Their basic diet was a mixture of cassava, iguana, manatee, turtle, landcrabs, pineapple and other fruits and fish. War followed upon war as the years of tropical heat and toil rolled by. Brimstone Hill, the 'Gibraltar' of the West Indies, was erected at the end of the seventeenth century. Nevis was sacked by the French in 1706. Brimstone Hill surrendered to the French after a month's siege in 1782. It was restored when St Kitts was ceded to the British in 1783. Privateers were so plentiful that sailors used to complain that there was more hazard crossing from island to island than from England to St Kitts. Frequent appeals were made for help to Barbados in early years, with little success. The early settlers were occupied in establishing a system which had been designed in London. Some successful planters returned to England, leaving the management of their plantations in St Kitts to attorneys. The islands were not desirable places to live in permanently. By 1744 the legislature of St Kitts claimed that one half of the property on the island was owned by absentees. Children were sent to school in England, yet some magnificent mansions were constructed by the wealthiest landowners.

Before the end of the eighteenth century St Kitts had a population of 4,000 whites and 26,000 negroes, of whom only 300 blacks and mulattoes enjoyed conditions of freedom. On Nevis there were 600 whites and 10,000 negroes. Because of the discovery of hot springs on Nevis and the popularity of spas in the eighteenth century, Nevis enjoyed some decades of popularity as a fashionable watering place. According to one writer in the early twentieth century, on Nevis there was to be had an 'unending circle of gaiety. There were morning rides to the hills, picnic parties on Mount Pleasant, fishing expeditions to Newcastle Bay'. The imagination boggles, however, at the description given in a newspaper of 1707 of 'Clarindas, Belindas and Elviras' coming out of church on Sunday 'patched and painted, hooped and farthingaled *à outrance* with fly-caps, top knots and commodes, tight laced bodies, laced aprons and fluced (the eighteenth-century equivalent of 'flounced') petticoats, accompanied or followed by the pretty fellows who wore square-tailed silk and velvet coats of all colours, periwigged and top hatted, silk stockinged and shoed with red-heeled shoes, their sword knots trailing almost on the ground, and their canes dangling from the fifth button'. Nothing like this could be imagined today, not even during Trinidad's carnival: least of all would it be likely to happen on Nevis, an island where for more than a century the spa has been silent and in ruins.

The glamour and fashion of eighteenth-century St Kitts and Nevis lasted only until the last quarter of the eighteenth century, when the decline of the planter aristocracy began. By the middle of the following century the class was extinct and London was soon to see the last of the St Kitts heiresses. Sugar has nonetheless continued to support the people of St Kitts in a state of life which would have been much worse without the industry which was made more efficient by the building of a narrow-gauge railway in 1911. Cotton has also been grown there and on Nevis, an island which also supplies St Kitts with some vegetables and cattle. As far back as 1880 the suggestion was made that Nevis might once again become the sanatorium and fashionable watering place of the West Indies.

Both Nevis and St Kitts have, however, been handicapped by poor communications and by the difficulties of adjusting traditional white oligarchic rule to modern trade-union oriented 'labour democracy'. The small size of St Kitts and its flamboyant labour leadership have not helped to smooth over difficult problems which might have found speedier solutions under a lasting Federation.

The charms of St Kitts and Nevis are very real and progress has already been made on both islands with the provision of attractive establishments for visitors who enjoy relaxing on undeveloped islands. The beaches of St Kitts occur in sheltered bays and are generally of black sand. On the peninsula small beaches of quartz sand are found, while there are coral reefs and white sandy beaches at Conaree on St Kitts and at Newcastle on Nevis.

St Kitts hopes to enter the 'big league' of tourist resorts with the development of 850 acres at Frigate Bay on the south-east coast. A marina is to be constructed there capable of serving 300 craft, an irrigated 18 hole golf course is being laid out, and there is accommodation for nine hotels, 1,500 residential apartments, banks, offices, cinemas, and shops. Like Antigua, St Kitts has passed legislation permitting the operation of casinos in approved hotels. Coleridge described Nevis in 1825 as 'perhaps the most captivating of any island in the West Indies. From the south and west it seems to be nothing but a single cone rising with the most graceful curve out of the sea, and piercing a fleecy mass of clouds which sleeps for ever round its summit. It is green as heart can conceive, perfectly cultivated and enlivened with many old planter's houses of a superior style and churches peeping out in the most picturesque situations imaginable. A complete forest of evergreens grows like a ruff or collar round the neck of the high land where cultivation ceases.' He found the mean temperature of Nevis and Montserrat lower than in any other of the Antilles and recommended that 'if a man would bring his resources with him, especially a wife, he might live in a delightful retirement in many of the sweet hill recesses of either of these islands.'

Nevis has an area of 50 square miles or about 32,000 acres of which no more than 15,000 are fit for cultivation. Its highest point is 3,596 feet above the sea.

Nevis and St Kitts are separated by a strait about two miles in breadth, but the normal sea route between Charlestown and Basse-Terre is about 12 miles.

Nevis was the birthplace of Alexander Hamilton, who left the island as a boy and became one of the best known Americans. His father, who later settled on St Vincent, was a Scotsman of aristocratic lineage and his mother of French descent. Nelson, who hated Americans for defying British Navigation Acts, married his wife Frances Herbert Nisbet, a widow, in Nevis. She was the daughter of the President of the Island Council and her first husband had been a doctor of medicine. A tablet on the old pillars of the gateway leading to the site of the Montpelier House records that on the 11th day of March 1787 Horatio Nelson the Captain of H.M.S. *Boreas* was married to Frances Herbert Nisbet in Montpelier House. Prince William Henry gave the bride away. The official record of the marriage is kept in the parish church of St John at Figtree Village. Coleridge called Figtree Church 'the most perfect thing I ever saw', adding: 'it is situated half way up the mountain, and looks down upon a wide expanse of sea, the town, the ships, the whole length of St Kitts and the top of St Eustatius above all'. On a 64 acre coconut plantation, Beachlands, restored by Mrs Mary Pomeroy to resemble an eighteenth-century great house, Nisbet Plantation Inn offers a place where the modern traveller 'can recapture the atmosphere of Nelson's Nevis and enjoy a mile long private beach'. On the south-east side of Nevis an old Sugar Mill estate has been converted into the Golden Rock Hotel which looks out to Antigua, Redonda and Montserrat and provides a cabin cruiser for fishing.

Nevis needs a larger airport if it is to achieve full development as a tourist resort. Only small planes carrying about a dozen persons at a time can land on the airstrip. But for its attachment to St Kitts, Nevis might already have been much more highly developed as a tourist resort for middle-income travellers. At least this view is shared by those Nevisians who advocate separation from St Kitts. Because of isolation, Nevis, like Virgin Gorda and some of the Grenadine islands, is becoming almost an exclusive resort for those who can afford to pay rates which go as high as 100 United States dollars a day. Pinneys Beach is the best on the island and three hotels were under construction there at the time of writing.

Anguilla, which the United Kingdom recognised as one of the three components of the single government of St Kitts, Nevis, Anguilla, lies about 60 miles north-west of the mother island of St Kitts. It is about 16 miles in length and varies in breadth from three to one-and-a-half square miles. Its area is 35 square miles and the Dogs and neighbouring islets are dependencies. Sheep, goats, salt and cotton are the traditional products of the island, which also is blessed with white coral sandy beaches that are likely to be exploited soon by tourist and resort developers who are transforming these former 'slums of Empire' into havens of sunshine and pleasure for persons escaping from the huge metropolis which is the Eastern United States, and from the overcrowded beaches of traditional resorts in highly developed countries. At the time of writing Anguilla was still so much an unspoilt island that the official tourist brochure was notifying visitors to Savannah Bay that permission was required 'from Mr J. Webster to cross his land to the beach'. At Jukes Hole similar permission was required from Mr Hodge and at Shoal Bay 'one of the finest beaches in the Caribbean, extremely white sand, clear water edged with reef, the shore tree lined', from Mr Harrigan. As if all these friendly inviting beaches, which only need the courtesy of a simple request to welcome visitors, were not enough, Anguilla invites those with 'the explorer's spirit' to visit their islands of Dog, Prickly Pear East, Prickly Pear West, and Sea Island, small islands lying to the north and north-west, still unspoiled, where 'fishing is great fun'. And for men with rifles who happen to be on Anguilla there is good duck shooting, once permission has been obtained.

The Caribs who called Anguilla by the happy sounding name of Malliouhana knew a 'fun' island when they saw one.

Montserrat is named after the mountain in Spain on which

is built the monastery in which St Ignatius Loyola decided to form the Society of Jesus. Eleven miles long and seven miles wide its area is 32½ square miles. The island which lies 27 miles from Antigua is of volcanic formation and is very rugged and mountainous. The hills are covered with forest. Chance's Mountain in the southern part of the island reaches up to 3,000 feet. Coleridge, who got a 'ducking' on landing at Montserrat and who found the island's administration so run down that the President of the Council was in a state of 'unworthy destitution', nonetheless found his heart swell with love and sorrow 'at the thought of never seeing Soufrière again'. His morning ramble there on horseback took him up a winding road where 'snowy amaryllis dropped her long and delicate petals like a love-sick girl; the thrice gorgeous hibiscus was unveiling his crown and feathers of scarlet, and the light limes and darker orange trees ... were exhaling their perfumed incense to Him who made them so beautiful and good.' From the Savannah, where a circuitous and overarched path descends to the vale of Soufrière he could see to the south the broad and irregular eminences of Guadeloupe, to the north Redonda shining like an emerald in the blue waves, and 'beyond the great pyramid of Nevis cut off from sight at one third of its summit by an ever resting canopy of clouds. The wind was so fresh, the air so cool, the morning dew so healthy and spangling that I might have forgotten but for the deep beauty that was around me, that I was still within the tropics.'

One hundred and fifty-five years later it is still as true that early morning and late evening are the two most delightful and most temperate periods of a tropical day, especially during the winter months.

The Irish colonised Montserrat in 1632. The French captured the settlement in 1664 and held the island for four years. The French recaptured it again in 1782, but it was returned to England a year later. From 1668 until 1861, Montserrat had a Legislative Council and Assembly. Several constitutional experiments were tried between 1861 and the demise of the Federation in 1962 when Montserrat reverted to being a colony of the United Kingdom. Many crops have also been tried – sugar, sea island cotton, tomatoes, onions and limes – while exports have included lime oils, lime juice, cotton seed, oil, cattle and vegetables. Hurricanes have devastated Montserrat on several occasions, notably in August 1899, August 1924 and September 1928. Earthquake shocks were frequent between 1933 and 1935 causing much damage to stone and mortar buildings. Montserrat has suffered heavily from emigration. Small tropical islands have few opportunities for young men and women who know that the world is much larger than $32\frac{1}{2}$ square miles!

The government has refused to cut the links which bind it to the United Kingdom because it considers its resources unequal to the task of providing higher living standards for its people. Special efforts have been made to attract retired persons to settle. By the end of 1968 about 140 new homes had been built. Keeping the Union Jack and reducing personal taxation to a maximum figure of 20 per cent together with abolition of death duties has attracted new investment in Montserrat, where agricultural export schemes have continued to attract investors. One of the most publicised in recent years has been the 'dream of Father John Christiansen' from Arizona. This dream became a half million dollar investment in over 3,000 acres of land utilised for food production and cattle breeding. The enterprise is hoping to revive the reputation which Montserrat has particularly enjoyed for quality tomatoes. Maximum agricultural development in Montserrat will require more than the enthusiasm of private investors. No permanent improvement can be expected in any of these islands unless there is an all-out effort to build an active regional agricultural department which can generate enthusiasm for farming as a way of life. Without farmers rooted in the soil, development in Montserrat is likely to be speculative.

Montserrat is too small to stand on its own feet and its future as a tourist resort and 'settlers island' must depend on its integration into some larger regional grouping, whether political or economic; only then is it likely to obtain the men of calibre required to promote and maintain its growth.

Montserrat, Antigua and Barbuda are sufficiently close together to be promoted as holiday areas which offer sea-and-air voyages and enough variety for two or three weeks. Those who settle will increasingly demand better sea communications to neighbouring towns like St John's, Antigua, Basse-Terre, St Kitts or Pointe-à-Pitre, Guadeloupe. The greatest deterrent to settlement in 'out' islands is isolation from the more highly developed social, educational, cultural and other services which are expanding in the more highly developed places.

All the West Indies suffer from lack of freedom of movement of people and goods, but the remoteness of islands like Montserrat from the centres of West Indian development could be alleviated by the knowledge that large island destinations were within quick reach of daily planes and ships and that travel documents would not be required. Montserrat needs the security of integration with other islands, to which it is linked by sea, but from which it is artificially separated by the 'hangover' of European mercantilism.

The tourist potential of Montserrat has already been recognised by the Holiday Inns of Canada, while the Commonwealth Development Corporation now supplies electricity and power and may also build a hotel there. It is hard to imagine Montserrat ever being 'spoilt' or over-developed by tourism. Yet it has for some time stepped out of the classification of being a 'backward' island. It has an airport (with a tricky approach) at Blackburne capable of accommodating Avro 748's, two resort hotels, Emerald Isle and Vue Pointe, a nine hole golf course, a small yacht club, tennis courts, some good beaches, fine scenic views and easy access to 'fun sports' in or on the sea.

15 Coconut grove, St Kitts

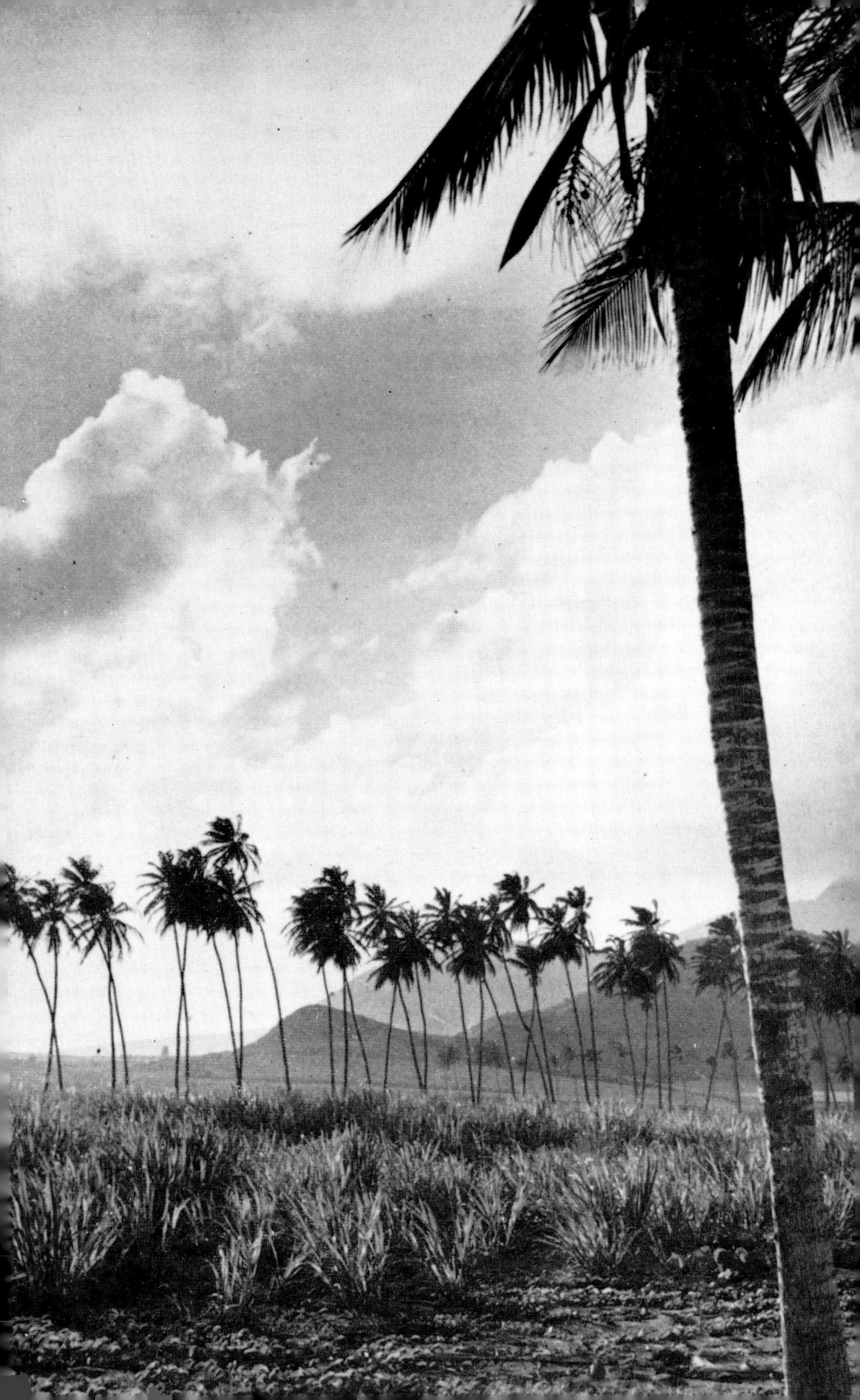

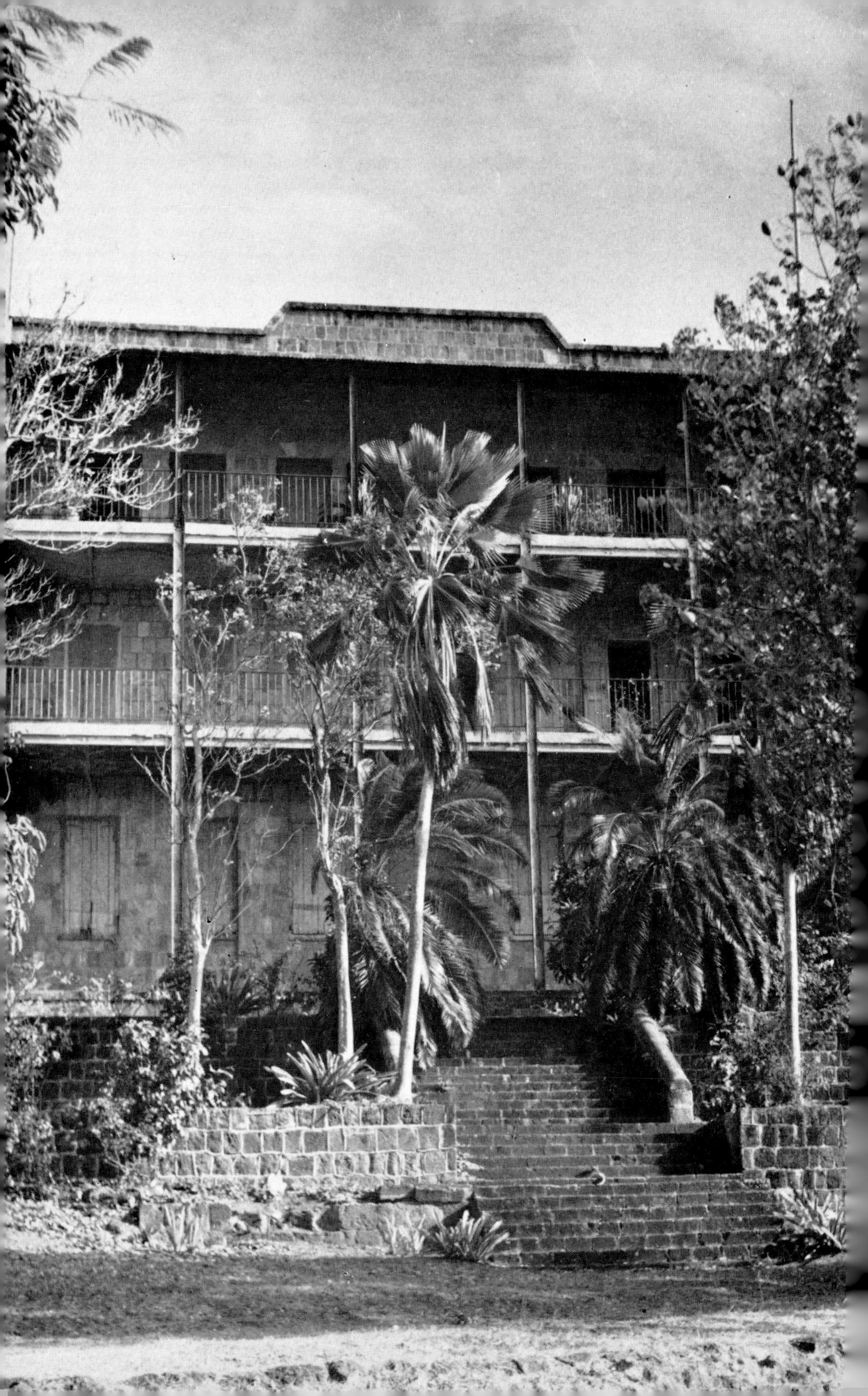

GENERAL INFORMATION

Antigua

Churches   Anglican, Roman Catholic, Methodist, Moravian and other denominations.
Climate   Mainly dry and sunny. Average annual rainfall 42"; average temperature winter 75°F, summer 85°F.
Clothing   Light summer dresses and sportswear for daytime. Gentlemen are required to wear jackets for dinner in some of the hotels. Short shorts are not recommended for wear in St John's.
Communications   Overseas telephone and telegraph.
Airlines   Airlines operating in Antigua are BOAC, Pan American, British West Indian Airways, Air Canada, Air France, ALM, Caribair and Leeward Island Air Transport.
Currency   Eastern Caribbean Currency $1.00 = 21 British New Pence = 50¢ US. Denominations: coins 1¢, 2¢, 5¢, 10¢, 25¢ and 50¢. Notes = $1.00, $5.00, $20.00, and $100.00.
Documents required   Citizens of the USA and Canada do not need a visa; required is proof of nationality, e.g. passport or birth certificate, a return or onward ticket and a smallpox vaccination certificate.
Electric current   220 volts A.C. 60 cycles. The Hodges Bay area and the villages of Parham and Cedar Grove are supplied with 110 to 120 volts A.C. 60 cycles domestic current from the A.C. plant at Coolidge field. Transformers converting 220 power to 115 volts must be used with most electrical appliances from North America.
Food and Drink   The favourite dishes are Pepper Pot, fungee or coo-coo (corn meal and okras) rice in many forms and souse (boiled pig head and trotters) served with lime juice, sliced cucumber and pepper. Lobsters are caught at the nearby island of Barbuda.
Holidays and Festivals   January 1st – New Year's Day, Good Friday, Easter Monday, Labour Day (first Monday in May),

16 The Old Bath House on Nevis

Whit Monday (first Monday after Pentecost), Queen's Birthday (first Saturday in June), Carnival Festival (between the last week of July and first week of August), Merchants' Holiday (first Monday in October – Banks and Government Offices remain open), State Day (November 1st), Christmas Day and Boxing Day.
Language English and English patois.
Laundry and Dry Cleaning One Hour Martinizing operated by Caribbean Cleaners Ltd.
Medical Facilities The Holberton General Hospital and clinics in all principal villages. Private medical and dental care also available.
Night Life Local artists, dancing to steelbands, orchestras and limbo dancers. A Casino at Marmora Bay.
Daytime Fishing trips operated by Lee Westcott, Crosbies. One day boat trips on the *Warrior Geraint*; Glass-bottom boating and scuba diving operated at Dickenson Bay. A tour on the colourful sugar locomotive 'Sunshine Chu Chu' arranged through Alexander Parrish Travel Service.
Pets and Animals Dogs and cats may not be brought into Antigua.
Sports Cricket and football. Golf at the Antigua Beach Hotel and the Half Moon Bay Hotel. Lawn tennis. Swimming, scuba diving, skiing, snorkeling at several beaches. Yachting centre at Nelson's Dockyard operated by V. E. B. Nicholson & Sons.
Shopping Hours Stores close half day on Thursdays, offices half day on Saturdays.
Special Events Yacht REGATTA in first week of June. St Vincent Antigua ocean race, charter yacht race from Guadeloupe, local yacht races.
Summer Carnival during week preceding the first Monday of August. Caribbean Queen and Calypso King competitions.
Son et Lumière twice weekly December to April, Mondays and Fridays at 9.30 p.m. English Harbour.
Casino At Holiday Inn, Mamora Bay.

Time   Local time is one hour ahead of Eastern Standard Time.
Tipping   Most hotels add a 10% service charge to the bill.
Transportation   Taxis and self-drive cars available. Self-drive cars may be rented at $12 US per day. Presentation of driver's licence and a charge of 60¢ US entitles to Antiguan's driver's licence valid for a period of six months. Apply to Traffic Dept., Police Headquarters, St John's.
Water   Rain water stored in cisterns and catchments is drinkable; tap water is also drinkable.
What to See   IN TOWN The Anglican Cathedral, the Court House, the Market Place, Industrial School for the Blind, Rum Distillery and a view of the city from Michael's Mount. OUT OF TOWN Fort James, Sugar Factory, Antigua Pottery Factory, Edible Oil Factory, Monoliths at Greencastle Hill, Monks Hill, Nelson's Dockyard, Clarence House, Shirley Heights, Devil's Bridge, Indian Town, Parham Church and a circular drive over Fig Tree Hill.
What to Buy   French perfumes, cashmeres, English tweeds, Irish linen, Sea island cotton material and clothing, English tobacco, Wedgwood and English bone china, Swiss watches and clocks, liquor, English and European cameras, locally made straw handicraft, pottery and hand-screened fabrics.
Other Information   BANKS Branches of Barclays, Royal Bank of Canada, Canadian Imperial Bank of Commerce, US Virgin Islands National Bank, Bank of Nova Scotia. All are on High Street. Banking hours: Monday to Friday 8 a.m. to noon; Saturdays 8 a.m. to 11.30 a.m.

St Kitts – Nevis – Anguilla
Churches   Catholic, Anglican, Methodist and other denominations.
Language   English.
Climate   Temperatures range from 68°F to 89°F.
Passports   For a stay of up to six months, for nationals of United Kingdom and British subjects, Canada and the U.S.A. no passport, but suitable identification (birth certificate or

naturalization papers) and possession of return ticket. A valid international certificate of vaccination less than three years old, must be shown on entry.

Customs Personal belongings are admitted duty free. Also admitted duty free: 200 cigarettes or 100 cigarillos or 50 cigars or ½ lb. tobacco, one bottle of spirits and one bottle of wine and a reasonable amount of perfume in use.

Currency Eastern Caribbean Dollar $1.00 E.C. = 50¢ US and $1.00 US = $1.95 E.C. (these figures are approximate).

Electricity 220/230 volts, 60 cycles AC. A transformer is usually needed for appliances from the United States and Canada.

Driving Before driving any vehicle, a local driver's licence should be obtained from the Traffic Department at a cost of $1.00 E.C., and this is valid for three months. All vehicles are driven on the *left* hand side of the road. Gasoline is sold by Imperial Gallon (1.2 American gallons).

Taxis Taxi fares are statutory, i.e. 45¢ per mile in St Kitts, 50¢ per mile in Nevis and 55¢ per mile in Anguilla. After first 15 minutes waiting, a charge of 50¢ per 15 minutes is payable. Association rates are for organised excursions mainly. Fare from Golden Rock Airport to Basseterre is $2.00 (E.C.), $1.03 (US), and from Newcastle Airport to Charlestown the fare of $5.00 (E.C.) $2.56 (US).

Buses There is as yet no bus timetable. The Bus Termini in St Kitts and Nevis are on the Bay Front. There are no tour buses on the islands.

Air Transport LIAT (Leeward Islands Air Transport) runs daily services between St Kitts and Nevis (duration of flight five minutes).

Sea Transport Motor launch between St Kitts and Nevis daily except on Thursdays and Saturdays.

Where to Stay Accommodation listed by the Tourist Board gives Nevis 155 rooms, St Kitts 111 and Anguilla 56. So far Nevis has proved most attractive to holiday makers but the Frigate Bay resort development and the Liamuiga hotel on

St Kitts could make the 'mother' island more appealing to visitors.
Cruise Ships All cruise ships anchor in the roadsteads, and passengers are taken to piers by tenders. The Tourist Bureau in St Kitts is at the head of the pier. The Nevis Tourist Bureau is in Chapel Street, Charlestown.

Montserrat
Churches Anglican, Roman Catholic, Methodist, Seventh Day Adventist and other denominations.
Climate Average temperature winter 75°F., summer 85°F.
Clothing Same as in Europe, Canada, USA in summer.
Communications LIAT three flights daily, connecting with Antigua. Limited sea accommodation by West Indies Shipping Service and Saguenay Shipping Company.
Currency Eastern Caribbean.
Documents required by Visitors Passports US citizens need only round trip plane or sea tickets.
Electrical Current 230 volts, 60 cycles.
Food and Drink peculiar to Montserrat Mutton broth and Perkins punch.
Holidays and Festivals New Year's Day, Easter Monday, Whit Monday, first Monday in May, August Monday, Queen's Birthday, Christmas Day, Boxing Day.
Language English.
Laundry and Dry Cleaning None.
Local Courtesies and Customs Normal general courtesies always extended. No peculiar customs.
Medical Facilities 60-bed hospital, surgeon, five doctors on the island.
Night Life Dancing, discothèque, barbecues.
Other Tourist Activities Sightseeing, sailing, fishing, snorkeling, horse riding, tennis, golf.
Pets and Animals Requirements for bringing in: health and rabies-free certificates.
Food and Restaurants Two small 'eateries'. No restaurants.
Sports Water skiing, sailing hired sunfish, snorkeling.

Time Five hours behind GMT: one hour ahead of Eastern Standard Time.
Tipping Permitted.
Transportation Taxis available.
Water Soft spring water from faucet.
What to See Sulphur springs, Great Alps Waterfall, View from Fort St George, Carr's Bay, Galway's Soufrière, Runaway Ghaut, Harris' Lookout, St Anthony's Church.
What to Buy Low-priced liquors and cigarettes. Dress materials and local souvenirs.
For settlers Maximum income tax 20 per cent.

Chapter 9
The British Windwards

For many years before the formation of the Federation of the West Indies in 1958 the English Windward Islands were effectively governed by a Commander-in-Chief resident in Grenada and by four administrators in each of the islands of Dominica, St Lucia, St Vincent and Grenada. The attractive necklace of Grenadine islands was administered partly from Grenada and partly from St Vincent, which represent as it were the clasps of the string of pearls. Barbados, Trinidad and Tobago fall naturally within the group of windward islands and they were all associated politically in the year 1838. Tobago had previously been under Windward administration for 12 years between 1764 and 1784. Dominica was detached from the Leewards and joined, where it belongs geographically, the Windwards in 1940.

The Windward government was not created until March 1885. Previously many of the islands in the Windward chain, inclusive of Barbados, Trinidad and Tobago, had been governed as the 'Southern Caribbean Islands'. St Lucia was not included in this general government until 1838. Together the four islands and their dependencies have an area of 829 square miles, or approximately five times the area of Barbados.

Dominica, which has an area of $304\frac{2}{3}$ square miles, is the largest of the British islands in the Windward arc of islands which runs from the Anegada passage to Tobago. It is sandwiched between the French departments of Martinique and

Guadeloupe. Like these two islands Dominica is mountainous and picturesque. Imray's view on Morne Diablotin is 4,747 feet above sea level. Since the rainfall of the island is measured in feet (it exceeds 300 inches yearly in the mountains) the peaks are often concealed by clouds.

Its discovery on Sunday, 3 November 1493, explains how Dominica got its name. Unhappily the island is frequently confused with the republic that is part of the island of Haiti and which is generally known as the Dominican Republic.

The history of Dominica belies its peaceful name. The island has never totally been subjected by man. Caribs established limited footholds on it over several centuries and the English and French see-sawed for possession for hundreds of years, but the island spirit remains opposed to control. Nature in Dominica means giant trees, swollen torrents, large rivers, splendid vistas, rare birds, flowers and isolation. Dominica is not for those who love cities, bright lights or discothèques. Its main attraction is a Botanic Garden. It could become a hippie paradise. It provides a perfect background for Rousseau's noble savage, and attracts as settlers people who are sick of the 'rat race' of computerised and standardised societies. Dominica has an appeal for poets and painters and in Jean Rhys it produced perhaps the best West Indian novelist and one of the most understanding writers of the twentieth century.

Although part of the Carlisle grant of 1627, Dominica was never successfully reduced to English subjection. By the Treaty of Aix-la-Chapelle in 1748 with other windward islands it was declared 'neutral' and the Caribs were left in possession. The French took the opportunity offered by the 'neutrality' to settle and establish plantations to such an extent that the English attacked the French settlement in 1756 and took partial control of the island. The Peace of Paris in 1763 gave Dominica to Great Britain and eight years later a separate government was established under Sir William Young, Bart. Several French settlers obtained secure land tenures and remained under British administration.

The French under the Marquis de Bouillé, governor of Martinique, captured Dominica for France in 1778 and held it for five years during which there was great distress because of the maladministration of the Marquis Duchilleau. The English were attacked again in 1795 by French Republican forces under Victor Hugues who had successfully driven British troops from Guadeloupe. Local resistance made Hugues' attempt fail, but in 1805 the French General La Grange attacked Roseau which was then accidentally set on fire. The British paid the French £12,000 to evacuate the island and the Governor Sir George Prevost set up his headquarters at Prince Rupert's near Portsmouth.

Dominica was joined to the Leeward Islands government from 1833 until 1940. Serious riots, arising out of tax collections, led to loss of many lives in 1893 at La Plaine on the windward coast. Five years later the British government contributed £15,000 towards road construction.

Coffee was at one time a flourishing crop, but many estates were abandoned in the nineteenth century because of blight and pilfering by maroons. Other crops have suffered severely from disease, but limes have been exported for many decades. A few miles outside Roseau is the plantation which supplies the famous Roses lime juice. The higher slopes of Dominica are well suited to the cultivation of coffee, oranges, nutmegs, spices and tropical fruits which require humid conditions. Dominica is volcanic. An eruption in the great crater occurred on 4th January 1880 when ash, two to three inches in depth, settled on houses in Roseau. On the Grand Soufrière hills there is a geyser and boiling lake 2,300 feet above sea level. The island has many thermal, chalybeate, sulphur and other medicinal springs, and abounds in rivers, reputedly one for each day of the year. Some have fish. Green in all its hues is the colour of Dominica's lands, sapphire blue the colour of the deep seas which surround it. The sun makes gay rainbows that dance in the rain, and cascades tumble from mountain streams into bamboo ringed pools.

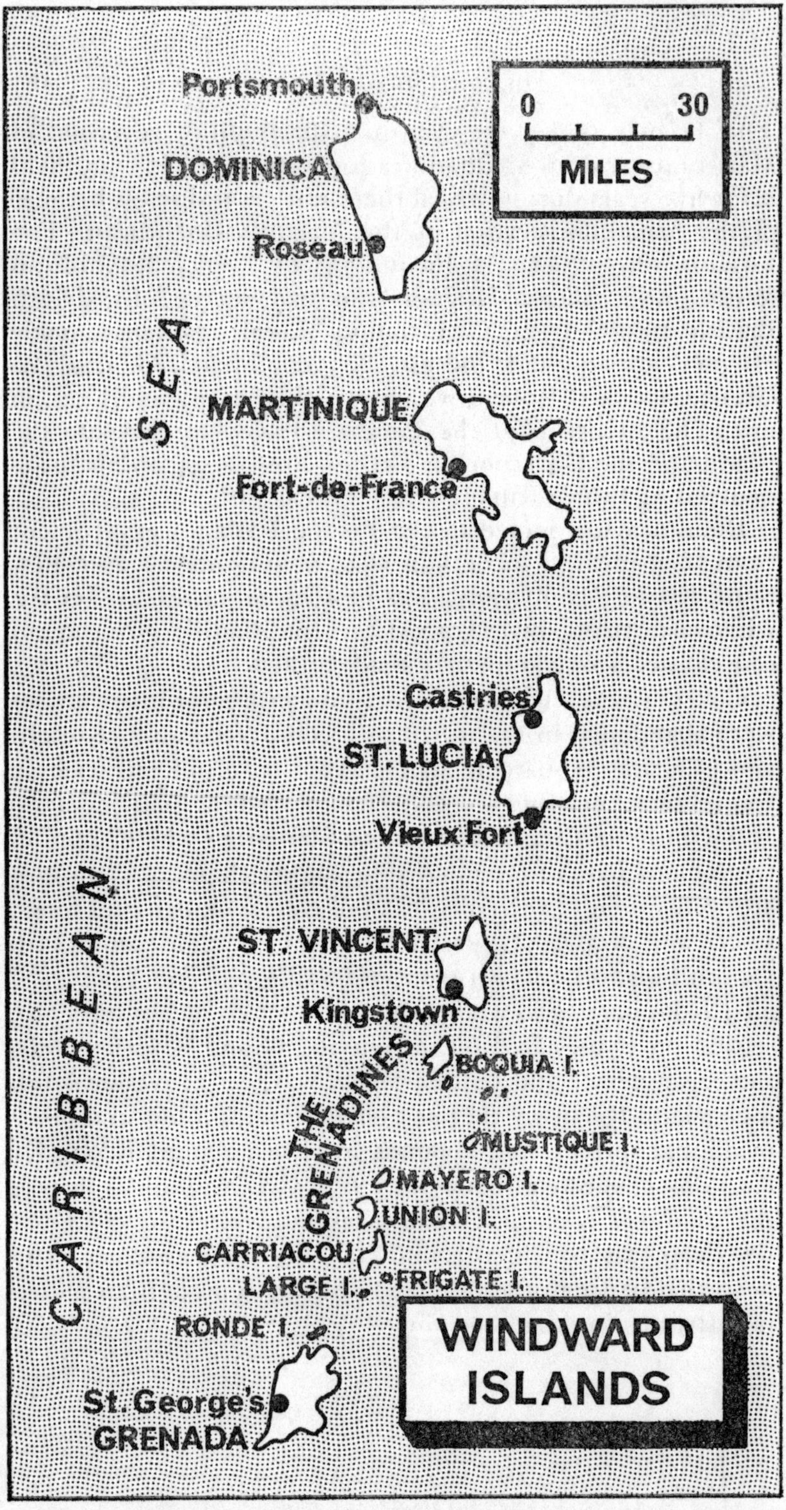
0
30
MILES
Portsmouth
DOMINICA
Roseau
SEA
MARTINIQUE
Fort-de-France
Castries
ST. LUCIA
Vieux Fort
CARIBBEAN
ST. VINCENT
Kingstown
THE GRENADINES
BOQUIA I.
MUSTIQUE I.
MAYERO I.
UNION I.
CARRIACOU
LARGE I.
FRIGATE I.
RONDE I.
St. George's
GRENADA
WINDWARD ISLANDS

The people of Dominica are individualists largely because so many own plots of land. Catholicism, the religion which for centuries emphasised the blessings of life on the land, has implanted a special mark on the Windward Islands.

Dominicans, St Lucians, and the people of Grenada have a distinct air of equality, if not superiority about them. People with great faith in another life are not too concerned with the difficulties and disappointments of daily living, leaving Our Lady and the Saints to look after their real needs. This earlier peasant faith is changing as the Catholic Church draws closer to Protestant practices and ideas, but many more decades will pass before Dominicans will lose their special graces as persons, each of whom is 'unique in the sight of the Lord'.

There have been some disadvantages from Catholic practices. Sir Hesketh Bell in his diary of 1901 noted a drawback in having Government House so near to the Catholic Churchyard from which unpleasant smells would be borne on the breezes reaching his gardens. (Sir Hesketh also recorded in 1901 the death of Wilfred Clive, who was overpowered by sulphurous fumes in the Boiling Lake when on holiday from Madrid.)

Sir Hesketh Bell was a great lover of Dominica and did everything he could to promote its interests. To encourage tourism he once climbed the mast of a steamship with a little Kodak camera and 'snapped' a photo of Roseau and the mountains which was used on Dominican stamps for decades. He also persuaded the Royal Mail Company to supply Dominica with a small coastal steamer and took the initiative in approaching insurance companies to obtain protection for planters whose crops were liable to damage from hurricanes.

Poulets de montagne, like *escargots* are beloved of Frenchmen; so the frogs of Dominica have been relentlessly hunted for centuries. So long as there are streams and mountains the 'mountain chickens' will probably survive, in Dominica, but frogs eaten in the West Indies today may have travelled thousands of miles before they arrive on those few West

Indian tables which specialise in French cuisine. One lover of Dominica's mountain chickens was Adlai Stevenson, who made a visit to the island in the late 'fifties.

The face of Dominica may be changed by the development of timber cutting. The authorities will have to ensure that the exploitation of timber which began in August 1968 is carried out with the long-term needs of agriculture in mind. Only if such precautions are taken is it likely that the investment in timber felling by a group of Canadians who are authorised to cut over one billion feet of timber over 21 years will be profitable for Dominica. Certainly the danger of soil erosion in an island whose soil slopes down towards the sea is real.

Because of its geographical position between Martinique and Guadeloupe and its dependencies, Dominica can also look forward to a share in the resort hotels which are being constructed by international hoteliers in the islands. The Fort Young hotel has provided a base for modern hotel growth and there is reason to believe that the 'Sunday island' will become more popular as new waves of tourists arrive in the West Indies to explore new islands not yet discovered by themselves. Because it escaped the tourist invasion of the 'sixties Dominica stands to gain by an influx of new visitors during the 'seventies. But roads will have to be improved and the airport modernised and extended. The approach to Melville Hall airport is impressive from the air. To get there from Roseau in a hurry may require nerves of steel. One hardened traveller still remembers with awe the experience of telling a Dominican taxi driver to 'make the airport in under one hour'. The taxi driver said 'hold on' and the nightmare recurs every time the traveller remembers the switchback journey up and around and down from the clouds.

'Green gold' and 'tourist gold' are the riches of St Lucia, the beautiful Helen of the Eastern Caribbean. No island is more beautiful, none (for its size) less developed or more in need of a modern road system. The beauty of St Lucia is the beauty of nature.

It was spotted as a tourist resort by the Jamaican hotelier Abe Issa, whose report to the West Indies Federation on the potential of East Caribbean tourist development was chiefly responsible for the formation of a consortium of Commonwealth Development Corporation and Jamaican and North American investors to build beach hotels in Antigua, Grenada and St Lucia. The St Lucian hotel on Reduit beach forced a pace of tourist development which was far ahead of the infrastructures required from air services, road transportation and general amenities. Development also preceded the elimination of sandflies which, together with flies and mosquitoes are the flaws in most West Indian island paradises. Yet Helen is a charmer and the growing numbers who choose the lovely island with a French atmosphere and British traditions seldom are perturbed by problems which no existing administration in the Windwards is likely to solve unaided.

Columbus saw St Lucia nearly ten years after his first voyage of discovery on 15 June 1502. The island has an area of 233 square miles. Its circumference is 150 miles. It lies 24 miles south of Martinique, with which it has many social and commercial contacts, and 21 miles east of St Vincent. French is still spoken by educated persons, the Catholic bishop is a Frenchman and a radio station in St Lucia broadcasts French commercials for Martiniquan business houses.

The Caribs held St Lucia until the King of France granted the island to Messieurs de l'Olive and Duplessis. English people who settled in 1639 were murdered by the Caribs a year later. The King of France in 1642 ceded St Lucia to the French West Indian Company who sold it eight years later for £1,000 to Messieurs Houel and Du Parquet. Unable to expel the Caribs the French made a treaty with them in 1660.

Preliminary to the expedition of Barbadians despatched by Lord Willoughby in 1664, St Lucia in 1663 had been 'purchased' from the Caribs by Thomas Warner, whose mother was a Carib woman and whose father was the pioneer English governor of St Kitts. By the peace of Breda in 1667 St Lucia became French again and seven years later was made a dependency of Martinique. Between 1713 and 1723 the island was disputed by French and English claimants. In 1718 the Regent of France granted it to Marechal d'Estrées and in 1722 King George I of England gave it to the Duke of Montague. In 1723 the English were forced to evacuate St Lucia which was declared 'neutral'. By 1744 the French had regained possession of the island and held it until 1748 when it was again declared neutral. French control was reasserted in 1756, but Admiral Rodney and General Monckton obtained a victory which put St Lucia under the British flag once more until in 1763 it was reassigned to France, under whose dominion it remained until 1778, a year in which England once more established a foothold. In the spring of 1782 Rodney, with a fleet of 36 vessels, set out for Gros Islet Bay to win his famous victory against Count de Grasse off the Isles des Saintes. The victory did not make St Lucia an English possession for long because English diplomats at Versailles a year later gave it back to France. As a consequence of this diplomacy the strategic position of St Lucia greatly helped French revolutionaries, who rampaged through the islands defying the English whose countrymen had declared war against France in 1793. The fate of St Lucia during the French revolutionary wars is part of a Caribbean struggle for possession between French and English forces in which also Guadeloupe and Martinique, Dominica, St Vincent and Grenada were pawns which often changed hands. In the West Indies an ex-innkeeper from Guadeloupe, Victor Hugues, became Commissioner of that island in 1794 and established himself as 'the Robespierre of the Isles' controlling French armies and navies in the war to death against the English. Queen Victoria's father planted a British flag on Morne Fortuné in April 1794, but the French were in possession of St Lucia a year later while the English took refuge in Martinique. A final encounter gave the English victory on 24 May 1796 when the Republican forces surrendered to the

27th Regiment, whose flag is still flown each year on that day to commemorate the second capture of Morne Fortuné by British forces.

The English again gave 'Helen' back to the French by the Treaty of Amiens in 1802, but a year later the island surrendered for the last time to British forces under General Grinfield on 22 June 1803. It remained under absolute British rule till 1 March 1967 when it obtained local 'independence' or qualified 'dominion' status in association with Britain.

The economic independence of St Lucia, as of the other Windward islands, is chiefly supported by Geest Industries Ltd. who supply 50% of British bananas and who developed the exports of the Windwards from 19,700 long tons in 1954 to over 170,000 tons 13 years later. Banana production came in the nick of time for St Lucia when sugar production had declined because of serious discord between employees and plantation and factory owners. The relatively healthy banana industry of the Windwards today owes as much to the unifying force of the Windward Island Banana Growers Association as it does to the highly modern marketing and distributing organisation of Geest Industries.

The beauty of St Lucia ought to be cultivated and shared as a permanent asset for all the East Caribbean chain of islands. The island is large enough, and varied enough to attract visitors from within the region, thereby making it less dependent, especially in the summer months, on tourists from outside the Caribbean. Barbados is an outstanding example of the benefits which can be derived from attracting summer visitors from Guyana, Venezuela, Trinidad and the Windward islands. St Lucia, which is a larger island than Barbados, and with more variety of scenery, should seek to follow the balanced growth which has been Barbados' objective at least until recent years.

The best model for St Lucia and other islands to follow is Bermuda, where the character and architecture of the island have been preserved and where the industry is regulated primarily for the benefit of the Bermudians.

Yachtsmen confirm the accuracy of St Lucia's motto: 'a reliable shelter for ships'. There are good harbours at Castries, Marigot and Pigeon Island and protected anchorages at Cul de Sac Bay, Anse La Raye, Soufrière Bay and Vieux Fort.

St Lucia possesses in the two Pitons near Soufrière the most impressive and perhaps the most frequently photographed natural features in the Caribbean. The twin cones Gros Piton (2,619 feet) and Petit Piton (2,461 feet) rise steeply out of the sea like giant sugar loaves. Sad tales are told of English sailors who have attempted to scale their height only to fall to deaths caused by the fangs of the deadly *fer de lance*, St Lucia's least attractive resident which is fortunately not often seen by visitors. The drive-in volcano from which the fishing village of Soufrière is named ought to be the major reason for visiting St Lucia because hot sulphur baths are available there, even though under primitive conditions. With the development of Vieux Fort, which must follow upon the rehabilitation and expansion of the runways constructed by the Americans during World War II, it is possible that the Soufrière baths may be more sought after than the sea of St Lucia by middle-aged visitors. St Lucians have never failed to 'avail' themselves of the restorative qualities freely available to those who want to use the mineral waters. For those who seek privacy a hut filled with a tub is available for a modest fee.

St Vincent, the Grenadines and Grenada form a single holiday area, even though lively seas divide them. Twenty-one miles south-west of St Lucia, St Vincent lies about 100 miles west of Barbados, from where it can be seen on very clear days and from high points. The island is only 18 miles long and 11 miles wide. Because of shortage of land in the valleys terraced cultivation had to be introduced on mountain slopes, in order to feed a prolific rural population.

The Caribs were well entrenched on St Vincent when Columbus is believed to have seen it on 22 January 1498. They remained entrenched long after it was granted to the

17 Soufrière 'volcano', St Lucia

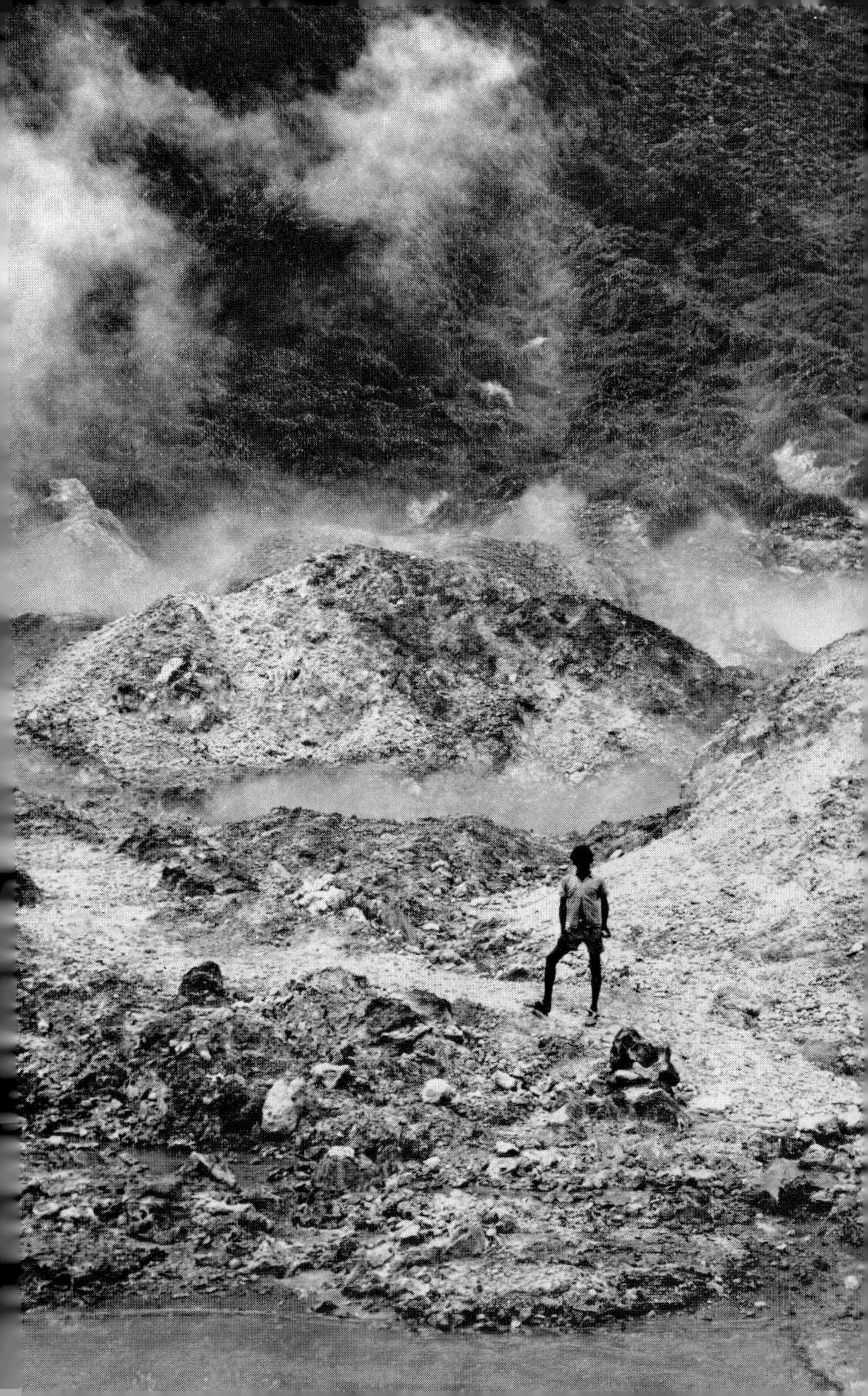

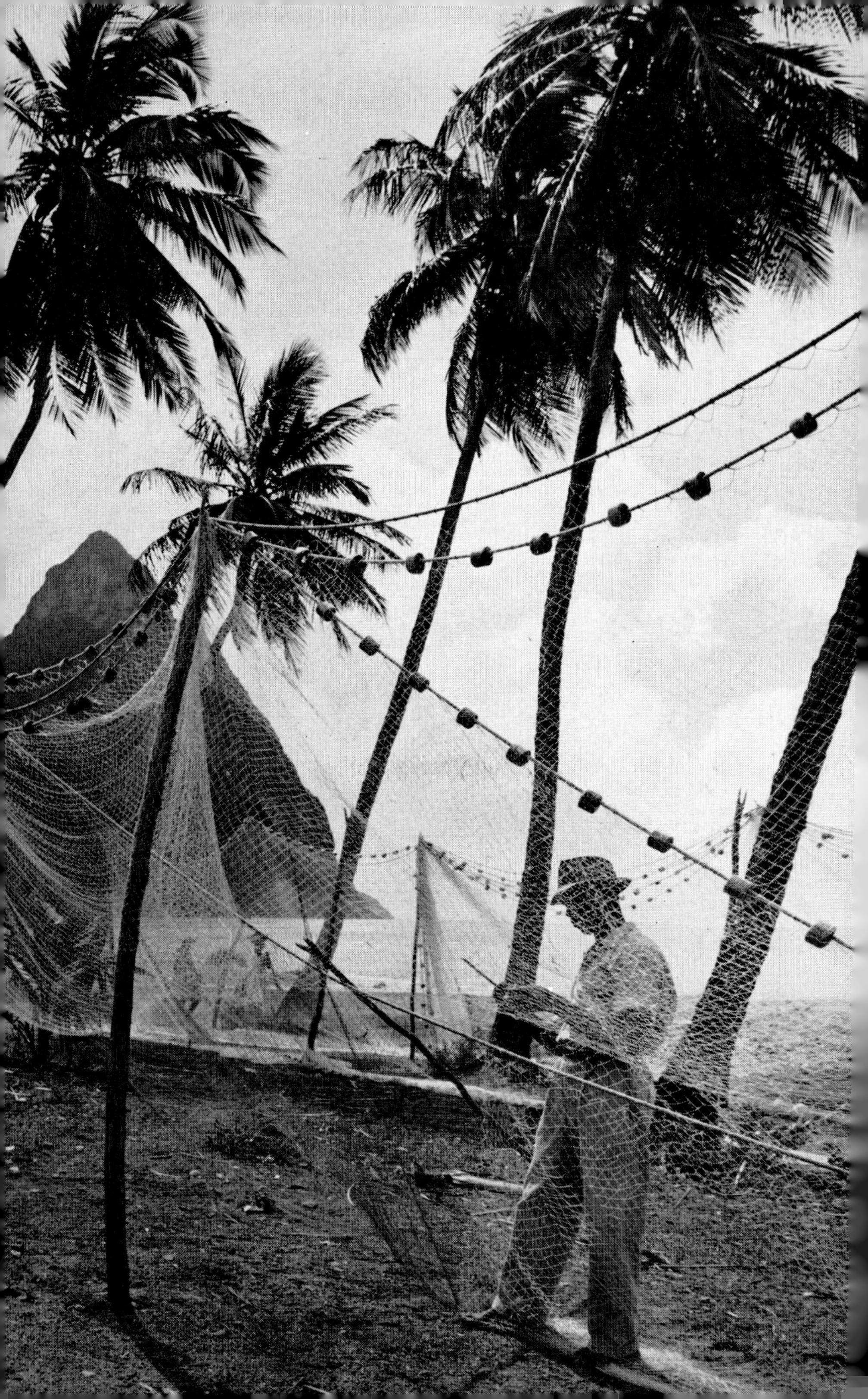

Earl of Carlisle by Charles I in 1627. Officially declared 'neutral' by French and English in 1660 St Vincent was granted to Lord Willoughby in 1672. No settlement was then made and both the English and French agreed to abandon it, with Dominica, to the Caribs on condition that these Indians would make no claim on other islands. Between 1722, when George I granted St Vincent and other islands to the Duke of Montague, and the year 1740 nearly 1,000 white settlers and 3,000 slaves established themselves on the island. The Treaty of Aix-la-Chapelle eight years later declared St Vincent neutral once more, but from 1756 the island was disputed by French and English until General Monckton seized it for England in 1762. Eleven years later the Caribs signed a treaty acknowledging the King of Great Britain as the sovereign of St Vincent. In return they were granted a large part of the island.

For six years the island remained under British rule, then the French captured it the year before the awful hurricane which devastated most of the islands in 1780. Britain was restored to possession in 1783, but the French revolutionaries under Victor Hugues assisted by warlike Caribs murdered, plundered and burnt the island mercilessly in 1795. After relief by Sir Ralph Abercromby's forces in 1796 the authorities decided to banish the Caribs and on 11 March 1797 over 5,000 were put on ships at Bequia and transported to the island of Ruatan in the Bay of Honduras. To obtain labourers for teh sugar plantations after the emancipation of slaves the government of St Vincent imported Portuguese and subsequently East Indians.

The sugar industry of St Vincent died in 1962 and bananas soon after became the dominant economic activity, overtaking arrowroot. St Vincent has achieved the reputation of producing the finest sea island quality cotton in the world and its former reputation should favour the island if recent efforts to revive the production of West Indian cotton are successful. Arrowroot plantations may be seen all along the 18 miles drive on the Windward coast. St Vincent produces

18 The Small Piton rising behind the fishing nets, Soufrière, St Lucia

a large portion of the arrowroot starch which is an important ingredient of the baby foods which are sold all over the world.

Coconuts are also grown extensively on the island on lands which are unsuitable for the other crops such as vegetables, tobacco, nutmegs, black pepper, hot pepper, mangoes, avocado pears, grapefruit, citrus, ginger, onions, white potatoes, ground nuts, pineapples and passion fruits. The growth of tourism in the Grenadines and the neighbouring islands offers attractive prospects for the further development of these crops, which however require special skills and export markets and distributive organisations if they are to be economically rewarding.

For lovers of natural beauty St Vincent is a satisfying island. Its Botanic Garden, which preserves a specimen of the breadfruit family descended from Bligh's importation of 1793, is the best tended in the East Caribbean. From Fort Charlotte a splendid view of the capital city of Kingstown is obtained, while the windward coast offers exciting drives over twisting mountain roads below which lie fertile valleys and unspoilt seaside villages. Soufrière, an active volcano, which killed many thousands of people in 1812 and 1902, today has a magnificent crater lake surrounded by steep green sides. It is often obliterated by rain and mist and the top has to be approached on hands and knees during bursts of rainfall. Raincoats are also needed for the long tramp through dense tropical forest, darkness and heat.

Château Belair Bay, which lies under Soufrière, and Cumberland Bay on the west coast are adequate anchorages for yachtsmen. Other anchorages are near to the Aquatic Club and Young's Island, an 'away-from-it-all' luxury resort where the guests are invited to swim across from the mainland if they want to 'go native' before arrival.

Between May and October the black fish, a whale between 12 and 15 feet long, is harpooned off the north-western village of Barrouallie. Each whale produces, in addition to meat, between seven and 20 gallons of oil.

Although small, Kingstown has some interesting survivals

of old Colonial architecture. At least one façade is being preserved to retain an old-world character that is fast disappearing throughout the West Indies.

St Vincent is known throughout the West Indies as the homeland of Cyril Barnard, whose race horses are kept in air-conditioned stables and exercised on 35 acres of fenced paddock on Orange Hill estate near the foothills of Soufrière. Horses from the Barnard stables are frequent winners on the race courses of Barbados and Trinidad.

Until Princess Margaret's honeymoon visit, Bequia was an island escape for West Indians from St Vincent and Barbados. They went there to get away from their own 'developed' towns, to walk barefoot on sands, talk with boat builders or sit gazing out to the horizon until their island schooners were ready to take them back to St Vincent or their own islands.

Bequia also gained notoriety when the Earl of Avon owned a beach house at Friendship Bay. The island has a backbone of hills 900 feet high, beautiful sandy beaches, rocky cays, wooded valleys and sloping hillsides. It is possible that the name Bequia is a corruption of the French word Béké which is used in Martinique as a description of white Creoles or French-born residents. It may even be possible that this name was applied to 'white' Barbadians who early emigrated from Barbados to St Vincent, Bequia and the Grenadines.

Today Bequia is on the tourist map and smart hotels provide their own sleek yachts to bring guests across the nine-mile channel which separates Kingstown from Port Elizabeth, the capital village. Only about six miles long and one mile wide, Bequia cannot develop into more than an expensive piece of real estate, but the wave of tourism which now beats upon it is unlikely to recede until the whole character of the schooner-making island is changed. No longer will it be possible for visiting yachtsmen to be impressed by the wall paintings of the Virgin giving a model sail boat to her young son Jesus. Bequia will no longer be an island of boat builders and fishermen.

The tourist wave which beats on Bequia must also surge

throughout the chain of Grenadine islands. Already there are expensive hotels and luxury houses on Prune island (also known as Palm) where LIAT (Leeward Island Air Transport) has regular stops. On Mustique, banker Hugo Money Coutts, who pilots his own plane on to rough landing strips, and the Hon. Clive Tennant are developing the 1,250 acres of the privately owned island. A proper airstrip ought by now to be in operation. Petit St Vincent and Petit Martinique are also being rescued from oblivion by hotel developers.

The 33 islands and cays which comprise St Vincent and its Grenadines have a total area of 150 square miles and vary in size from 85,000 acres to a few yards in diameter. Only St Vincent and seven of its dependencies are inhabited.

The Grenadines altogether comprise 125 islands with truly unspoilt bathing beaches and natural harbours. It would require a whole winter to visit and explore them all. They hang together like pearls on a necklace nearly 70 miles long, so close together that wherever you sail there is always an island visible in the distance. With crystal-clear water, dazzling white beaches, and green covered hillsides they defy the stock descriptions of the image makers. They are God's masterpieces, protected by their tiny land surfaces from invasion by travellers en masse, but are vulnerable to settlement, or yachting visits from the very rich who are never satisfied and always on the look out for new hideaways, as far away as possible from the places where their fortunes were made.

King George V and his brother Prince Alfred who visited the islands on the *Bacchante* in the year 1880 described them as made of grey and red rocks, and saw in them resemblances to 'the Cyclades of the Grecian archipelago or the islets of the inland sea of Japan'. One of the most picturesque interiors of a church in the West Indies is to be found on the little Grenadine island of Mayero. From the outside of the church there is a breath-taking view of Union island, where according to an official publication, vessels 'will shoot into the anchorage' at Chatham Bay if they follow the precise instructions given in the manual. Union island, which has perpendicular mountains over 100 feet high, has been likened to Saba but is less confined. Tradition says that the Union islanders are descended from Africans who were shipwrecked and who never worked as slaves. The survival of genuine African dances there seems to support the statement.

From Cannouan, which has a solid Anglican church as well as a Catholic chapel, an excellent view of Tobago Cays is visible from the top of the hill behind the village of Charlestown Bay. Doctor John Lewis of the Bellairs Research Institute of McGill University in Barbados has made several pleas for the preservation of the four tiny Tobago Cays as a natural land and sea park. The cays are protected from the great Atlantic rollers by the Horseshoe Reef which is about two miles across and has an axis of nearly three miles. The channel on the sea side goes down to one hundred feet. Swimmers have to be wary at the crest of the elkhorn coral, which is as dense as a forest and perilous for the bottoms of boats. Behind the crest in shallow waters coral sea fans abound and at least one hundred species of many-hued small fish. The residents of the islands are red-necked ramier pigeons, seabirds on the cliffs, land and soldier crabs and iguanas, green and brown, who are as at home in the sea as on land and swim easily from island to island.

Carriacou is the largest of the Grenadines with an area of 8,467 acres. It is seven miles long and two and a half miles wide. The dividing line between St Vincent's administration and Grenada's actually makes the northern extremity of Carriacou a part of St Vincent. It is more logical to ignore this and to regard the sea between Petit St Vincent and Petit Martinique which are one mile apart as the real boundary between the two states. Because of the location of the boundary the inhabitants of Petit Martinique are labelled by some people as 'smugglers', but yachtsmen who have spent many months sailing between the islands are of the opinion that most of the smuggling occurs through transhipment at larger ports in the West Indies.

The sign on a shop in Petit Martinique 'In God We Trust, cash for all others', is at least a tribute to the canny business sense of the islanders whose attitudes are also influenced by the Catholic school and church. Schooners are built on Petit Martinique and Carriacou and some of the islanders still believe that each vessel launched in the sea has a 'soul of its own'. This explains perhaps the coincidence of a Catholic priest blessing a new schooner at a ceremony where a goat is sacrificed to provide the ship's soul.

The emerald islands of the Grenadines take the colour of rubies when the red flamboyant is in bloom, while their sands glitter like gold and silver against topaz seas. Carriacou once had a thriving sugar economy, as an old document in the Rhodes Library at Oxford recalls. There no less than 50 well-known English families are recorded as being proprietors in Carriacou and eight on Petit Martinique, in the year 1776. Carriacou has been compared by one Englishman to England at its best in the summer, and Hillsborough Harbour likened to a miniature St George's Grenada. The shooting season runs from September to February, and fishing is all year round. On a dark night some fish show their presence by phosphorescence in the water. Jackadan, a small island in Hillsborough Bay recalls the presence of the French on Carriacou. The bathing is superb on Sunday Island, and the thickly wooded Mabouya to the south of the bay is the nearest thing to a Rovers Boy Camp to be found in the West Indies. From Chapeau Carré, 960 feet above sea level there is a view of the swamps of Carriacou, which attract the land crabs used for the delicacies of 'crab backs', and also migrant birds. Also visible from the hill top are the oyster beds near Harvey Vale. Rain water which for centuries was caught in all the islands is still the main source of supply of drinking water in the Grenadines. On Carriacou large cisterns are used as catchments for rain which is precipitated from the roofs of buildings. At Windward on the eastern side of Carriacou light-skinned fisherfolk and boat builders of Scottish descent survive as they have survived on the windward coast of

Barbados, St Vincent, Grenada and other islands, as if the Atlantic sea reminded them of their long-lost original homelands. The French left Carriacou with no less than 73 miles of good roads which have given it a proper push forward since hotel developments are more likely than cotton, limes, cattle raising or fishing to improve the living standards of its inhabitants.

All the islands which lie between Carriacou and the north coast of Grenada are as picturesque as their names, but the sea surface is almost always agitated. The waters between Carriacou and Kick-em-Jenny are very deep and the shallow water off the island is under constant pressure from the currents coming from the northern tip of Grenada. During high winds heavy seas are common and wise sailors stay clear of Kick-em-Jenny, the island which can 'give a kick like a mule'. Even on the leeside of the Isle de Ronde, which is regarded as a pretty and safe place to anchor, there is almost always a constant roll. For those who want to see Carriacou without a sea journey, the airstrip at Lauriston Field is ten minutes flying time from Pearls Airport in Grenada.

Grenada is an island of superlative beauty. It was chosen by producers of 20th Century Fox as the backdrop for the film *Island in the Sun*, which did more than any other single post-war effort to project the scenic appeal of the East Caribbean islands. An Italian, who wrote that 'no person can impressively describe the heavenly beauty of this island' likened it to 'a piece of green cotton arising from blue water into a majestic chair of high mountains, always covered on top with white light clouds, as a kiss from the sky' and said that its 'dance of colours could send any painter mad'. Grenada is about 21 miles long and 12 miles at its greatest breadth. It lies 68 miles south-south-west of St Vincent and about 90 miles north of Trinidad. Its mountains are for the most part volcanic, the highest, Mount St Catherine, being 2,749 feet. It has many streams and mineral and natural springs.

Grand Etang, a lake on top of a mountain ridge 1,740 feet

above sea level and Lake Antoine have been formed from old craters. At certain seasons of the year Grenadians of African origin offer rice and other foodstuffs to the spirit who is believed to dwell in the Grand Etang. Annandale Falls is a favourite natural swimming pool for the young where cool fresh water from a river drops white as snow from a dark green forest, as it might have done in the garden of Eden. The roads of Grenada are narrow and twisting and are best negotiated by local drivers who know the rules and the courtesies of the island, so important at bridges where only one vehicle can pass at a time.

Grenada's crops are harvested mainly from trees, nutmeg, cinnamon, banana, cocoa, coconut, citrus and others which make the island appear to be a wild, tangled garden of fruits and spices. Because trees take many years to come to fruit-bearing size the island took more than a physical buffeting from the hurricane Janet, which hit it full force in 1955. Several years elapsed before new trees could be grown. Many non-fruit-bearing trees cover the slopes of the interior where the land resembles a huge conservatory which has outgrown the restraints of its caretakers, everything growing lush and matted. Birds thrive in the wooded habitats and the forest is most appreciated by those who love birds, walking and communing with the God of Nature.

At Westerhall Point, eight miles from Pearl's airport and four miles from the picturesque town of St George's a British architect, Beresford Wilcox, and his Norwegian wife Kari have given Grenadians an example of the best way of developing sea bordering land to be seen anywhere in the East Caribbean. There 'naked Indian' or gommier trees, and wild Antiguan frangipani are preserved among 20,000 others which have been planted over 110 acres that roll down to five separate beaches and coves amid patterns of carved fallen tree trunks, volcanic boulders and neatly tended green turf which makes vivid contrast with her flowering bougainvillaea shrubs. There the music of the mocking bird and the cheeps of banana quits are more melodious than the twanging of electric guitars and there the turtles will waddle on to the beach to lay their eggs on lands from which the mongoose has been banished, like Adam from Eden. At Westerhall community living is possible, children using a single school bus to go to an international school, and everybody preparing shopping lists for Friday's excursion to St George's.

Throughout the West Indies you will find men and women of great individuality. A Catholic priest once told me how he had proposed to a lady on behalf of one of his bashful parishioners. A film executive during the making of *Island in the Sun* had to do business with a Grenadan man whom he finally ran to earth in his bedroom the worse for drink and talking to a game cock which he had taken upstairs to bed for company. It was on the way to Westerhall that I realised the full personality of my driver Henderson Harris whom his friends called 'Rat', for good luck, he said. The car had come to a standstill in an old estate yard. Henderson, or 'Rat' for luck, got out, ceremonially shut the door, and walked across to a field from which he selected a stone large enough to kill a man. Slowly retracing his steps he approached the car, jerked up the bonnet, held it aloft with one hand and with all his strength banged it down on the battery leads. Then he let fall the bonnet with a clash, hurled the stone into the field, opened the door, slid gracefully into his seat, switched the key and pressed the starter. The car roared into life. Henderson grinned all over his face and spoke. 'Forgive me,' he said, 'but the man who drive this car before me is a car-killer. That man treat a car real bad. He ent say a word how bad this car is. It really need a good overhaul.' And slipping into gear he rolled on the way to Westerhall Point.

At Annandale Falls I had already noted his ability to sum up a situation in pithy words. At the far entrance to the falls was a locked gate, and we had taken the precaution of obtaining a key in advance. But there was no need, for as Henderson observed with his sly grin 'anybody can walk around the side'. The language of the people in the West Indies comes from the earth. It is full of the raw material of life. Few modern writers could invent, for instance, a description of political corruption as basic as that given me by a street cleaner in Bridgetown when he said 'I know what sweeten the goat mouth does burn underneath its tail'.

The people of Grenada have many vivid expressions to describe rare moments of life. No Barbadian could find words more suited to translate an act of God than the Grenadan who said: 'What is to is, must is'. For many years Grenadans, like the St Lucians and the people of Dominica spoke in a patois largely composed of words of French origin. The song which the women banana loaders of St Lucia used to sing all day to ward off fatigue contains a refrain which goes:

Ola, Ola Bois ti boy la cassé

In St Lucia's English this would read 'Fly up, Fly up, de little boy arm break'.

It has been suggested by people who admire the clear diction of the middle classes of Grenada that they speak English with great precision and clarity, precisely because English had been taught as a second language and was not the tongue they spoke at home. The suggestion is fascinating but there is no doubt whatever that the educated people of Grenada do speak an English which is easily understood by people born in England. In Barbados on the other hand the slow Somerset drawl, coupled to American idiom and the basic Afro-English of the sugar plantations makes communications even with North Americans far from simple. Many visitors to Barbados complain of the difficulty of making themselves understood, while the Barbadians in turn have learnt how to give the impression that they have fully understood when they have understood nothing at all because the 'mistress' or 'the master speak too great'.

When Columbus saw Grenada on 15 August 1498 and called it Concepcion the Caribs were in possession. They continued in possession for more than a century and successfully foiled an attempt of London merchants to establish a settlement on the island in 1609. Forty-one years later

Martinique's governor Du Parquet was more successful and established a colony on the site of the modern St George's. Seven years afterwards he sold Grenada to the Comte de Cerrillac for 30,000 crowns. The new owner tyrannised the colonists, who eventually executed him after a trial. France annexed the island in 1674, but in 1762 the British captured it and it was acknowledged as a British possession by the Treaty of Paris in the following year. The French recaptured it in 1779 and held it until 1783, when by the Treaty of Versailles it was returned to Britain. More blood flowed during the French revolutionary wars. Rebels massacred the Lieutenant Governor and other British subjects. In 1796 the rebellion was put down by Sir Ralph Abercromby. From 1766 Grenada possessed a Legislative Council and an Assembly. A Single Chamber legislature was enacted in 1875, but two years later crown colony government was established. On 1 June 1885 Grenada became headquarters of the Governor of the Windward Islands which then included St Lucia and St Vincent. Upon the liquidation of the Federation of the West Indies, Government House became the residence of the Administrator of Grenada until 1967. A Governor was appointed for 'the self-governing independent state' of Grenada which like other islands became 'associated' with Britain. The first Governor of Grenada is a native-born lady, Dame Hilda Bynoe. Like Martinique and Antigua, Grenada is a centre for yachtsmen, and has a modern marina and efficient dock services in the inner harbour of St George's.

After Barbados, St Lucia and Tobago, Grenada has the greatest tourist potential in the East Caribbean and is already well supplied with luxury and first class hotels. The problem of the Isle of Spices will be not in too little but in 'too much' unplanned and uncontrolled development, some of which has already happened because West Indian politicians are too easily persuaded that gardens of Eden cannot be spoilt.

GENERAL INFORMATION

Dominica

Churches Roman Catholic (majority), Anglican, Methodist Seventh Day Adventist, Reformed Methodist, Gospel Missions.

Climate Normal temperature ranges from 65°F to 90°F. Average 80°. Rainfall about 70 inches near Roseau, 300 inches in mountains. Lowest rainfall between January and May.

Clothing As for other Windward islands.

Communications Air—LIAT and Caribair. Sea—Geest and other lines provide limited passage accommodation.

Currency East Caribbean dollar.

Necessary Documents Passports are not required for *bona fide* visitors who are British subjects or citizens of the United States coming direct from their countries of origin, and in possession of adequate identification papers and valid return tickets, provided that duration of stay does not exceed six months.

Electricity 230 volts AC 50 cycles.

Food and Drink Dominica has fine oranges and other citrus fruit, bananas, and other fruits and vegetables. Fish are available at certain seasons, notably king fish, tuna and dolphin (dorado). Dominica is celebrated for mountain chickens. Imported liquors are relatively cheap.

Holidays and Festivals New Year's Day. Pre-Lenten Carnival, Good Friday, Easter Monday, May Day, Queen's Birthday (June), Whit Monday, First Monday in August, Dominica National Day November 3, 4, Christmas and Boxing Day.

Language The official language is English, but a French patois is widely spoken, though not written.

Laundry and Dry Cleaning Limited facilities.

Local Courtesies and Customs The social atmosphere is friendly and influenced by French customs and the Catholic religion. Every soul counts.

Medical Facilities Twelve doctors and two dentists were registered in 1968. Most doctors have private clinics. The Princess Margaret Hospital at Roseau has private rooms. There are cottage hospitals at Grand Bay, Marigot and Portsmouth.
Night Life In hotels.
Other Tourist Facilities Safari tours of the interior, fishing, water sports, relaxing, occasional exhibitions and performances by Arts Council. A small museum in nucleus form. Two cinemas in Roseau.
Other Sports Spectator sports are cricket, football, basket ball, netball, and lawn tennis in private clubs. Dominoes.
Tipping Accepted.
Time One hour ahead of Eastern Standard Time, five hours behind London time.
Where to Stay Fort Young in Roseau, Castaways Beach Resort (14 miles from Roseau), Island House and Springfield Estate.
Harbour A small harbour has been approved for Woodbridge Bay near to Roseau.
What to Buy Dominican handcrafts, local cigars, W. A. Gilbey's local gin and whiskey (bottled at River Estate near Roseau).

St Lucia

Churches Majority Roman Catholic. Other denominations: Anglicans, Methodists, American Baptists, Seventh Day Adventists and Salvation Army.
Climate Temperature varies from 70°F to 90°F. Rainfall from 60 inches on north and south coasts to 160 inches in the interior.
Clothing As for other Windward islands.
Communications A jet airport at Beane Field Vieux Fort will give St Lucia direct services from North America and Europe. Vigie Airport is serviced by BWIA, LIAT and Carib-

air. Sea communications are provided by Geest and other steamships with limited passenger accommodation.
Currency East Caribbean dollar.
Electricity 240 volt AC 50 cycles.
Food and Drink Creole and French style cooking, wines from France and Martinique.
Holidays and Festivals January 1, 2 Le Jour de l'An celebrations on Columbus Square, Pre-Lenten Carnival, March 1st Statehood Day, Good Friday, Easter Monday, May 1st Labour Day, Whit Monday, Queen's Birthday (June) Parades, Corpus Christi, Religious Processions, July 14 Bastille Day celebrations, August First Monday Emancipation Holiday, August 30 Fête La Rose, flower festival in honour of St Rose de Lima, September 1st Hunting Season opens, October 2 Thanksgiving holiday, October 17 Fête La Marguerite Flower festival in country districts, December 13 St Lucia Day holiday, Christmas, Boxing Day.
Language English is official language. Creole or patois is spoken.
Laundry and Dry Cleaning Adequate facilities in hotels.
Local courtesies and customs St Lucians appreciate good manners. It is useful to have a guide or chauffeur in the country districts.
Medical Facilities Castries has a hospital and there are small district hospitals at Soufrière, Dennery and Vieux Fort.
Night Life In hotels and clubs.
Other Tourist Facilities Shopping, sightseeing, yachting, trips to neighbouring islands.
Pets and Animals Approval must be obtained from the Department of Agriculture in advance of importation. Veterinary certificates are required from official agencies in the country of origin. No dogs or cats allowed from countries where rabies is endemic.
Sports Tennis courts are available at clubs and some hotels. Water skiing, swimming and skin diving. Cricket, basketball, football and netball are spectator sports. Hunting and fishing are male sports. The new hotels offer a wide variety of sport-

ing activities and swimming pools near the beach. Cap Estate on the north has a golf club. Yachtsmen are welcomed by the St Lucia Yacht Club. Yacht services are provided in Castries harbour and cruises and rentals organised by Carib Cruises P.O. Box 183 Castries, St Lucia. St Lucians are keen fans of cockfighting. Fights are usually staged in the winter months.
Time One hour ahead of Eastern Standard Time: five hours behind London time.
Transport Comfortable cars for land journeys and yachts and motor boats for expeditions by sea. Local drivers and skippers are recommended for maximum enjoyment. Drive on the left ashore. Between Vigie Airport (Castries) and Beane Field airport (Vieux Fort) taxi fare is $21 US per car of four persons. Seats in a five-seater twin engine plane between the two airports cost $10 US each. Drivers of cars are warned that any person driving a car is responsible for the first £50 in damages caused by an accident.
Water Is chemically treated, filtered and disinfected in Castries. Untreated water should not be drunk.
Stores Business places in Castries close between 12.30 p.m. and 1.30 p.m. for lunch, Monday to Saturdays. Stores close half day on Wednesdays.
Banks Banks close at midday daily except Saturdays (at 11 a.m.).
What to Buy Imported British goods, St Lucia straw hats, dolls, pottery, hand printed fabrics, madras 'Têtes'.
What to See Castries from points overlooking town. Morne Fortune, Paix Bouche claimed by St Lucians as a possible birthplace of Josephine whose father had an estate there. This claim has not been documented and is not accepted in Martinique. Anse Ger, where there are 400 rock-cut basins on windward coast. Vieux Fort, which is being developed into a major hotel centre. Soufrière, where the guillotine was set up by French revolutionaries. Above Soufrière is the drive-in volcano. The Pitons are close to the village. Marigot Bay, landlocked and settlers resort, a yachtsman's heaven. Reduit Beach where an artificial causeway connects the mainland to

Pigeon Island. Hotels, shops and other amenities are being constructed on the causeway. Cap Estate a picturesque home, hotel, golf and shopping resort.

St Vincent

Churches Anglican, Methodist, Roman Catholic, Seventh Day Adventists and several other Christian denominations.
Climate The prevailing North East Trade Winds temper the healthy climate to an average 80°F. The annual rainfall is about 80 inches.
Clothing Lightwear summer and sports clothing is generally recommended for men and women. Cocktail wear for formal occasions. All clothing suitable for wear in the island can be purchased locally.
Communications There is a telephone service in the island with links to the Grenadines. Cable and Wireless (W.I.) Ltd. also operate an efficient overseas service. The local Government Radio Station WIBS, features a daily variety of programmes. Commercial stations operating from Trinidad and Barbados also have a large listening public in St Vincent. Geest and other shipping lines offer limited passenger accommodation by sea. Air communications are provided by LIAT and Caribair.
Currency Eastern Caribbean Dollar.
Electric Current There is a good Hydro electric power supply throughout St Vincent, operating at 220/30 volts and 50 cycles, for domestic purposes.
Food and Drink There are a multitude of local vegetables, fruits and fish. Breadfruit is very popular, as a vegetable dish. Passion fruit juice punch is rapidly earning for itself a name as *the* drink of St Vincent.
Holidays and Festivals New Year's Day, January 1st, St Vincent's Day (Discovery Day) January 22nd, Pre-Lenten Carnival, Easter (popular time for boat excursions to the Grenadines), Whit Monday (approximately seven weeks after

19 The Roman Catholic church, Kingstown, St Vincent

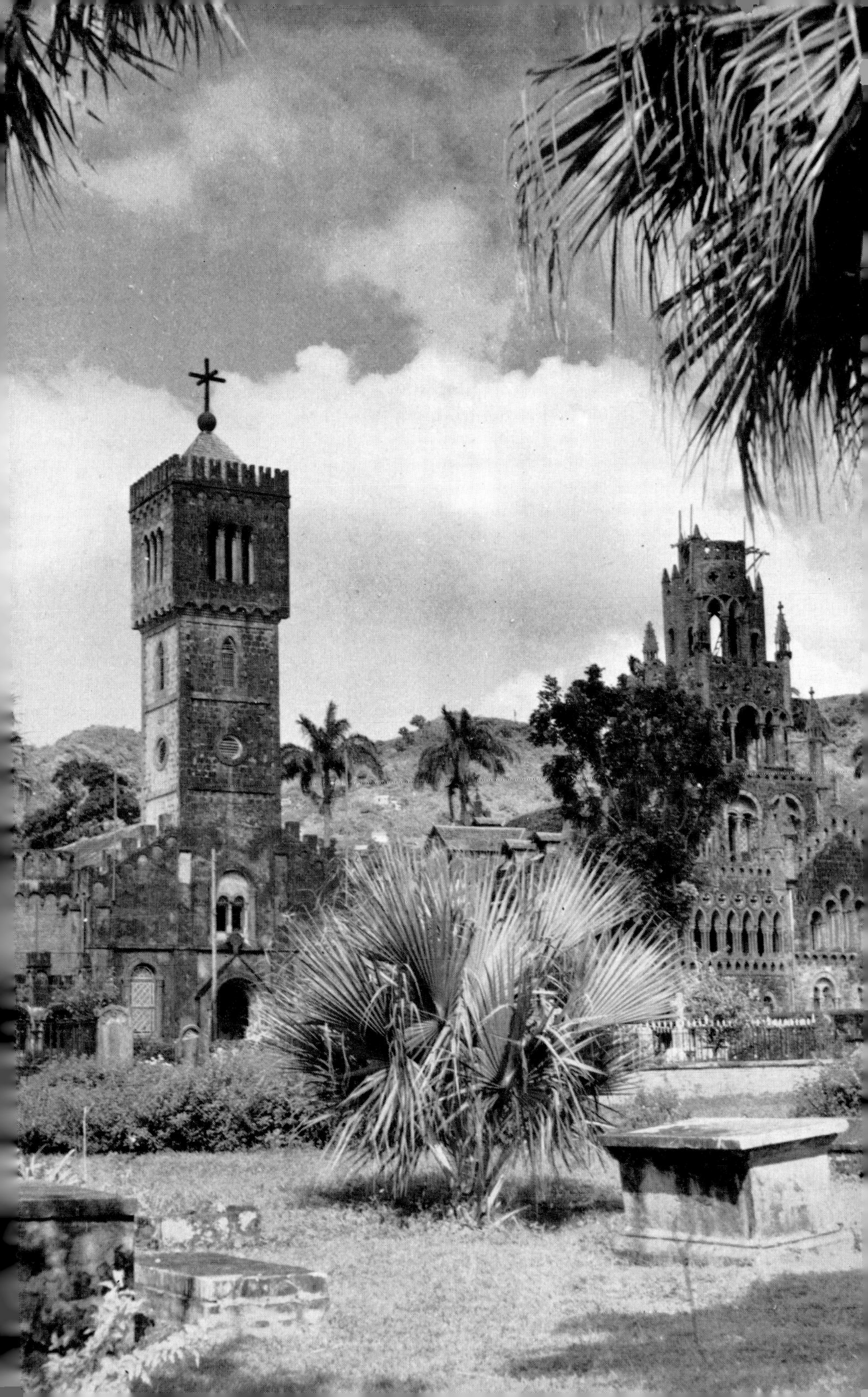

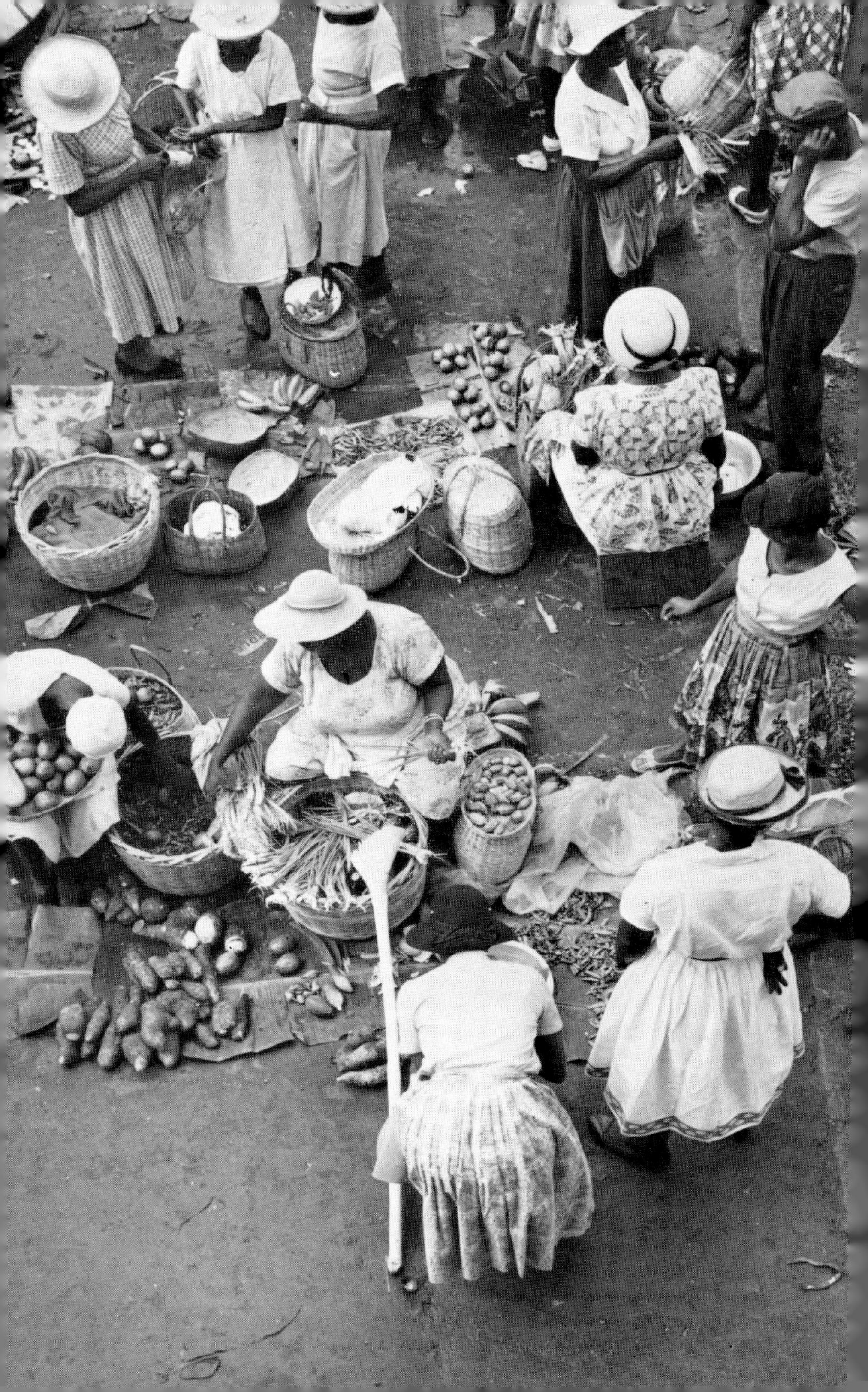

Easter) Annual St Vincent/Bequia yacht race and fishing boat regatta; Corpus Christi (Holiday given to facilitate celebration of this important Catholic feast day), August Monday Holiday (first Monday in August), Christmas and Boxing Day.
Language English.
Laundry and Dry Cleaning Hotels provide facilities but also available in Kingstown.
Local Courtesies and Customs It is popular practice to exchange greetings with visitors even if you are not introduced.
Medical Facilities There is a General hospital in the capital Kingstown, attended by Surgeons and Physicians. Qualified doctors and dentists render efficient island-wide service privately and as Government officers. Georgetown and Bequia have small hospitals.
Night Life There are a few night clubs in or around Kingstown. Except for private parties, dancing usually is the popular form of entertainment.
Other Tourist Facilities There are a few cinemas. Organised tours of the island and trips to the Grenadines.
Pets and Animals 'No animal shall be imported into the territory except in accordance with the terms of a permit granted by the Superintendent of Agriculture who may grant or refuse such permit as he deems fit and in granting such permit may include therein such conditions as he considers necessary.'
Restaurants There are a few restaurants in Kingstown but most hotels offer facilities.
Sports Cricket and soccer are the main spectator sports. Swimming, boating, yachting, deep-sea and spear fishing and skin diving are favourite sports. Tennis courts are available at the Kingstown Tennis Club where temporary membership can be arranged. The mountains can also be a challenge to the mountain climber.
Time One hour ahead of Eastern Standard Time, five hours behind time of London.
Tipping Accepted.
Transportation Local U-Drive cars are available in large

20 *Open-air market, St George's, Grenada*

numbers and rates are reasonable when compared with other West Indian islands. Just bring your driver's licence with you, have the numbers noted by the Police and remember to keep on the left.

Water There is a good clean island-wide, pipe-borne water supply throughout St Vincent. In the Grenadines cisterns and catchments provide the water supply and there is a desalination plant on Petit St Vincent.

What to See Visit the Kingstown Public Library and see the relics of Carib Indian stone implements. Botanic Gardens and Fort Charlotte are both worth visits. Central Arrowroot Factory at Bellevue. Black whales at Barrouallie between May and October.

What to Buy Local handicrafts can be bought from many stores in straw and mahogany.

Other Information Airports at Arnos Vale and Prune Island (Palu) and Mustique.

Other Tourist Facilities The Grenadines which are administered by the island government of St Vincent are rapidly being developed as settler and holiday islands. The Palm Island Beach Club on Casuarina Beach, Palm Island is managed by John Caldwell (author of *Desperate Voyage*). Guests can visit nearby islands or go fishing in the 45 foot ketch *Outward Bound*, or the 24 foot sport fisherman *Caribonito*. Air service between Palm Island, St Vincent and Grenada is seven days a week. There is also daily air service to Mustique, the three mile long island made famous by the wreck of the French liner *Antilles* in January 1971. Resort homes and hotels are being constructed on Mustique, Petit St Vincent, Union Island and on Bequia (160 rooms). A motorboat leaves Bequia daily for Kingstown (the capital of St Vincent) at 6.30 a.m. and returns at 2.45 p.m. (one hour earlier on Saturdays). One way fare between Bequia and Kingstown is $1 E.C. In Kingstown on the waterfront an old warehouse of Georgian style has been renovated and named the Cobblestone Inn after the old cobblestone walkways and arches. Part of the reconstruction is reserved for boutiques and stores selling quality goods. Not far from the capital Young Island Hotel is situated on a small island very close to the mainland, a short distance from the airport.

Grenada

Churches Roman Catholic, Church of England, Methodist, Presbyterian and other denominations maintain churches in the capital and in other towns and districts over the island.
Climate Year-round average temperature of 80°F.
Clothing Most suitable wear is the usual type of cool summer clothing. Sportswear is very popular, as most of the social entertainment is of an informal nature.
Communications Grenada is served by Leeward Islands Air Transport from Puerto Rico through the Leeward and Windward Islands, Trinidad and Tobago; by BOAC from London with connexions at Barbados or Trinidad; by BWIA from Canada, New York and Miami, and by Air Canada from Montreal and Toronto with similar connexions. All Air Lines calling at Barbados and Trinidad may be used with onward journeys by LIAT in 45 and 35 minutes flying time respectively. Limited passenger services by sea are available from London, New York, Miami and Montreal.
Currency $1.00 US=$1.99 EC; $1.00 Canadian=$1.86 EC; £1=$4.80 EC; 1 New Franc=.36 EC; 1 Bolivar=.44 EC.
Necessary Documents No passports are required of citizens of the United Kingdom, Canada or the United States who are visiting for a period not exceeding six months, provided they can produce evidence of citizenship such as birth certificates or naturalisation papers, and tickets to an onward destination. For periods in excess of six months and for permanent residence written application to the Premier is necessary.
Electrical Current Rating 230 volts at 50 cycles.
Food and Drink Sea Food and a profusion of fresh tropical fruit and vegetables. Rum and Planters Punches are popular.

Holidays and Festivals January 1st, two Horse and Yacht Races, Carnival two days before Ash Wednesday, Easter Horse and Yacht Races, May 1st, Labour Day Processions, Whit Monday, Corpus Christi Religious Processions, Queen's Birthday Celebrations (June), August 3, four Emancipation Day Holidays, August 15, National Day Parades, November 8, Remembrance Day, December 25, Christmas, December 26, Boxing Day.
Language English is the official language.
Laundry and Dry Cleaning Limited facilities.
Local Courtesies and Customs Ladies are advised not to wear short shorts or too scanty clothing in the town or public places.
Medical Facilities There is a General Hospital in St George's, and two cottage hospitals in outlying districts, which all provide satisfactory medical and surgical care. Private doctors and nurses are also available on call. Grenada is free from all venomous insects, animals and reptiles.
Night Life See up-to-the-minute movies, at either of St George's two cinemas or at the larger hotels. The Pyramid Night Club in the resort area caters for occasional evening entertainment. Dances are held throughout the week to steel-band music or local orchestras at the larger hotels.
Other Tourist Facilities Watersports play an important part in the visitor's programme. Swimming, water-skiing, sailing, fishing, snorkeling, scuba diving are all available and Grenada is now becoming a centre of Game Fishing in the Southern Caribbean. Sunset cocktail cruises are popular favourites. Yachting is also one of Grenada's outstanding pastimes and no visit to the mainland is complete without a cruise among the scenic Grenadines—a yachtsman's paradise. A completely modern and up-to-date marina offers efficient services to visiting yachtsmen.
Other Sports These include tennis, horse racing and golf. The Woodlands Golf Course—nine holes—is located within a couple of minutes drive from the resort hotels.
Tipping In Grenada there is a government tax on hotel

rooms and a 15 per cent service charge.
Time One hour ahead of Eastern Standard time, five hours behind London time.
What to See The town of St George's on foot. Visit Forts George and Frederick, the Anglican Church, York House. Drive to one or more heights overlooking town and harbour outside St George's. Drive to Westerhall Point, Levera Beach, Sauteurs, Grand Etang, Annandale Falls, Morne Jaloux Ridge. Visit Carriacou. Carriacou (13 square miles, population 10,000) lies 20 miles north of Grenada and 40 miles from St George's, the capital. Flying time from Pearls Airport (Grenada) to Lauriston airstrip (Carriacou) is approximately 10 minutes. At L'Anse aux Epines (pronounced Lansopeen) the Calabash and Horse Shoe Bay hotels are unique for their settings and architectural designs. On the way to the Calabash visit the Red Crab an English type 'pub' run by a Pole. British draught beer, shove-ha-penny board and snacks at reasonable prices. Look out for gaily painted buses with signs like Poor Me, Good Hope and As Usual.

Chapter 10
The Independent Islands

Trinidad, long the crossroads of the Americas, today advertises itself as the hub of the Caribbean. Dr Eric Williams, the distinguished historian who has been Prime Minister of the joint state of Trinidad and Tobago since independence from Britain was proclaimed on 31 August 1962, firmly believes in the necessity for an autonomous Caribbean economy and is no less firmly dedicated to the fostering of Trinidadian and Tobagonian nationalism. In pursuing the objective of his People's National Movement Dr Williams is greatly assisted by the abounding self-confidence and effervescence of the young people of Trinidad, who comprise the most obviously identifiable inter-racial and inter-Caribbean society to be found in any of the West Indian or other islands. Today's citizens of Trinidad have been born of ancestries as widely divergent as Irish, Portuguese, Lebanese, Chinese, Indian, Pakistani, East and West African, French, Spanish and English. No less than 10% have originated in neighbouring Caribbean territories.

The welding of so many different nationalities and communities into a single unit of citizenship encourages the people of Trinidad to see themselves as bridge-builders for an integrated Caribbean region, which a growing number of West Indians now believe to be indispensable if the peoples of these former European settlements are ever to achieve the maximum development of their physical, economic and human resources.

The riches of human resources drawn from so many continents are the real wealth of Trinidad and should protect the island from policies of isolationism, which are less likely to succeed because of the island's geographical location and function as the crossroads of the Americas. Only four and a half hours jet flying time from New York and eleven from Amsterdam, Trinidad is also on the direct air route to Santiago, Caracas, Rio de Janeiro and other South American cities. As the only oil producing country in the West Indies, Port of Spain, Trinidad's bustling industrialised capital is a major bunkering station for ships travelling between North and South America, to Europe across the Atlantic Ocean and to Pacific ports through the Panama canal. The significance of oil as a primer of Trinidad's industrial development and commercial supremacy over the other islands in the East Caribbean may be gauged from the fact that the Texaco Oil Refinery at Pointe-à-Pierre is the largest in the Commonwealth. Before Trinidad's emergence as a major oil-refining country the island had become famous internationally for its exports of Trinidad asphalt or *epuré*. The asphalt industry, which relies on deposits of natural asphalt from the Pitch Lake, the largest single source in the world, got off to a flying start in 1888 when A. L. Barber of New Jersey and J. W. Previté of London with other business men founded the Trinidad Asphalt Company. It is not surprising that Trinidad with its long experience of the petroleum industry, should be the first of the Commonwealth South Caribbean islands to set up a steel mill, the site for which was announced as Point Lisa on 1 February 1970. Jamaica in the Northern Caribbean has had a steel mill for several years.

Trinidad had an average rate of growth of 9.7% between 1951 and 1961. Besides expansion of oil refineries other heavy manufacturing industries such as fertiliser plants, metal works, a dockyard, cement factory and motor car assembly plants have been established, while there is rapid growth in the manufacture of textiles, garments, building materials and several light consumer products made for the home and

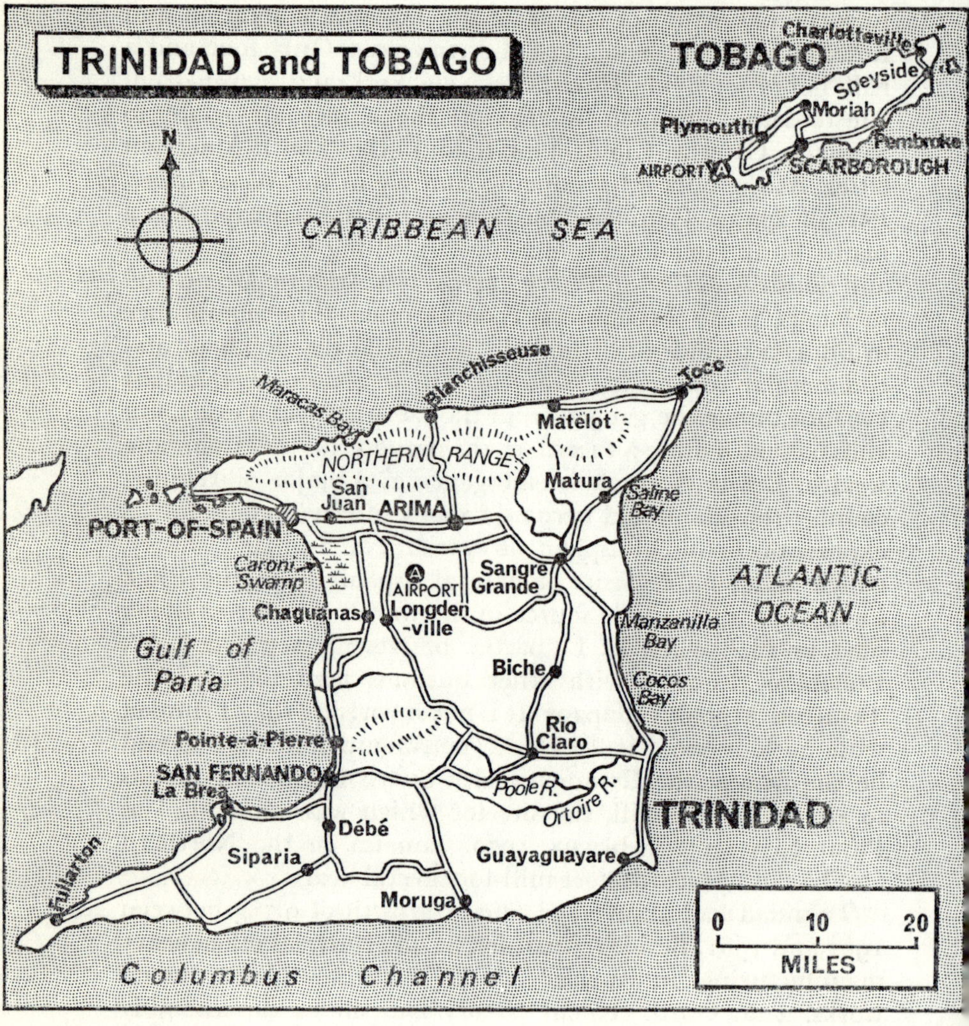

TRINIDAD and TOBAGO
N
TOBAGO
Charlotteville
Speyside
Moriah
Plymouth
Pembroke
AIRPORT
SCARBOROUGH
CARIBBEAN SEA
Blanchisseuse
Toco
Maracas Bay
Matelot
NORTHERN RANGE
Matura
San Juan
ARIMA
Saline Bay
PORT-OF-SPAIN
Caroni Swamp
AIRPORT
Sangre Grande
ATLANTIC OCEAN
Chaguanas
Longden-ville
Manzanilla Bay
Gulf of Paria
Biche
Cocos Bay
Rio Claro
Pointe-à-Pierre
SAN FERNANDO
La Brea
Poole R.
Ortoire R.
TRINIDAD
Débé
Siparia
Guayaguayare
Fullarton
Moruga
0
10
20
MILES
Columbus Channel

West Indian markets, which have been opened by the Caribbean Free Trade Area Agreement.

Since 1965 Trinidad has had a Productivity Centre which provides training at all levels in modern management and helps to promote industrial skills among local entrepreneurs. A Labour College named after Captain Cipriani started in 1966 and is helping to develop a responsible labour movement. Stability in industrial relations is further encouraged by an Industrial Court. A Central Bank established in 1964 is actively promoting the development of a money and capital market in Trinidad.

The population of Trinidad and Tobago exceeds one million persons and is expected to reach one and a half million by 1980 if the high rate of growth continues. About half the population is under 20 years and 40% live in the urban areas; about 300,000 in Port of Spain and its suburbs, and about 100,000 in and around San Fernando, which is the heart of the oil-refining industry. Tobago, which is 26 miles distant from Trinidad, has less than 4% of the population.

Despite Trinidad's gigantic strides into the modern 'developed' world the spectre of unemployment hangs over the island like a storm-cloud, black and threatening and depressing. At Christmas of 1969, the leaders of the Catholic, Anglican, Methodist, Presbyterian, Moravian, Lutheran and Salvation Army religious denominations appealed to government and people of Trinidad to 'join hands: not point fingers' in a national effort to reduce the unemployment figure of 15% of the labour force or 20% of the entire population, which they described as a 'horrible plague'.

The depressing unemployment figures in Trinidad are made worse by the fact that Trinidad is likely to be the chief beneficiary of the Caribbean Free Trade Area Agreement, since its industrial progress exceeds that of any other neighbouring member territory in the South Caribbean. Unemployment in Trinidad must discourage freedom of movement into an island which is nonetheless regarded by the inhabitants of the Windward and Leeward islands as a highly developed country. It is also likely to foster the kind of racial tensions which must be the inevitable consequence of separatist racial ideologies such as Black Power, and which can be exploited by movements which are opposed to racial integration of people.

The figures of unemployment in many West Indian islands are perhaps higher than they would be if there was not resistance to certain types of work. It is likely that the figures in Trinidad are also inflated for the same reasons. On the other hand unemployment would still be serious even if all the vacancies for workers were filled from Trinidad's local resources of manpower.

Trinidad and Tobago have a road network of 2,500 miles. By 1985 every 15 Trinidadians will own at least one motor car. An electricity supply grid extends to nearly every part of Trinidad and a 20-mile undersea cable supplies Tobago. Buses are gradually replacing rail transportation.

Trinidad lies about 16 miles to the east of Venezuela. Its average length is 50 miles and its greatest breadth 37 miles. Its area is 1,864 square miles, slightly smaller than the county of Lancashire in England. Chacachare, the most westerly of Trinidad's Bocas Islands is only seven miles distant from Venezuela in the Gulf of Paria which separates Trinidad from South America. There is a strong tendency for Trinidad to establish close relations with Venezuela, in the same way that the Republic of Guyana is actively seeking to establish close relations with Brazil.

The north coast of Trinidad is rugged and rock bound but there are numerous bays and scenic sites. On the northern tip, Chaguaramas, the site of a former United States Naval Base, is being developed as a major resort. The beauty of Trinidad is to be found chiefly in its hills, rivers and forests. Three ranges of hills run roughly from east to west, the most northerly rising to 3,083 feet at El Cerro del Aripo. The central range runs south west from Manzanilla Point to San Fernando, and the Southern runs parallel and near to the south coast. Trinity Hills, first seen by Columbus when he discovered Trinidad in 1498, are near to the south-east coast.

Trinidad was a cocoa-growing island under the long Spanish régime which became effective from 1532 and lasted until the island fell to British forces on 18 February 1797. Some years before that date Trinidad received many French settlers who were fleeing from San Domingo and other French territories which had been harassed by French Revolutionaries. Trinidad was formally ceded to the Crown of Britain by the Treaty of Amiens in 1802. Spanish law was not repealed entirely until 1845: the Cabildo, which was the Spanish institution of government, had been replaced five years earlier by the Port of Spain City Council. In 1848 Trinidad was divided into divisions, counties, districts and wards. In 1888 borough councils were established in San Fernando and Arima. Tobago was amalgamated with Trinidad on 1 January 1889.

Trinidad has announced the intention of becoming a Republic in the future, but at the time of writing Her Majesty, a Senate and a House of Representatives represented the supreme authority of Parliament in the affairs of the unitary state of Trinidad and Tobago, an independent member of the Commonwealth of nations which was once united in membership of the British Empire. The House of Representatives is elected by registered Commonwealth citizens who are 21 years or over. The Supreme Court consists of a High Court of Justice and a Court of Appeal.

Tobago was occupied by Caribs when Columbus discovered it in 1498. Dutch, English and French claimed and occupied the island during the years which elapsed from the first settlement in 1632 until 1748, when, by the Treaty of Aix La Chapelle, Tobago was declared neutral. Fifteen years later Tobago was ceded by France to England by the Treaty of Paris. But the French under the Duke of Bouillé captured it in 1781 and it was officially surrendered to France two years later. The British recaptured it in 1793 but returned it to France in 1802. A year later the British Commodore Hood and the British General Grinfield reconquered it and it was finally ceded to the British Crown in 1814.

Sugar growing in Tobago began in 1770 when there were about 200 whites and 3,000 negro slaves cultivating 5,000 acres of land. In that year John Paul Jones, who was then a British subject, appeared before the island's Court of Vice-Admiralty on a charge of ill treating the carpenter on his ship. From 1803 Tobago enjoyed a reputation for the prosperity of its sugar industry and rich Tobago planters became prominent as absentee owners in England, at least for a time, before their profits were squandered by the overseers and attorneys they left behind to look after their properties.

The planters of Tobago were financed from a London firm which went bankrupt in 1884; this failure brought the economy to a standstill. Land sold for as little as ten shillings an acre, a price which delighted Negro peasants who knew how to live off the land, and enjoyed the satisfying sense of ownership which alone gives full meaning to patriotism anywhere. It was because of the failure of the sugar industry that the British government decided to make Tobago a 'ward' of Trinidad in 1889. Trinidad's interest in its ward began to be noticeable when in 1957 a new programme of reconstruction and development was announced.

The potential of Tobago as a holiday island is as great, if not greater, than that of Barbados. For this reason some Tobagonians have expressed the desire to be separated from Trinidad. If all the island governments are ever prepared to hand over sovereignty to a West Indian unitary government, a good case can be made for Tobago and all the other islands to manage their own affairs at municipal and borough council level. So far there is little reason to believe that the unitary state of Tobago and Trinidad is in danger of separation. The programme of development which has been planned for Tobago should give added meaning to the island's motto *'pulchrior evenit'*.

It is hard to see how Tobago, which has only 116 square miles, could become more beautiful than nature made it, yet this can happen when hotel resorts are properly landscaped and architect's eyes blend with the magnificence of unspoilt scenery which is both abundant and accessible in Tobago. At Buccoo Reef, as at Tobago Cays, the West Indies have marine reserves for tropical fish and sea-water plants. The water is waist deep only, so almost anyone can see the life underfoot.

On Little Tobago live the Birds of Paradise, the most famous but by no means the only birds which may be seen by visitors to Tobago and to the small islets which lie around its coasts. St Giles island is the roosting place for the magnificent frigate bird which is known throughout the islands as a Man of War bird, hawk or cobbler (Cobbler's Cove, an attractive beach resort in Barbados is named after this bird). Frigate birds also frequent the 70 by 40 yard sugarloaf-shaped Smith's island, half a mile distant from Tobago on the south-east coast. There live the sooty and nodding terns and occasionally the red-billed tropic bird. In the cocoa areas of Tobago bush-shrikes, woodhewers, Bonaparte's woodpeckers, bare-eye thrushes and other species are common. At 1,000 feet above sea level Lawrence's swifts may be seen and a little higher may be heard the best songbird of Trinidad and Tobago, the musical singer. A rare humming bird, the Blue-throated Sabrewing frequents the hill forests of Tobago, where may also be seen the red-bellied, insect-eating Trogon and the black-and-white coated thrush.

An early promoter of Tobago, Captain John Poyntz labelled Tobago in 1683 (the first example of a tourist brochure?) as the 'glory of the Caribes'. He had seen almost all of His Majesty's foreign plantations 'having viewed them all, have chosen this island of Tobago to take up my Quietus est in'. His anxiety to attract settlers may have led him to exaggerate the properties of the green turtle for medicinal purposes. According to Poyntz the flesh of the green turtle was a 'medicinal food for the Gonhorea, the Yaws and the French pox, there is not in nature a food more effectual'.

Trinidad is known as Iere or the Land of the Humming Bird, but it has many other species of bird life. The one which every visitor who leaves the city streets is bound to see or hear is the Keskidi, whose high-pitched note resembles the French words: *qu'est-ce-qui-dit?* The best known song birds are the God's bird, a little rosignol, the semp or simple, spotted tarode, ringed neck acravat, grass bird and cardinal bird. The Caroni swamp is a bird sanctuary and there live the Scarlet Ibis, which Trinidadians wrongly label as flamingo, a bird not known on the island. The Ibis is a vivid scarlet except for black tipped wings. About two feet high with long curved bill it splashes colour across the dark green vegetation and murky swamp water. Other birds to be seen in the swamp are the snowy egret, the little blue heron, the roseate spoonbills, ducks, teals, jacanas, flycatchers, the yellow-throated spinetail, black-crab hawks, white-tailed buzzards and long-winged harriers. A curious bird in Trinidad is the Poor-me-one, a large night hawk whose 'songs of distress' are comprised of a series of six notes arranged in interval of three, dying away in a low sound from the throat.

In the mountain districts of Arima, Blanchisseuse, and Caura the anvil bird beats out bell-like peals which are repetitive of the sounds 'boc-boc-boc-boc-tin-tang'. These reverberations echo like the chimes of a distant church bell across the valleys and give rise to the bird's common name of Campanero or bell ringer.

The Tourist Board of Trinidad lists as edible the wild pigeon, wild turkey, wild duck, crao, ibis, quail, wild dove, water fowl, ramier, ortolan, parrot, merle, guacharo and diablotin. The last two are not recommended for eating since they resemble after cooking a 'lump of fat'. The first place for flavour is given to wild turkey and crao.

From 1 October to 31 March hunting is permitted in Trinidad and Tobago. In the forest hunters seek the agouti, armadillo, deer, lappe, quenn or 'wild hog'. The alligator or cayman is caught in large rivers. On private lands all-year-round owners and their servants are permitted to hunt the manicou or opossum, the mongoose and the squirrel. A wide range of wild birds may also be hunted during the open season.

While Trinidad is best known as the land of Carnival where life is sometimes described as a 'continual preparation for the next', there are many other occasions which have special significance for the islanders. The Muslim festival of Hosein with parades of colourful tadgeahs at St James, Port of Spain; the Hindu Holy Festival in honour of Spring; the procession of the Black Virgin at Siparia, the lighting of candles in cemeteries on All Souls Day; Divali the Hindu Festival of lights; the Christmas Crib in the Botanic Gardens; and the Moslem feast of Eid-ul-Fitr are religious occasions which demonstrate deep-rooted attachments of Trinidadians to the faiths of their forefathers.

Racing, cricket, hockey, athletics, football, yachting and golf are the major spectator sports of the sport-loving Trinidadians, who live on the West Indian island which has the reputation of loving 'fête for so' and from where jump-up and steelband music has riffled like the trade winds through every inhabited West Indian island, setting up eddying ripples of sound and taking infectious laughter into almost every capital of the Caribbean, Western Europe and North America.

The island named after the deepest Christian mystery, the Trinity, has been for at least one hundred years the best known of all the West Indian islands, except for Jamaica. More than ever today it dominates the thinking of the East Caribbean and will long continue to influence the pattern of developments which is being woven on the tapestry that comprises the former West Indian possessions of Great Britain.

Barbados is the respectable West Indian island, despite attempts by some hotel operators to advertise it as the most swinging in the Caribbean, and the desire of some tourists to 'have a ball' and 'to do their thing' in calypso style. Outside the tourist spots, however, teeming Barbadians go their own way, minding their own business.

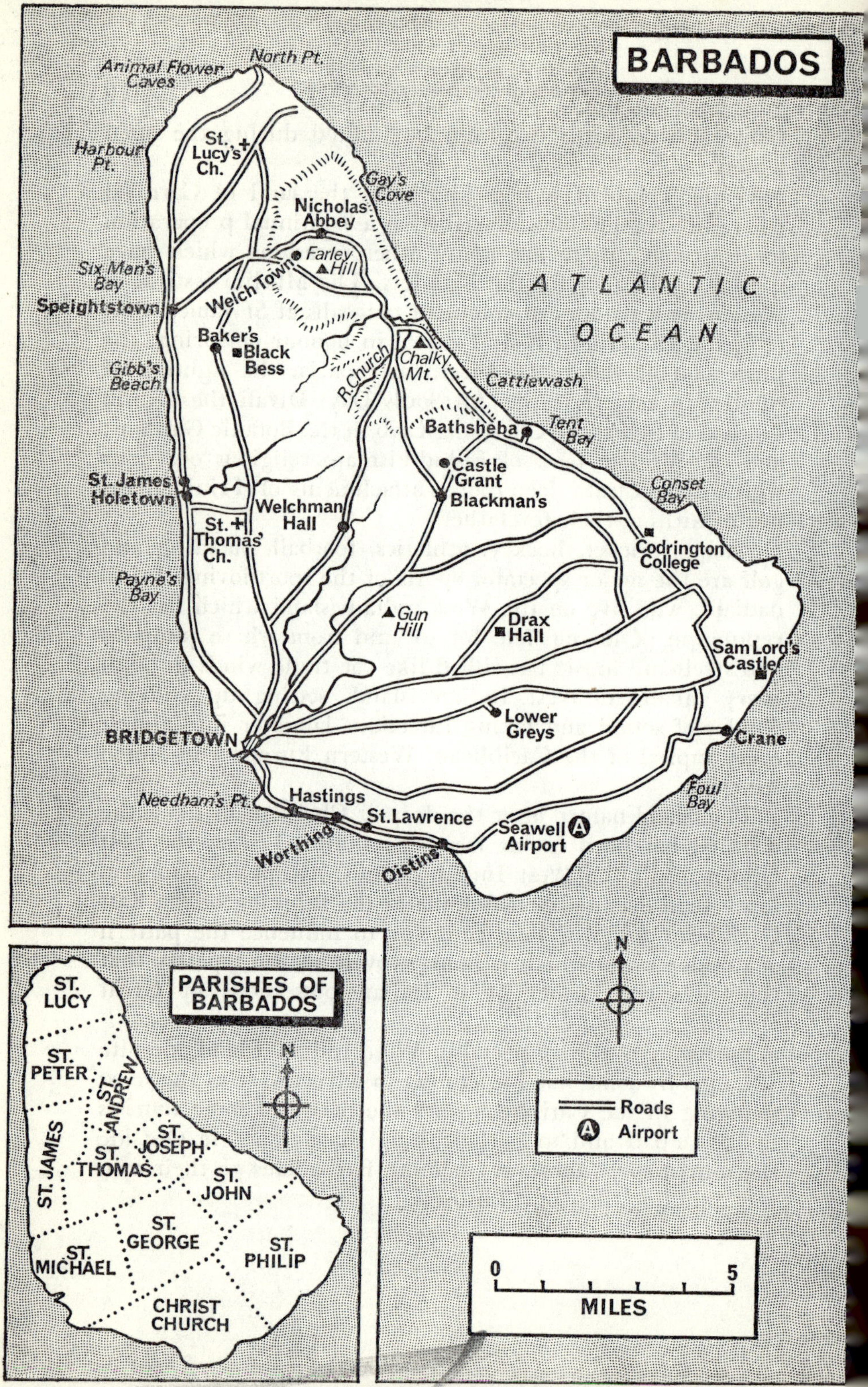
BARBADOS
North Pt.
Animal Flower Caves
Harbour Pt.
St. Lucy's Ch.
Gay's Cove
Nicholas Abbey
Farley Hill
Six Men's Bay
Welch Town
Speightstown
ATLANTIC OCEAN
Baker's
Black Bess
Gibb's Beach
R. Church
Chalky Mt.
Cattlewash
Tent Bay
Bathsheba
Castle Grant
St. James
Holetown
Blackman's
Conset Bay
Welchman Hall
St. Thomas' Ch.
Codrington College
Payne's Bay
Gun Hill
Drax Hall
Sam Lord's Castle
Lower Greys
BRIDGETOWN
Crane
Foul Bay
Needham's Pt.
Hastings
St. Lawrence
Seawell Airport
Worthing
Oistins
N
PARISHES OF BARBADOS
ST. LUCY
ST. PETER
ST. ANDREW
ST. JAMES
ST. JOSEPH
ST. THOMAS
ST. JOHN
ST. MICHAEL
ST. GEORGE
ST. PHILIP
CHRIST CHURCH
N
Roads
Airport
0
5
MILES

21 The Old Guard Room on Savannah, Barbados

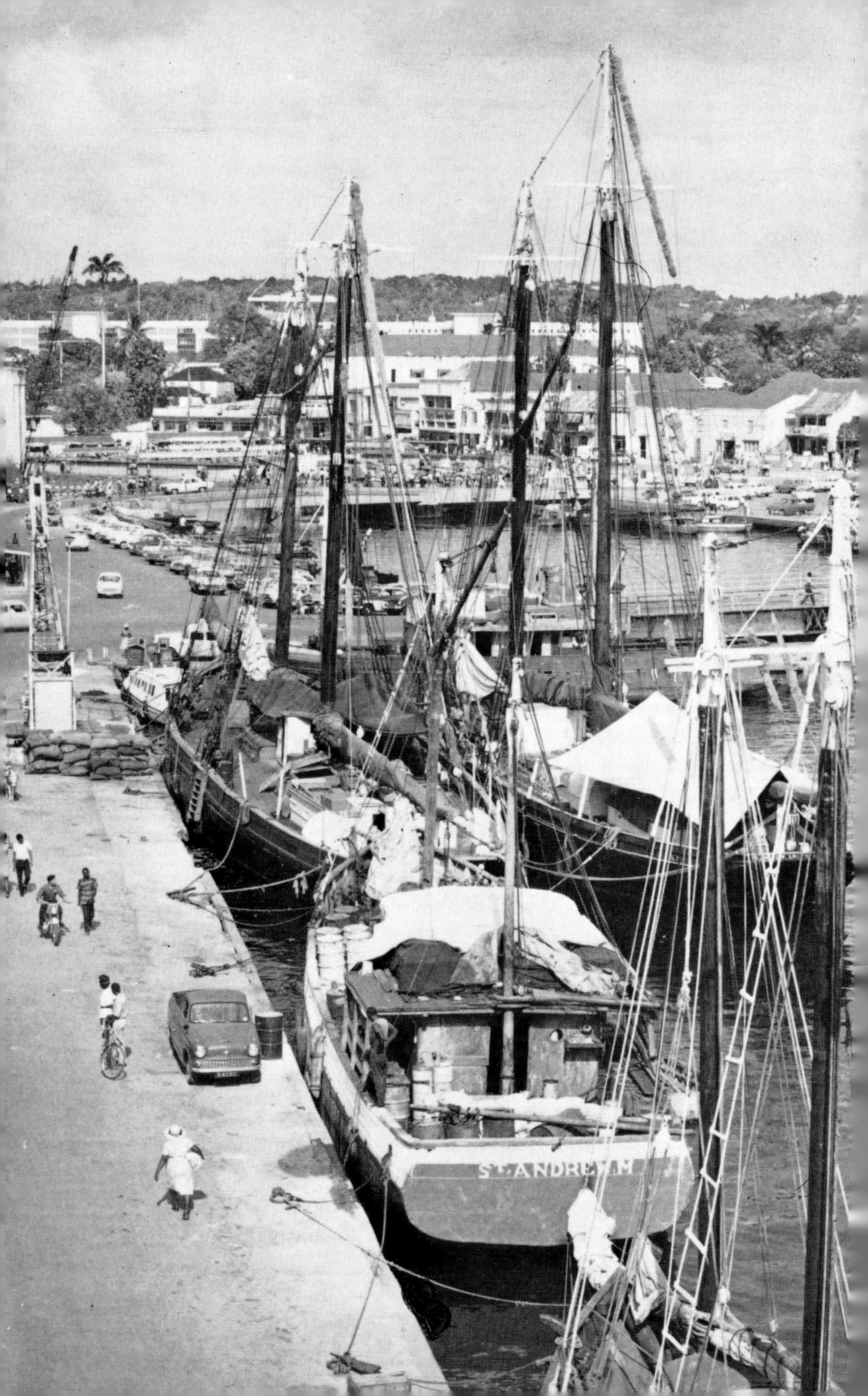
ST. ANDREW M

Nothing should surprise a visitor in Barbados, where it is common to see men asleep on city pavements, white millionaires preaching unnoticed at street corners, brothels open for business in daylight hours, and cars parked along busy thoroughfares. Barbados was a permissive society long before the word was invented and the greater number of its citizens were born out of wedlock. To be a Barbadian is to be a singular person.

The Barbadian special creed begins its recital with a definition that their small Atlantic, 21 by 14 miles, 'slightly-larger-than-the-Isle-of-Wight' island is 'Christ's own land'. The implication is clear. If only Barbados had been discovered before the year of our Lord's birth, it would have been the obvious birthplace for Him. The Barbadian creed, with its uncritical praises of a small overpopulated island is probably most deeply held by those Barbadians who have never left its shores or who have returned to leave their bones there after many years of exile abroad. For Barbadians, like all small islanders, have got to emigrate in order to survive. There is no other possibility but emigration for an island which was developed so early that people began going to the United States as soon as the sugar industry was well established in the mid-seventeenth century. Barbadians have emigrated ever since. The relatively high standard of the island's educational system since the late eighteenth century was consciously designed to ensure that children born of Barbadian parents had opportunities to compete overseas with children who had been born in more developed and larger countries. Recognition of education as the 'open sesame' which could pass human beings along the roads leading out of an Atlantic rock into the hearts of countries where history was being made, is perhaps the real explanation of the average Barbadian's superiority complex. The Barbadian, like any other small islander, has to prove that, although he lives on an isolated rock, he knows as much or more than the 'superior' visitor whom he envies with all his soul, although he will never admit it. The bumptious personal aggressiveness of Barbadian

22 *Bridgetown, capital of Barbados*

politicians at election times stems from their built-in need to advertise the fact that the lowliest cane cutter—and no one is more lowly in Barbados—is as good as the plantation owner, and certainly superior to any visitor from England, Canada, the United States or China. It is also taken for granted that the Barbadian is superior to all other West Indians, and naturally a cut above Latin Americans who live in countries whose people have never enjoyed the blessings of the English parliamentary system, English Methodism or the spiritual distinction of having Anglicanism as the recognised religion of the state.

At least this was Barbados before 30 November 1966, when the slightly-larger-than-the-Isle-of-Wight island became a sovereign independent state as the Union Jack was lowered immediately after midnight. Thus ended 339 years of continuous dependence on England, and of unswerving loyalty, since 1688, to the monarch who sat on the English throne. (Before 1688 both the factions who were striving for power in England were represented in Barbados, where those who ruled were sometimes 'loyal' to Royalists, sometimes to the Commonwealth.) The restored Stuart, Charles II, ended all hopes Barbadians had entertained of achieving Dominion status after the Restoration, by making it quite clear to Deputy Governor Codrington, the Council and Assembly of Barbados, in a despatch of 22 November 1671 that any idea of home rule was contrary to his concept of an English Empire. 'Distance of place,' wrote the King, 'shall shelter none from our Justice and Power'. English governments, hundreds of years later, were hoping to give independence to the Federation of the West Indies which broke up in 1962. The visit of Mr Iain McLeod, when Secretary of State for the colonies, to the Federal headquarters was to say 'hurry, hurry, hurry' to West Indian leaders. Hindsight shows the message to mean 'if you do not hurry up with independence as a group, you may have it thrust upon you as separate nations'. At least this is how the exodus of Jamaica, followed closely by Trinidad, and later Barbados appears to West Indians today.

The last thing that anyone in the West Indies believes should ever be done is to 'hurry', so nothing came from Mr McLeod's advice except a growing conviction among the small West Indian cliques who held power that England had made up its mind to 'thrust independence' upon the islands as quickly as their leaders were ready to accept it. This realisation sparked the efforts which were made in Barbados to seek independence for Barbados within a federation that would include the Leeward and Windward islands, where hopes of ever becoming 'first class' citizens of a West Indian country had been dashed to the ground when the Federation was dissolved by the United Kingdom in 1962. This decision was taken against the wish of the remnants of a Federal Parliament which had been bereft of the majority of its elected members who had come from Jamaica and Trinidad.

Many factors caused the failure of the second attempt to salvage the wreck of the first experiment in West Indian nationhood a 'second eleven' federation with headquarters in Barbados. The immediate consequence of this failure was an agreed decision of the United Kingdom and of Barbados' then 'colonial' government to set a date for independence.

The sovereign nation of Barbados has not added any acres to its slightly more than 166 square miles (nearly 100 acres had been added before when the deep-water harbour was reclaimed from the sea in 1961). Its density of population, more than 1,300 to the square mile, has continued to increase, despite a falling off in birth rates and a continuous high level of emigration. The sugar industry continues to be the island's major employer of labour despite a tremendous surge forward in the construction of hotels, apartments, settlers' homes and the spread of subsidiary services required by the most highly developed tourist industry in the Caribbean south of Puerto Rico.

The reasons for Barbados' attractions as a tourist resort are physical. The island lies completely surrounded by the

Atlantic Ocean about 100 miles further east than any other so called 'Caribbean' territory. The trade winds have no obstruction all the year round, although it is hotter and more humid in the long summer months which begin in the spring and last almost until Christmas time; for Barbados is an island of perpetual summer.

The water of Barbados comes from natural reservoirs lying under its surface. Enough is there to keep the island adequately supplied with fresh water until A.D. 2000, when the price of distilling sea water should be cheap enough to remove the fears of drought from the entire region. Except for the Scotland district, where there are high hills rising to over 1,100 feet and occasional cliffs between the north and south-east, Barbados is an island of valleys and low ridges, sloping gently towards the coastline. From the air its fields of sugar cane and 'ground provisions', the colonial description of all crops other than cane, resemble neatly drawn squares on a large chequer board, while abundance of trees and well-tended gardens whisper of a 'civilisation' which is conspicuously absent when one flies over the deep forests and highlands of most of the other Caribbean islands. On the ground the whisper of civilisation is maintained, although the very small size of the capital city of Bridgetown is surprising. Traffic accordingly snarls up in narrow lanes through which pedestrians, cyclists and other living creatures pick their way even against the frantic signals of modern policemen and -women. Roads lead everywhere in Barbados, but the islanders converge on Bridgetown, especially on Fridays and Saturdays. Other towns than Bridgetown are there none, although at one end on the north-west coast, Speightstown, and at the other on the south, Oistins, are both honoured by the description of townships, and do provide important shopping and other facilities for residents of their districts. Very little planning has taken place in Barbados since the Royal Engineers left the island in the latter part of the nineteenth century. Most of the buildings of architectural merit had been constructed before 1900, when the cult of the ugly seriously took hold of Barbadians. Only since the late 'forties has the influence of the jerry builders and the slapdash mason been challenged by modern architects and contractors. Town planning is a word frequently heard on Barbados, but only completely new towns can be 'planned' on an island which has developed a continuous strip of coastal suburbs extending from the airport in the south to the fishing village of St Peter on the north west.

A new city could easily be built around the nucleus provided by the university college campus on Cave Hill which looks down on Bridgetown's deep-water harbour. Unfortunately there is little public demand for such a town and the area is quickly becoming another sprawling centre devoid of the normal services which are associated with city life. The majority of Barbadians move along their roads on feet and on bicycles and there is also a diminishing but noticeable number of donkey and other animal- and hand-drawn carts. Traffic on the busiest street can be halted by box carts carrying long planks of lumber or stacks of boxes, while the speed on busy highways (never more than 30 miles per hour!) is frequently reduced to the pace of a stubborn mule who has all the time in the world.

The public utility companies of Barbados seem to find it necessary to keep digging up the sides of highways throughout the year, thereby adding to the frustration of drivers. Along the country roads, on the other hand, driving can be very pleasant provided that you blow your horn frequently at blind bends, keep away in to the left and never exceed the 30 m.p.h. speed limit!

It is said that Barbados is a microcosm of the world and it is true that in Barbados the bustling salesman is a reality, yet no less real than he is the Barbadian 'individualist' who will verbally disapprove of anyone in a hurry ('you can't wait' is a favourite expletive which pedestrians regularly hurl at motorists who overtake). 'Time,' as one employee of the island's water works told me, 'is a word that does not exist in my vocabulary.' There are many others who live by this precept as though 'Take your time' is the golden rule for self-preservation in the tropics.

When visitors compliment Barbados on the quality of its people, what do they mean? Not all mean the same thing. Some compare Barbadians favourably with surly West Indians whom they have encountered elsewhere. Others consider that Barbadians particularly and West Indians generally are very pleasant when compared with non-smiling Arabs or mysterious, withdrawn Orientals. Some Americans find Barbadians refreshingly free from those racial antagonisms which are prevalent in too many parts of the United States.

Is there then a special Barbadian quality, a recognisably Barbadian character? The answer is not easy to make. Barbadians derive from many racial 'mixes' and there are worlds of difference between their very many class structures. Some islanders say that on Barbados there are at least as many differences of social layers as there are religious sects (over 50). It is certainly true to say that there are very wide ranges of income groups. Some Barbadians, inclusive of whites, are extremely poor and live in 'tenantries' which are mainly rows of wooden hovels in varying stages of decay clustered together off main roads. It is estimated that 40% of Barbadian dwelling houses (homes they cannot be fittingly called) are without water and the underprivileged families living in them cannot afford to pay electricity bills. On the other hand no one can deny that there has been substantial progress in general housing conditions over the past three decades, and even more obvious progress with health and academic educational services. What has chiefly lagged behind all other social services and may even be deteriorating is the availability of public amenities for the ordinary citizen.

All the real beauty which has been added to Barbados since the tourist waves began pounding in the early 'sixties has been reserved for the relatively rich settlers and temporary visitors. They have well-combed beaches, gay flowering shade trees, green grass lawns, luxury swimming pools, modern bars and outdoor dance floors, expensive hotel restaurants and above all enough money to pay the constantly rising prices of everything on sale.

Those Barbadians, who have earned higher salaries arising from increased prosperity caused by new investment, also have well-tended houses, gardens, clubs and recreation grounds. But people's parks, promenades, civic beaches, well-equipped community centres and other public amenities are quite inadequate and hard to find.

No one will recommend ordinary visitors to patronise a Barbadian rum parlour or a small shop catering chiefly to people who are without motor cars. Tourist development on a densely populated island has grown apart from the life of the islanders. It needs to be re-oriented in such a way that the visitors can join with the islanders in appreciating amenities which are common to all. Only then will native resentment of tourist development disappear, and such resentment has been increasingly noticed by visitors in recent years.

The resources of Barbados are people, coral stone, sea, sand, sun and some fertile acres of soil. Until 1966 its economy was dependent on policies arranged by local oligarchies working closely with English civil servants in Barbados and in London. Today its future depends on the continuing prosperity of a region which has considerable potential only for tourist development and some opportunities for agriculture, fisheries, light industries and services.

Politicians are tempted, especially at election time, to display over-confidence in their several capacities to stop the Sisyphean rock of too many people chasing too little resources from rolling back down on their toes. Yet a growing number of people believe that economic salvation for West Indian peoples can be attained only by efficient utilisation of the sum total of the resources of all the islands. Highly developed Barbados and still more highly developed Trinidad are plagued with social and economic problems, yet the majority of other islands stretching along the 600 miles of East Caribbean sea closest to the Atlantic ocean lag far behind Barbados and still further behind Trinidad, which in turn lags far behind Puerto Rico and Venezuela.

How can the task of development be accomplished without massive injections of money and without the most efficient control of expenditure? The political fragmentation of former European possessions into sovereign states freed the owners from accusations of 'imperialism'. But the resulting sovereign countries require much more than 'freedom' in order to keep their new citizens well-fed, well-educated and industrious. They need dedicated men and women who put the interest of a region before the individual interest of each separate island. This need has not yet been met in the Caribbean islands and some of the smaller islands are painfully learning how slow it is to travel alone.

West Indian problems, however, need not concern the ordinary tourist, who is only looking for brief days of sun, fun and relaxation on Barbados or Tobago. These two islands stand head and shoulders above all others for giving the value which people from overpopulated cities seek, even though they are poles apart in their development.

Barbados is a sophisticated island, Tobago a natural Paradise only now entering upon major developments like international airports and convention hotels.

An Englishman once said of Barbados that it had the charm of old pewter. By this he meant that much which made England famous had been preserved during the centuries in Barbados. He meant especially old churches, old plantations great houses, village cricket greens, and English customs. Today the charm is fading as fast in Barbados as is the habit of afternoon tea. Another Englishman, a former chairman of BOAC, found a rare quality in Barbados. Writing in the Bajan magazine for March 1956 he said: 'There is a serenity in the Barbadian sun that is a balm to the mind as well as to the body. It stems from the pageantry of its past: the Regency roots have thrown out a fine labyrinth of courteous traditions, and that indefinable charm of manner that is so appealing to the visitor. Barbados is not primarily a holiday island. So many resorts and tourist centres nowadays have only one objective, which is to make all that they can out of the fleeting visitor. Barbados has an industry of its own. It is a productive island trading energetically and efficiently with the outer world. The tourist is welcomed with the courtesies appropriate to a guest and is not looked upon purely as a source of get-rich-quick income'. How true would these words be in Barbados today? The island has changed much since 1956 but you may still find some of the charm of old pewter, some Victorian dignity surviving among its peasant folk, some old-world courtesies practised by its older people. Yet the character and quality of the Barbadian *has* changed. The overall physical attractions instead have improved greatly as hotels, resort areas and apartments have been landscaped on places where sour grass, agaves and stunted shrubs once grew wild and where strange, thin-coated Barbadian sheep and goats used to graze freely. New shopping areas have been developed and the quality of merchandise multiplied. There are now more places for visitors to go for dinner and entertainment and more sea sports to enjoy. A week's stay in Barbados can be relaxed or active, but the island is no longer 'away from it all'. More tourists visit Barbados in the summer months than in the winter, even though the large hotels have higher occupancy in the winter. The summer is boom time for the guest houses, apartments and lower priced houses. Great new hotels with convention halls, 18 hole golf courses, dozens of resort and housing developments, condominium apartments and cottage homes are proliferating in Barbados as fast as town planning approval can be given and workmen found to build them. More people keep coming to the small, favourite Caribbean island each year because the island retains its reputation for being unique, and for giving value.

So long as the sugar cane grows and the island remains a large tropical garden the uniqueness of Barbados will be unchanged. For those who throng the beach-side apartments, hotels, guest houses and private homes will not then feel too 'squeezed in' during their brief holiday visits. Should the whole island become one piece of real estate with high-rise hotels leering up along the coast lines as they do in Miami, San Juan or Genoa then the little England of the tropics will disappear. Barbados would then have as much character as a VIP lounge in a modern airport; comfortable, but not unique. Then it might be true that the only people who would have any idea of what Barbados used to be like will be those who spend most of their holiday hours at the Museum, where those traditions which made Barbados the ever British island are safely embalmed for posterity together with excellent pieces of furniture, and other reminders of a vanished way of life.

The Portuguese called the two islands they saw in Carlisle Bay, Pelican and its main island, 'the bearded ones'. The Portuguese title was anglicised into 'the Barbudoes', much in the same way as Shakespeare called Bermuda 'the Bermoothes' and as the archipelago to the north is still known as 'the Bahamas'. It matters little whether Barbados, as the island is finally known, was named for bearded trees or bearded humans. Like another island with a similar name, Barbuda, to the north, Barbados has trees growing down to the coastline all along the western coast, which would have been the one most seen by visiting sailors during long centuries that elapsed between the period of Spanish discovery of the West Indies and English settlement of Barbados in 1627. The boast that Barbados knew no other flag than the English is irrelevant today. The island cannot wipe its slate of history clean, any more than external influences can alter the people's fundamental character. The chips of yesterday are still visible on every Barbadian shoulder, as they are on every Trinidadian shoulder, but the new concepts of Caribbean identities and integration change almost daily and what would have seemed true of yesterday can appear today in some completely new guise.

The changes which are making Barbados so different from the island it was in 1956 are still in motion. By 1980 the island will be even less recognisable—but so will many other places.

The East Caribbean islands are going to suffer many 'sea changes', but they will never again in this century be considered as 'slums of empire'. Modern air transportation and new investment have seen to that, and Barbados, like Trinidad, and to some extent Antigua, is a natural port of call for ships and planes, whether they come from the Americas or from Europe.

The day is not far distant when earth stations in Trinidad, Barbados and Jamaica will permit TV viewers to receive instantaneous transmission of world happenings while they actually happen. Already anyone can telephone from these three islands to the furthest points of the world, putting girdles round the earth in less minutes than Oberon demanded from Puck.

Some European and American visitors will be able to dial their home numbers direct as some Caribbean visitors already can. Whatever may be the consequences of political alignments or new trading associations, visitors to Barbados, Trinidad and Jamaica will very soon be enjoying the advantages of tropical holidays without losing immediate touch with the modern world. And gradually these lines of inter-dependence will tighten around all the islands, drawing them closer to one another and to the whole inhabited globe. Before these things come to pass millions of visitors will have discovered for themselves the real charms of the East Caribbean islands in the sun, on which the Elysian trade winds from across the Atlantic ocean blow as fresh today as in the morning of the world.

GENERAL INFORMATION

Trinidad and Tobago

Religions Christian, Jew, Mohammedan, Hindu.
Climate Minimum temperature 67°F., maximum 97°F. Annual mean temperature 79°F. Mean relative humidity about 82%. Rainfall average about 64 inches a year.
Clothing As for other islands.

Communications AIR Trinidad is headquarters for British West Indian Airways, and is served by BOAC, KLM, Pan American, Air Canada, SAS, Air France, LAV (Linea Aeropostal Venezolana), Caribair, LIAT, and other airlines. SHIPPING Many large international lines connect Trinidad with other islands, the United States, Canada, Europe and Venezuela.

Currency Trinidad dollar equals 58 US cents, 62 Canadian cents; $1 US = $1.71 Trinidad and Tobago; $1 Canadian = $1.58 Trinidad and Tobago; £1 = $4.80 Trinidad and Tobago; 1 Bolivar = 35 cents Trinidad and Tobago. Rates fluctuate.

Documents Required Identification as citizen of the United Kingdom, Canada and permanent citizen of the United States and possession of a round trip ticket to country of citizenship. Valid passports required by citizens of other Commonwealth countries.

Electrical Current 60 cycles AC 115 or 230 volts.

Food and Drink Special dishes: curried beef, callaloo soup, pigeon peas pelau, rice calypso, pastelles, souse, rum drinks; English pub with draught beer at St Anns (Pelican Inn). Trinidad has good restaurants and a wide variety of menus borrowed from many countries. Kam's at 12 Maraval Road specialises in sea foods and there are several places serving East Indian, Chinese, and European cuisine.

Holidays New Year's Day, Good Friday, Easter Monday, Labour Day May 1st, Corpus Christi, Discovery Day August 4, Independence Day August 31, Christmas Day, Boxing Day (December 26).

Festivals Carnival, calypso steelband competitions and celebrations, Hosein, a Moslem Festival, Festival of la Divina Pastora, Arts Weeks, Divali: Hindu Festival of lights, Christmas Crib at Botanic Gardens, Eidul-Fitr: Moslem Feast, Kartik Nahan: Hindu Festival, Ramlilla: Hindu Festival.

Language Official is English, but other languages reflect the mixed origins of the people.

Laundry and Dry Cleaning Available.

Local Courtesies and Customs Trinidadians are impossible to put into single categories. Generally speaking the people are polite and friendly. On Tobago there is a more intimate relationship, as might be expected of an agricultural community. The Tourist Board issues a booklet entitled *How to Meet the People of Trinidad and Tobago.*
Medical Facilities Up to date.
Night Life Night Clubs and hotels on both islands.
Other Tourist Facilities Tobago's Chamber of Commerce and Tourist Bureau has several active service clubs, inclusive of Lions and Rotary, and Clubs for Bridge, Chess, Drama, Fencing, Golf, Judo, Hunting, Horticulture, Music, Natural History, Photography, Flying and Rifle Shooting. Social clubs include American Women's, Canadian Women's, Chinese Association, Himalaya Club, Portuguese Association, Syrian Lebanese Women's Association.
Pets and Animals Prior permission and import licenses required, from Chief Veterinary Officer Port of Spain.
Sports Racing, football, cricket, hockey, cycling, athletics, yachting, boxing, rugby, netball, tennis, basketball, golf, fishing, hunting, riding.
Time One hour ahead of Eastern Standard Time: five hours behind London.
Tipping Acceptable; normally service charges are added to bills.
Transportation Taxis and sightseeing services with driver guides. Trinidad (1,864 square miles) has a mile of road for every square mile of territory.
Water Good.
What to See in Trinidad Royal Botanic Gardens and Emperor Valley Zoo, National Museum and Art Gallery, Chamber of Commerce building, Old Deanery, Anglican Cathedral, Crescent Estate Pineapple Farm, Bamboo Grove Fish Farm, Champs Fleurs tobacco factory, brewery. Drives to Maracas Bay and Las Cuevas Bay, Blue Basin Mount St Benedict Monastery, Maracas waterfall, Caura Valley, Valencia Forest, Caroni Bird Sanctuary, Chaguanas, Toco,

Montserrat Hills, Pitch Lake (300 feet deep at centre, has disgorged 35 million tons of asphalt in 75 years. Level is dropping at the rate of six inches per year).
What to Do Four-hour combined drive and boat trip to offshore island or fishing. Day tour from Port of Spain to Tobago.
What to See and Do in Tobago Visits to Botanic Garden outside Scarborough, Buccoo Reef and Nylon Pool, Bird of Paradise island, four-hour single tour through Mount St George. Drive to Fort King George, Fort James, Mt Irvine Bay, from Scarborough to Crown Point along Windward coast to Man of War Bay.
What to Buy FROM DUTY FREE SHOPS Watches, china, perfumes, cameras, binoculars, pipes, perfumery, silks, jewellery, cashmere, English bone china, Trinidad calypso records, miniature steel-drums.
Shopping Hours 8 a.m. to 4 p.m. daily except Saturdays (half day). Food fairs later on Fridays.
Banks Open Monday to Thursday 8 a.m. to noon; Fridays 8 a.m. to 3 p.m.; shut Saturday, Sunday and holidays.
Information From Tourist Board of Trinidad and Tobago, Port of Spain, Trinidad.

Barbados

Religion Christian of many denominations, Jew, Moslem, Hindu.
Climate The most easterly of the Caribbean islands. Ideal Mediterranean summer temperatures in winter months. Average yearly temperature between 78° and 87°F. Humidity is highest in rainy months June to November.
Clothing As for other islands. Luxury hotels require jackets and ties for dinner.
Communications Air communications by VIASA, KLM, Air France, Pan American, Air Canada, BOAC, BWIA, Caribair, LIAT and private charter. Regular sea communica-

tions to Europe, North America and other West Indian islands. Excellent telecommunications.
Currency East Caribbean dollar equivalent to Trinidad and Tobago dollar. Rates fluctuate but $1 EC is approximately equal to 58 cents US or 62 Canadian cents. $4.80 EC=£1 sterling.
Documents required Passports except for *bona fide* visitors who are citizens of the United Kingdom, United States and Canada in possession of return ticket and staying no more than six months. West Indian police permits are accepted for West Indians who are citizens of their countries.
Electrical current 110 volts AC.
Food and Drink Sangaree, green swizzles, rum cocktail and planters punches are traditional Barbadian drinks. Turtle soup, eddoe soup, bonavist and pumpkin soup are specialities of Barbados. Flying fish, dolphin, turtle steaks, melts, roes, sea eggs, lobsters and shrimps are seasonal sea-foods. Other Barbadian foods, cassava cake, corn pone, conkies. Special local dishes not available at all hotels are pudding and souse, jug-jug (made largely of pigeon peas) and roast suckling pig. Mangoes, pawpaws, shaddocks, bananas and banana figs are seasonal fruit. Local preserves are guava cheese, coconut sugar cakes, shaddock rind, cherry jam. Home-made coconut ice cream is delicious.
Holidays and Festivals New Year's Day, Good Friday, Easter Monday, Labour Day (May 1st), Whit Monday, First Monday in August, First Monday in October, November 30 Independence Day, Christmas and Boxing Day. Additional holidays are added for special occasions.
Language English is the official language, but the majority of the population use vigorous and sometimes not easily understood Barbadian dialects.
Laundry and Dry Cleaning Adequate and prompt.
Local Courtesies and Customs Barbadians like to be greeted as equals. They resent visitors who take their pictures without permission. The islanders are proud of their reputation for being the friendliest people in the West Indies. It is bad

manners to wear beach clothes in the city or in inland shops.
Medical Facilities   Good.
Night Life   Plentiful, but entertainment normally limited to calypso songs, limbo and fire-eating dancers, and belly dancers. Hotels have good indoor and outdoor dance floors and there is a discothèque at the Tamarind Cove and at Black Rock. Local bands are lively.
Other Tourist Facilities   Cinemas (two drive-in), occasional theatrical and musical performance, cocktail cruises with dancing, bridge and bingos. Occasional festivals, flower shows, open houses and gardens. Fashion shows, goat races on beaches, and exhibitions and art shows.
Pets and Animals   England is the nearest quarantine station. Permits to import have to be obtained from the Chief Veterinary officer.
Food and Restaurants   Luxury hotels serve food to international standards. The Ocean View Hotel, La Bonne Auberge and Windsor enjoy higher than average reputations and are not expensive. West Indian buffets at Sam Lords and Miramar are recommended. For men, who have to be invited by a member, the Bridgetown Club offers a unique gastronomic experience of food and drink.
Sports   Two nine hole golf courses at Rockley on the south coast and Sandy Lane on the west coast. An 18 hole golf course is under construction near the airport and others are projected. Water sports are well organised and include sub-aqua exploring, water-skiing, speedboating, sailing, fishing and cruising. The Yacht Club and Sailing and Cruising Club sponsor yacht races. Dominoes, darts, table tennis, bridge are popular people's pastimes. Participating sports are golf, tennis, show jumping, polo, riding, rifle shooting and in summer months bird shooting. Spectator sports are cricket, football, athletics, hockey, basketball, rugby, motor car rallies, horse races.
Time   One hour ahead of Eastern Standard Time: five hours behind London.

23 *The harbour at Charlotte Amalie, St Thomas*

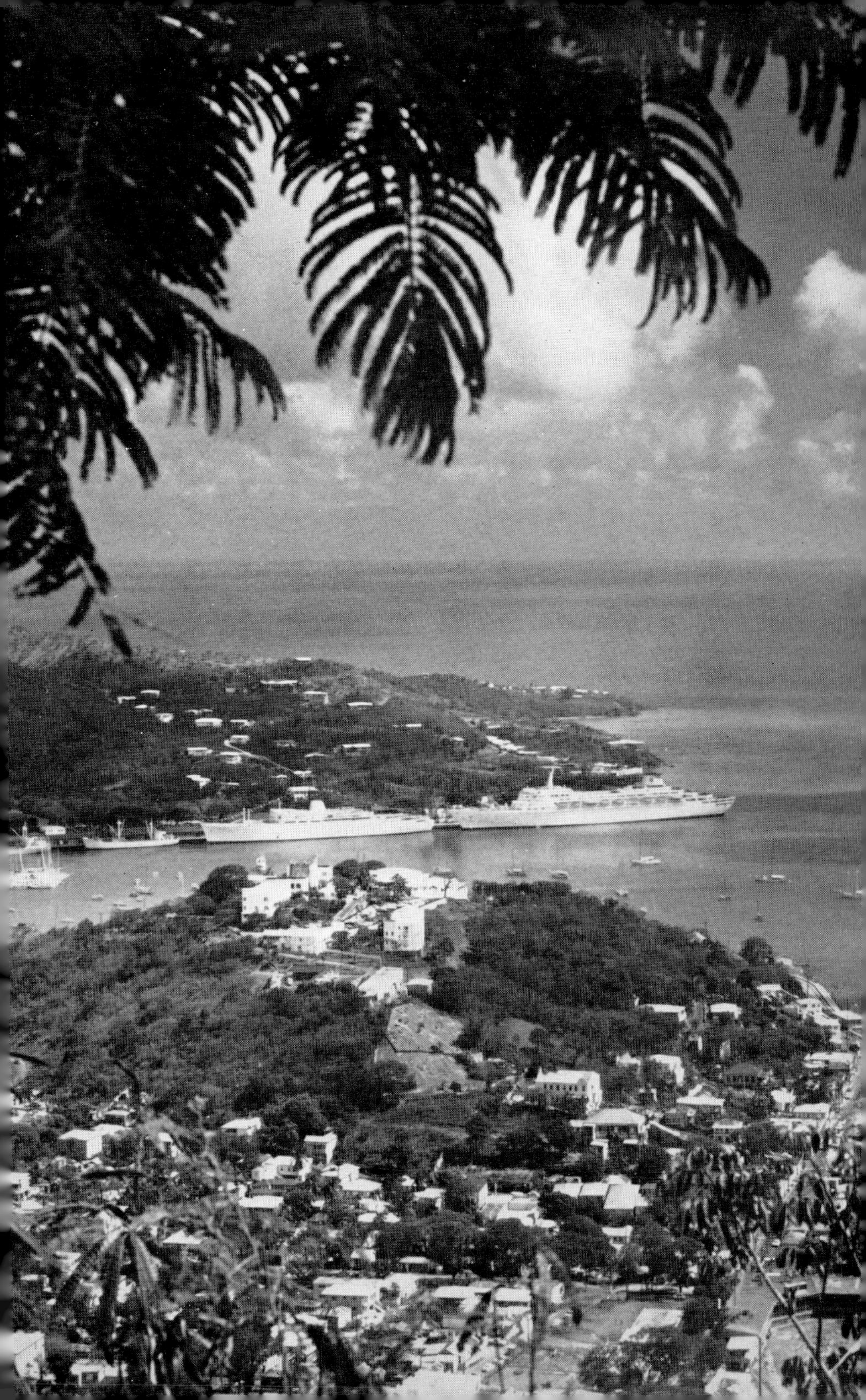

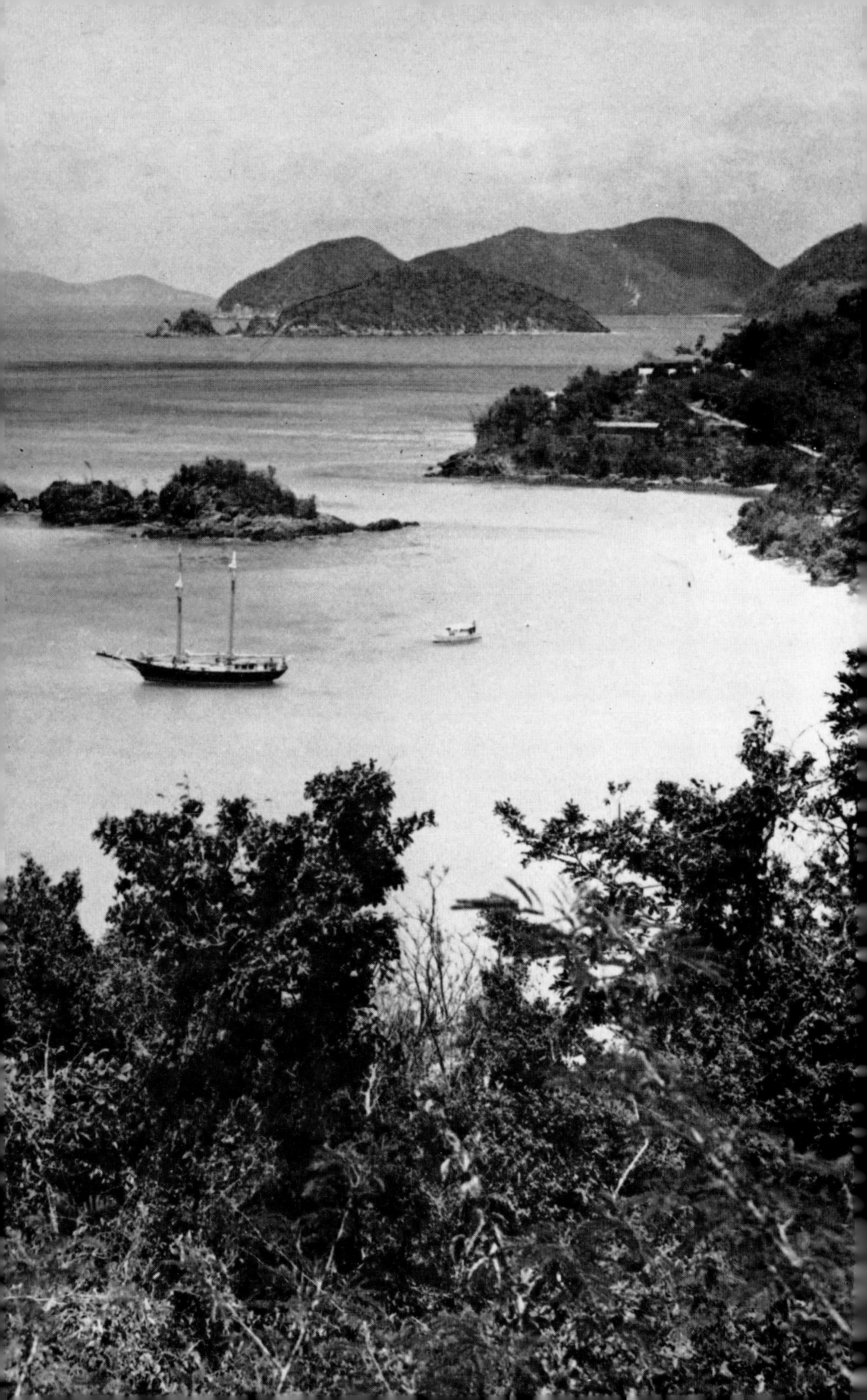

Tipping Always welcome. Service charge normally added in hotels and restaurants.

Transportation Hired cars and taxis charge reasonable rates. Roads are adequate for rigid speed limits 30 m.p.h. in country, 10 m.p.h. in towns. Scooters, bikes and mokes are available. Buses can be used but never have seats during rush hours.

Water Barbados has adequate supplies of safe drinking water from taps.

What to See BRIDGETOWN Old Jewish cemetery, Italianate drinking fountain opposite Carnegie Free Library, inside of Parliament buildings, statue of Lord Nelson, inscriptions inside St Michael's Cathedral, Inner Careenage. Near Bridgetown: Barbados Museum. IN COUNTRY Welchman Hall Gully, Cotton Tower, St John's Church and panorama, Cherry Tree Hill panorama, East Coast road, Coach Hill, Codrington College, Andromeda Gardens St Joseph, Gay's Cove, Animal Flower Cave, Tent Bay Fishing Village, Benjamin West painting in St George's church, Catholic Church at Villa Maria St Peter. OVERSEAS Airtrips by day to neighbouring islands.

What to Buy Local records and duty free liquor, jewellery, cameras, china, perfumes, silks, cashmere, English bone china, and other goods imported from Europe. Local souvenirs in wood, straw, pottery and rope, shellwork.

Information From the Tourist Board, Bridgetown.

24 Trunk Bay, St John

Chapter 11
The Virgins

St Thomas, St Croix, St John, Tortola, Virgin Gorda,
Jost van Dyke, Beef Island, Anegada

When in the third week of November 1493 Columbus saw the cluster of 100 small islands and islets dotting the 40 miles east of Puerto Rico and running down through the Anegada passage for a distance of 60 miles he called them Las Virgenes, in honour of the legendary Saint Ursula and her companions. Columbus may have believed he saw thousands of islands but he was not likely to have known that the traditional '11,000 virgin companions of a British King's daughter visiting Rome' were the invention of someone who confused the Roman letter 'M' on a tombstone with the Roman numeral 'M' which signifies one thousand. Instead of one thousand there were only eleven martyrs associated with Ursula whose bones show that she was an eight-year-old girl. The names had been taken from a tombstone near the Church of St Ursula at Cologne which was built on a site where in the early Christian centuries 'virgins' had died as martyrs.

Columbus, who lived at a time when Las Virgenes of St Ursula were supposed to be numbered in thousands, may be forgiven for imagining that there was no end to the dozens of islets which spread before his gaze in the virgin tropical dawn. The purity of the name 'virgins' however did not preserve the islands from the lusts and actions of sinful men. Their bays and creeks make them attractive hideaways for the sailing desperadoes or 'fall-outs' who lived by plundering the vessels of countries hostile to their own. With or without encouragement from their native lands Dutch and English made unsuccessful attempts to settle in some of the islands in the middle years of the seventeenth century, but little effective development had been achieved before the Danish West India Company established a settlement in 1672 on St Thomas. The Danes acquired St Croix later from the French (whose West India company had bought it and other Caribbean islands from the Knights of Malta) in 1733. In 1734 St Thomas, which had been controlled by the Brandenburg Company since 1685, was transformed into a Danish Crown Colony. From this period until the end of the Napoleonic wars the Danish Virgins and especially St Thomas thrived as a natural trading area during the bitter wars between France and England in the West Indies. After the Congress of Vienna had introduced new concepts of European relationships in peace time and the doctrine of nationalistic economic monopolies was being watered down, a decline in prosperity of the Danish islands led to heavy emigration.

As early as 1865 the first suggestion was made that the islands of St Thomas and St John should be sold to the United States. Later, in 1900, after the United States had become a Caribbean power through possession of Puerto Rico, another attempt was made to purchase all three of the Danish islands. Finally St Thomas, St John and St Croix were offered for sale to the United States in 1916 for 25 million dollars and after the Danish people had agreed by plebiscite the United States took possession of the former Danish Virgins on 31 March 1917. Included with the three islands were about 50 small islets and cays.

Acquired for strategic purposes because they guarded the Anegada passage the islands remained under the United States Navy Department until 1931, when government by a department of the interior was substituted. The Acts of 1936 and 1954 created the constitution of the US Virgin Islands which are now administered by a native-born governor. Six of the eleven senators of the single-chambered legislature are directly elected.

Charlotte Amalie, the capital city of St Thomas, has nearly half of the estimated population of 50,000 American Virgin Islanders. It has a splendid harbour equipped with oil reservoirs, shipyards and floating docks. Spread out over three hills, it is known to sailors as 'foretop, main and mizzen'.

St Thomas, which has an area of 32 square miles, lies between Culebra island and the island of St John, about 75 miles distant from San Juan the capital of Puerto Rico. St Croix, which is 82 square miles (almost half the size of Barbados which it resembles in some respects) is 40 miles to the south of St Thomas.

St Thomas is a rugged, deeply indented island of volcanic origin with steep hills that fall down sharply to the sea on all sides. Its highest peak, Crown Mountain, is 1,550 feet above sea level. The roads twist and turn and afford spectacular views of other Virgins. The town of Charlotte Amalie, the name of a Danish Queen, still retains Danish street names like Kogens Gade or Drenningens Gade. Danish influences are also evident in tiled roof buildings along the narrow streets which climb up from the open waterfront faced by white and pastel tinted villas. Magens Bay, which leads to the popular lookout at Drake's Seat on Mafolie Hill, is perhaps as perfect a beach as any to be found in the Caribbean. St Thomas by day is a bargain hunter's paradise, especially for Americans, each one of whom can take back to the mainland $100's worth of duty-free purchases bought in the islands inclusive of one gallon of spirits. By night the choice of entertainment justifies the island's description as the nightclub of the Virgin Islands.

St Croix is Alexander Hamilton's island. He was glad enough to leave it at the age of ten in search of adventure which led him to a pinnacle of American history. But the islanders know no more famous son and have given his name to the airport, and the store in which he worked as a boy while his mother, Rachel Sarah Fawcett Levine, is honoured

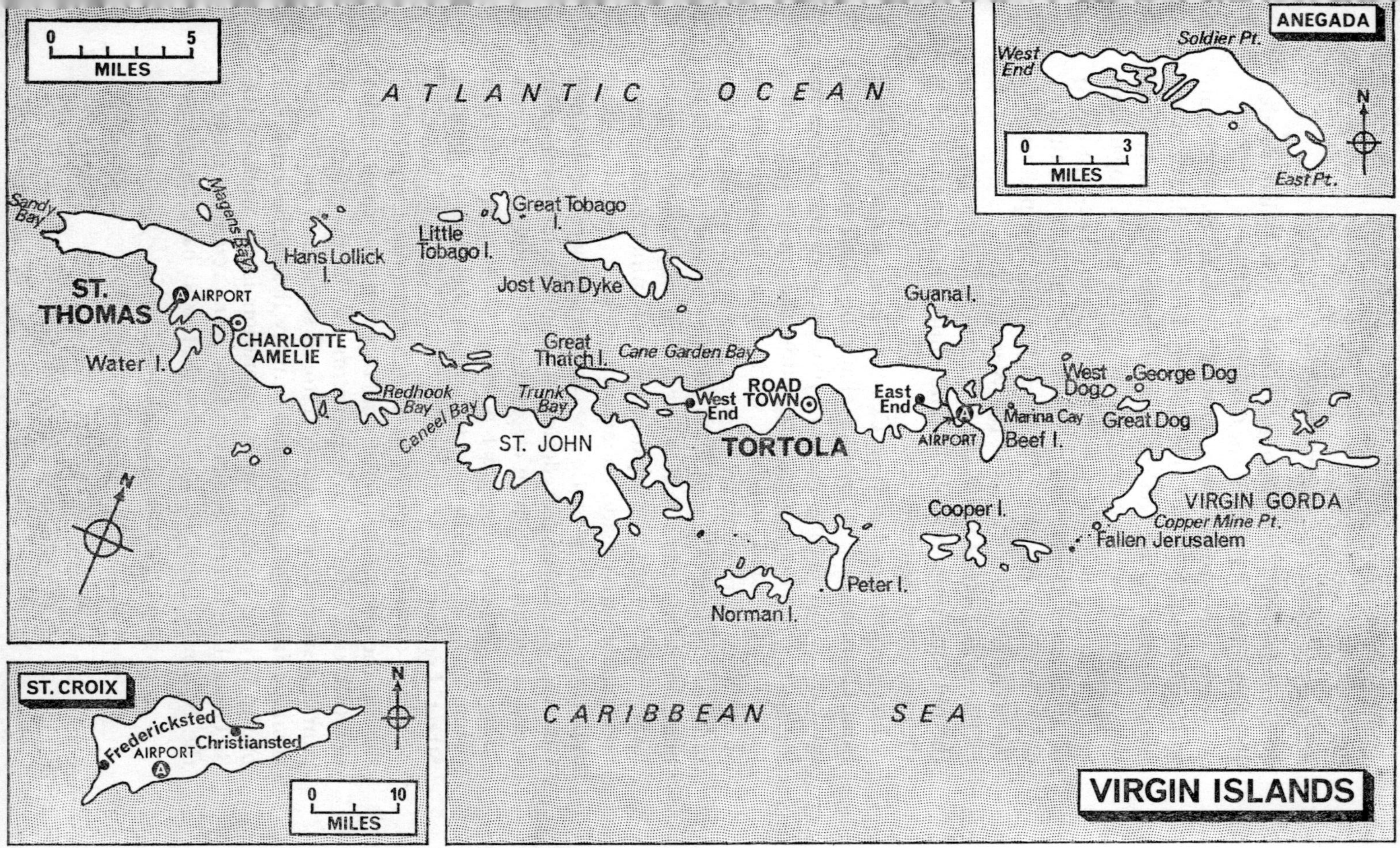
VIRGIN ISLANDS
ATLANTIC OCEAN
CARIBBEAN SEA
0 5
MILES
ST. THOMAS
AIRPORT
CHARLOTTE AMELIE
Water I.
Sandy Bay
Magens Bay
Hans Lollick I.
Little Tobago I.
Great Tobago I.
Jost Van Dyke
Redhook Bay
Caneel Bay
Trunk Bay
ST. JOHN
Great Thatch I.
Cane Garden Bay
West End
ROAD TOWN
TORTOLA
East End
Guana I.
AIRPORT
Marina Cay
Beef I.
West Dog
George Dog
Great Dog
VIRGIN GORDA
Copper Mine Pt.
Fallen Jerusalem
Cooper I.
Peter I.
Norman I.
ANEGADA
West End
Soldier Pt.
East Pt.
0 3
MILES
N
ST. CROIX
Frederickskted
AIRPORT
Christiansted
0 10
MILES
N

by a monument at the Grange, a typical West Indian residential house about a mile from Christiansted.

Nearly three times the size of St Thomas, the 84 square mile island of St Croix has rolling hills which reach the highest point (1,165 feet) at Mount Eagle in the north and slope gently down to coastal plains on the south. Sugar cane used to be grown in the centre of the island. The capital city of Christiansted may not unjustly be called a diminutive Copenhagen of the West Indies and is the best preserved of the architectural heritages of the West Indies.

The area around the docks is a natural historic site, while the old fort, museum, library and church are maintained as they were two centuries ago.

Fredericksted on the West Coast, 15 miles across the island from Christiansted, is another charming small town with a solid stone fort dating back to 1760. Many of the houses rebuilt in 1879 after a great fire retain the tradition of ornamental lattice and bandsaw work. Graceful stone arches along Strand Street survive from earlier centuries. About two miles east of Fredericksted is Whim's Greathouse, a neo-classic mansion which dates back to 1751 and which according to local guide books was owned in the early nineteenth century by a planter who made enough money to settle in England and then to buy a castle in Denmark where he became Chamberlain to King Frederick VI. The interior of the great house is furnished with an elegance which recalls Sam Lord's castle in Barbados, the great house of another West Indian planter who settled in England, where he died, in Jermyn Street London, on 5 November 1845. Whim's plantation Museum contains coppers in which cane juice was boiled during the process of conversion to syrup and sugar, and a pot still, casks and other implements for the manufacture of rum and sugar. A completely restored sugar mill of the type common in the late eighteenth century lies to the south east of the Great House. Whim's restoration is the work of the St Croix Landmarks Society, whose aims resemble those of the National Trust in Barbados, but who have far greater achievements to their credit, notably the establishment of the National Historic Site in Christiansted containing the Fort, the Customs House, old Scale House, Government House and the Steeple Building. Like the National Trust in Barbados the Landmarks Society invite visitors to make tours of notable houses and gardens during the months of February and March.

Midway between Fredericksted and Christiansted the championship Fountain Valley Golf Course was designed by Robert Trent Jones for David Laurance Rockefeller, whose Davis Bay development lies across the ridge from the golf course.

Sugar production was gradually phased out during the decade of the 'sixties while tourism and industrial development were being expanded. Hess oil began operation in 1966 with a $30 million plant adjacent to the Harvey Aluminium Plant which had a capital investment of over $65 million capable of producing 22,500 kilowatts of power and 1,500,000 gallons of fresh water per day, besides the production of alumina from bauxite. Harvey Alumina and Hess Oil have plans for further expansion on St Croix where light industries have also been introduced such as watch-assembly plants, textiles, pharmaceuticals and chemicals. St Croix has also been making a bid to recapture its former title of the Garden of the West Indies by means of truck farming and the adoption of modern techniques of vegetable growing by members of its sugar-cane-growing community.

Five miles north east of Christiansted, Buck Island, the modern version of Pocken-Eyland, is administered by the United States National Park Service and is renowned for tropical fish and coral, sponges and sea fans which may be seen at close quarters from an underwater trail which extends for 750 yards, 12 feet below the surface of the sea.

In 1956 the Congress of the United States designated St John, the 19-square-mile island three miles west of St Thomas, as a National Park. The land was donated by Laurence Rockefeller, whose resort at Caneel Bay Plantation has ten perfect beaches and offers complete privacy and the comforts of the simple life in a Garden of Eden setting. High upon Bordeaux mountain, bay leaves are still picked by islanders who ship them to St Thomas where they are used for the manufacture of bay rum, the traditional cooling lotion of the West Indies for external application. About 1,200 islanders live on St John where the traditional occupations of cattle grazing, bay leaf picking, farming, basket making and fishing have now been expanded to include those of gardeners, maids, guides and similar 'tourist' jobs. Coral Bay, which is seven miles from Caneel, lies under a cliff from which the Danes once kept watch on hostile ships approaching their islands. It is about three times as large as the harbour of St Thomas and looks out on to the British Virgin islands.

Tortola, which lies a few miles across the sea from St John and is about 20 minutes flying time from St Thomas, is the largest of about 16 inhabited British Virgin islands which comprise a total of 36 islands. The airport for Tortola is on Beef Island which is now connected to the principal island by the Queen Elizabeth Bridge. The collective area of the British Virgins is 67 square miles and the native-born population numbers approximately 12,000. Road Town, the capital of Tortola, is the seat of the Administrator who is responsible for the colony of the British Virgin Islands as representative of the Queen. The first British settlers arrived at Tortola from Anguilla in 1666 and by the early eighteenth century plantations of sugar, cotton and indigo were established on Tortola, Virgin Gorda (the Fat Virgin) and Jost Van Dyke. After the decline of the West Indian sugar economy which followed upon the end of the Napoleonic wars and the abolition of slavery in 1833 there was large-scale emigration of Europeans who were reduced to little more than 12 people by 1902. This European evacuation led to the creation of a landed peasantry among the descendants of the African slaves who remained. In 1946 the average land holding of the islanders was as high as 18 acres for each individual.

The tradition of land-ownership has bred among the islands a rugged individualistic attitude and a special sense of freedom and pride in being a native-born Virgin islander. In 1871 the Presidency of the Virgin Islands became a member of the Leeward Islands Federation, but its constitution was abrogated in 1902. In 1950 representative government was restored and continued after the dissolution of the Leeward Islands Federation in 1956, when the Virgin Islands were governed directly from the colonial office in London, having refused to join in the Federation of the West Indies. The guiding hand of London rests very lightly on the British Virgins today because of the close links which have developed between them and the United States Virgins during the first half of this century. Dual citizenship is common, the United States dollar is accepted as legal tender and it is possible to buy British Virgin Islands stamps printed in US values from the Post Office on Tortola.

The kinship between the families of both national groups of islands came about through free movement of British islanders who went to work, to do business or to study on the American islands. During the war years the movement became a flood when workers from the British islands flocked to work on the United States naval base on St Thomas. In the past decade the British islands have experienced their own waves of development as their attractions as tourist and tax havens have become better known. Between 1966 and 1968 the average growth rate of the economy had reached the unprecedented heights of 31% per annum and an average of 27% is still claimed.

Tortola, the largest of the British Virgins, has an area of 20 square miles and is ten miles long by three-and-a-half miles wide. Its steep and rugged hills reach their highest point at Sage Mountain, 1,780 feet above sea level. Its soils are shallow brown loam derived from volcanic material.

Because of their small size the islands can truly be described as unspoiled and are real havens for those who want to escape from the tourist atmospheres of other so-called tropical hideaways. There are good riding trails and footpaths for mountain hikes, the sea was made for sailors and underwater explorers, while the beaches and coves invite relaxation or exploration. The sea water in the 'Baths' at Virgin Gorda has been likened for its translucence to that of the famous Blue Grotto at Capri, but the pool at Virgin Gorda is considerably smaller in extent. The best known British Virgins are Tortola, Virgin Gorda, Anegada, Jost Van Dyke, Salt Island, Peter Island, Cooper Island, Marina Cay and Guana Island, but many others can be reached by boat excursions or during fishing expeditions.

Jost Van Dyke, a mountainous little island to the West of Tortola, is the birthplace of two famous men, Dr William Thornton and Dr John Lettsom.

Dr Thornton was born of Quaker parents on Jost Van Dyke, which he left at the age of five for England. He studied medicine at Edinburgh and Aberdeen and became an American citizen in Delaware in the year 1788. His design for the Capitol at Washington won him a lot in the new city (Number 15 in square 634) and a cash prize of 500 dollars.

Dr Thornton later designed two houses for George Washington on North Capitol Street and built the Octagon which is today headquarters of the American Institute of Architects. A scholar and a gentleman he enjoyed the friendship of Franklin, Washington, Jefferson, the Madisons and of other famous Americans of his day. Full of talent and eccentricity he was also a painter, a horse racer, and an experimenter with early paddle steamboats. He wrote an essay on teaching the deaf to hear and the dumb to speak and in a political pamphlet published in 1804 under the title of *Political Economy Founded in Justice and Humanity* he advocated the abolition of slavery. He deserves, at least in the British Virgin Islands, to be as well remembered as Wilberforce.

The second illustrious son of Jost Van Dyke, John Coakley Lettsom, also studied medicine at Edinburgh and graduated MD from Leyden in 1769, becoming FRS in 1771. An original founder of the Medical Society of London he is still honoured today by the Lettsomian lectures. One of his papers contains an original account of alcoholism and is claimed to be the first work on the drug habit. Dr Lettsom's name is also associated with the foundations of the General Dispensary in Aldersgate Street, the Royal Humane Society and the Royal Sea Bathing Hospital at Margate. It is one of the ironies of life that the man who supported Jenner's stand on vaccination should be chiefly remembered in the islands by the jingle:

> I, John Lettsom
> Blisters, bleeds and sweats 'em;
> If after that they please to die
> I, John Lettsom.

The humour is plainly that of a schoolboy!

Anegada, the most easterly of the islands, has been equipped with an airstrip and deep-water berth. The latter is of vital importance since the reefs around Anegada (or the 'drowned' island) have claimed over 200 wrecks.

Anegada has an area of 13 square miles and is being developed as a resort island by Mr Kenneth Bates of Lancashire. Mr Bates also added 60 acres of new land which have been reclaimed from the sea to Road Town the capital of Tortola. This project is known as the Wickham's Cay development and is one of the many developments on Tortola. Resorts are also being developed on Beef Island and Virgin Gorda where Laurance Rockefeller's 500 acre estate Little Dix, was opened in 1964.

Hotels have also been established on Mosquito Island, Guana Island and Marina Cay, the six-acre island which is the subject of Robert White's book on which a movie and TV show have also been based. At the northern end of the Anegada Passage (in which Prince Maurice was drowned) Sombrero, a low flat rock 25 feet above sea level, functions as a Board of Trade lighthouse.

Like the Grenadines at the lower end of the Lesser Antilles the British Virgin islands are attractive because of their small size and their remoteness from highly developed places. Their continuing appeal will depend on the ability of the developers to keep them unspoilt and their future will almost inevitably be linked with that of the American Virgins with whom they have important trading and social connexions: so close that a British visitor going to the United States Virgins is officially advised to obtain a United States visa before leaving home since they are most likely to pass through American territory during their stay.

GENERAL INFORMATION

United States Virgins comprising St Thomas (32 square miles), St Croix (82 square miles), St John (18 square miles) and about 50 neighbouring islets.
Language   English, some Spanish and Creole French.
Documents required   None for United States citizens, but proof of citizenship and smallpox vaccination required if from other than US ports of origin.
Currency   As for United States.
Electricity   110 V and 120 V AC.
Climate   Average about 78°F. Average rainfall 45 inches.
Time   Noon is 11 a.m. Eastern Standard Time.
Churches   Roman Catholic, Lutheran, other denominations, Jewish.
Clothes   Formal gowns for luxury hotels. Jacket and tie for men. Otherwise light summer wear.
Tipping   About 15%. Porters 25¢ to 30¢ per bag. No departure tax.
Transportation   Taxis (look for T on licence plates) and hired cars. Drive on left.
Water   Ask at hotels.
Food   Creole, American, European. Sea food.
Laundry   Good.
Medical Facilities   Government-owned hospital on each of three islands.
Sports   Deep-sea fishing, spear fishing, lobster diving, yachting and sailing, motor cruises, horseback riding, tennis, nine

hole golf course on St Thomas, Fountain Valley Golf Course on St Croix.
Spectator Sports Basketball, cricket, baseball, horse racing. Cockfighting on St Croix.
Gambling Legal lottery with monthly drawing.
Courtesies Brief shorts frowned upon.
Theatre New Island Centre, Christiansted St Croix, drama, musical comedies, orchestral and dance groups.
What to Buy World-wide imports including South American silver jewellery, Florentine leather goods, English woollens, liquors. Note that US residents returning directly or indirectly from the US Virgins are allowed $200 duty free goods (retail price) of which half must be spent in the US Virgins.
Sightseeing ST THOMAS Drake's Seat, Street of 99 steps, Danish 'conchshell' cemetery, dungeon of Old Fort Christian, Church of St Peter and St Paul, All Saints Church, Bretta centre off Main Street. Take glass-bottomed boat ride and aerial tramway up Flag Hill.
ST CROIX Twice-daily free tours of old Fort Christiansted, Steeple Building, Lutheran Church, Government House. St Croix's collection of pre-Columbian Indian relics in Golden Grove College, Kingshill, Fredericksted Fort. Underwater Trail 12 feet below surface of sea.
ST JOHN Virgin Islands National Park, Trunk Bay and Caneel Bay. Daily boat and amphibian flights.
Holidays All US holidays plus January 6 (Three Kings Day), March 31 (Transfer Day), June 22 (Organic Act Day), July 25 (Supplication Day), October 25 (Freedom from Hurricanes Day), November 1 (Liberty Day), December 25, 26.
Festivals Carnival times are between December 15 and January 6 on St Croix and for three days in the last week of April on St Thomas.

The British Virgins, comprising Tortola and 35 other islands and islets of which 16 are inhabited. Best known are Tortola,

Virgin Gorda, Anegada, Jost Van Dyke, Salt Island, Peter Island, Cooper Island, Norman Island, Marina Cay and Guana Island.

Language   English.
Documents required   International certificate of vaccination. Passports required for cashing travellers cheques, otherwise no visa or passports required for stays up to six months. A departure tax of $1 US for air travellers and 40 cents for those leaving by sea.
Currency   US Currency is official, although the islands are in the sterling area.
Electricity   120 V 60 cycles.
Climate   Average temperature of 79°F. Average rainfall 30 inches.
Time   As for American Virgins.
Churches   Anglican, Roman Catholic, Methodist and other denominations.
Clothing   Formal gowns, jacket and tie only at larger resorts. Otherwise light summer wear.
Tipping   Between 10 and 15%.
Transportation   Airport on Beef Island, Airstrips on Virgin Gorda and Anegada, Drake's Highway on Tortola links the east and western parts of the 10 mile long island. Virgin Gorda, Jost Van Dyke and Anegada have roads. Hydrofoils operate daily between San Juan and Tortola. Private launches are available for hire. Some hotels provide free bicycles. Horse and donkeys available for pleasure riding. Cars drive on left.
Water   Mostly from cisterns or wells. Limited public supply on Tortola.
Food   Mostly imported. Sea food and English roast beef recommended at Little Dix Bay, Virgin Gorda.
Laundry   Through hotels.
Medical Facilities   A hospital with X-ray and laboratory facilities, five medical practitioners and two dentists.
Sports   Yachting, fishing, scuba diving, water-skiing, horseback riding, picnics, motor boating.

Other Amenities   A cinema in Road Town, hotel dances, horse races on holidays.
Courtesies   Always remember that the Virgin islanders are proud of their islands.
What to See   Mount Sage (1,780 feet) on Tortola. The Baths on Virgin Gorda, scenic views of neighbouring islands.
What to Buy   Souvenirs from tiny gift shops.
Holidays   January 1, February 23, Good Friday, Easter Monday, May 24 (Commonwealth Day), Whit Monday, Queen's Birthday, July 1 (Colony Day), 1st Monday in August, October 21 (St Ursula's Day), November 14 (Prince Charles' Birthday), December 25, 26.
Festivals   First week in August, street parades, fireworks, horse races, aquatic sports, commemorating abolition of slavery. Christmas week, carol singing, torchlight processions, street masquerades.

Chapter 12
Puerto Rico

Puerto Rico stands at the most easterly point of the Greater Antilles which are the high peaks of a 1,300-mile chain of submerged mountains in the Atlantic ocean. Puerto Rico is the smallest of the Greater Antilles. The other islands of the group are San Domingo and Haiti (Hispaniola), Jamaica and Cuba. Puerto Rico's area of 3,315 square miles (3,435 including its adjacent island possessions) makes it very much larger than any of the islands of the lesser Antilles; the largest of which, Trinidad, has an area of 1,864 square miles.

On his second voyage friendly Indians in the lesser Antilles told Columbus of an island which they called Borinquen. He landed on that island on 19 November 1493 and christened it San Juan Batista. Much later, in 1508, Ponce arrived from Hispaniola to build a Spanish settlement at Caparra among the low hills which lie to the west of San Juan's harbour. Three years later this settlement became known as Puerto Rico. It was later moved in 1521 to the small island at the entrance to the harbour where old San Juan stands today. Gradually with the passage of time the island took the name of Puerto Rico, while the capital alone was called San Juan.

Because of its strategic position as a gateway to the Caribbean from Europe, Puerto Rico was exposed to constant attacks from the enemies of Spain – Caribs, French, English and Dutch. As early as 1533 La Fortaleza was constructed on old San Juan to act as a bastion, treasure house and residence of the Spanish Governor. Towards the end of the century the gunners of El Morro were ready to resist Sir Francis Drake's three-day fight to capture the Spanish treasure fleet in November 1595. The Earl of Cumberland was more successful in the summer of 1598, but was unable to establish his victory for more than two months because of plague and resistance from the islanders.

In 1624 Governor de Haro bravely beat back the efforts of a Dutch naval commander, Boudewijn Henrikszoon, who kept up a siege for several weeks. Puerto Rico was saved for Spain; so its privateers could take severe toll of British ships for many decades of the seventeenth and eighteenth centuries. One such, most feared by the English who called him the 'Grand Arch Villain', was a mulatto shoemaker turned pirate. His name was Henriquez and he harried the Caribbean seas for three decades. Spanish defences in Puerto Rico were strengthened by the completion of San Cristobal, which together with El Morro proved impregnable when Sir Ralph Abercromby, the conqueror of Trinidad, launched an English attack in 1797.

Abercromby's failure was the last determined effort by a European power to replace Spanish dominion in Puerto Rico. It was not until 1898, several months after American troops had landed at Guanica on the Caribbean shore line, that Spain's 400 years of possession of the gateway to the Caribbean ended. By the Treaty of Paris on 10 December 1898 sovereignty over Puerto Rico was ceded to the United States. Spanish sovereignty ceased to have sway from that date, but the effects of Spanish rule have survived to this day. Of these the Spanish language is the most obvious. Spanish is spoken at home, is the language of instruction in the schools, of literature and of most of the newspapers and radio and television stations. Debates in the Puerto Rican legislature also take place in Spanish. English is a required subject because it is essential for business, but it is a second language for native Puerto Ricans, whose Spanish heritage is also seen in the arches, balconies, patios and grilles of the buildings. Spain is also present in the little towns where the church looks across the plaza at the town hall as it does in several villages of Sicily. Spanish, too, is the deep-rooted tradition of the family and the observance of Catholic feast days with their colourful street processions. Every town has its own patron saint, but the greatest honour is reserved for the saint whom Columbus especially honoured when he changed the name of Borinquen – St John the Baptist. All-night vigils with bonfires are held on the night of June 23 and on the dawn of the saint's day, June 24, thousands of faithful Puerto Ricans wade into the water to re-enact the baptism of Christ, and, more mundanely, to assure themselves of good health during the coming year. St Patrick, whose anniversary occurs during the Lenten fast is especially honoured by the residents of the little village of Loiza Aldea because he helped the townsfolk there centuries ago to withstand the attacks of ants. Lent takes on a carnival atmosphere for about 10 days before St Patrick's day.

The Puerto Ricans are predominantly European in ancestry, with some Negro and Indian mingling of blood. The population approximates to $2\frac{3}{4}$ million, of whom 761,500 live in San Juan. Less than 20% of the Puerto Ricans in 1960 were classified as non-white. They are also predominantly Catholic in religion, only 20% belonging to the evangelical sects which came in with the Americans in 1898. Among Puerto Rican ancestors are also to be found French fugitives, who fled from Haiti in 1791, 1803 and 1811, and Spanish and Creoles, who came from neighbouring Santo Domingo when part of Hispaniola was ceded to France. More Spanish refugees poured in from Louisiana after it was sold by France to the United States in 1803 and more Spanish came from Venezuela in 1813 when Bolivar decreed the death of those born in the Peninsula. Puerto Rico had 51,216 slaves in 1846 when some Puerto Rican owners began voluntarily to free some. Abolition of slavery did not, however, become official until 22 March 1872, a holiday that continues in Puerto Rico. Americans began to move into Puerto Rico after 1898, but it was not until the 'forties that the political genius of Luis Muñoz Marin, founder of the Popular Democratic Party, allied to the executive ability of Rexford Tugwell, the American Governor, made possible reforms which were credited to the New Deal establishment of President Franklin D. Roosevelt. In 1942 Governor Tugwell appointed a Planning Board which launched Puerto Rico from 'Operation Lament' over a static agricultural economy into 'Operation Bootstrap', a blue print for switching the economy into a gear of industrialisation.

A Government Development Bank was also established in 1942 and its practical ally or arm was the Economic Development Administration or 'Fomento'. The 'stirring-up' of the economy took the form of building and industrial enterprises which private investors were not ready to undertake.

The success of industrialisation in Puerto Rico – some 1600 industries since 1947 – has had a dramatic impact upon the *per capita* average income, which rose from $121 in 1940 to $1,200 in 1969 and is expected to reach $2,000 by 1975. Unfortunately the gains from industrialisation have not been great enough to eliminate unemployment, which is officially put at 12% but is considered by some commentators to be much higher. Nor has the benefits of association with the United States prevented the formation of separatist movements or the periodic explosion of terrorist bombs. In July 1952 Puerto Rico achieved full internal autonomy as a Commonwealth, 'associated with the United States'. It has a senate of 27 and a House of 51 Representatives elected for four-year terms. The Governor is also elected for four years. Puerto Ricans also elect one commissioner to represent their island in the United States House of Representatives, but he has no vote. The first Puerto Rican Cabinet was appointed in 1941 and the first native governor in 1946.

Despite the existence of serious problems Puerto Rico has nonetheless captured the imagination of all the other Caribbean territories (except Haiti, Cuba and San Domingo) and each island has borrowed something from the Puerto Rican methods of developing industries and tourism. As a counterpart to the injection of American know-how, techniques, education and communications, the Puerto Ricans have been consciously striving through their Institute of Culture, formed in 1955, to emphasise their historical links with Spain, while at the same time striving to foster a modern Puerto Rican identity. The very success of Puerto Rico's leap into the modern world is likely to resuscitate the latent anxiety as to status which was partially shelved when Señor Luis Muñoz Marin focused Puerto Rican energies upon first raising desperately low living standards. The independence of Jamaica, and other British Caribbean territories, which looked upon Puerto Rico as a model, must have stirred new political aspirations, although independence is equated by moderates with Fidel Castro and his revolution, uprisings in Haiti and San Domingo or emergencies in Jamaica and Trinidad. The political future will become more clear after the next elections are held in 1972.

Puerto Rico measures about 100 miles from east to west and 25 miles from north to south. It lies 65 miles east of the Dominican Republic across the Mona Passage, 1,050 miles south-east of Miami, Florida, and 1,600 miles south-east of New York. It may be considered as half-way bastion of an outer ring of islands which enclose the Caribbean sea.

Puerto Rico has three geographical regions. Lowlands and coastal plains occupy 27% of flat or gently rolling lands where sugar and fruit crops are mainly farmed. 36% of the island forms the highlands where coffee and tobacco are the principal crops, supplemented by subsistence farming and pasturage.

Rolling hill lands between flat coastal plains and mountainous terrains account for the final 37% of land area. On the north-east and north-central sections there are limestone belts similar to those of the Cockpit area of Jamaica. Karst formations in the limestone belts are named after a Jugoslav province where limestone rock dissolved by water produced conical sink holes in the ground. In Puerto Rico the sinkholes occur chiefly between Aguadilla and Toa Alta. Between the sinkhole area at Aguadille and Loiza Aldea small hills are

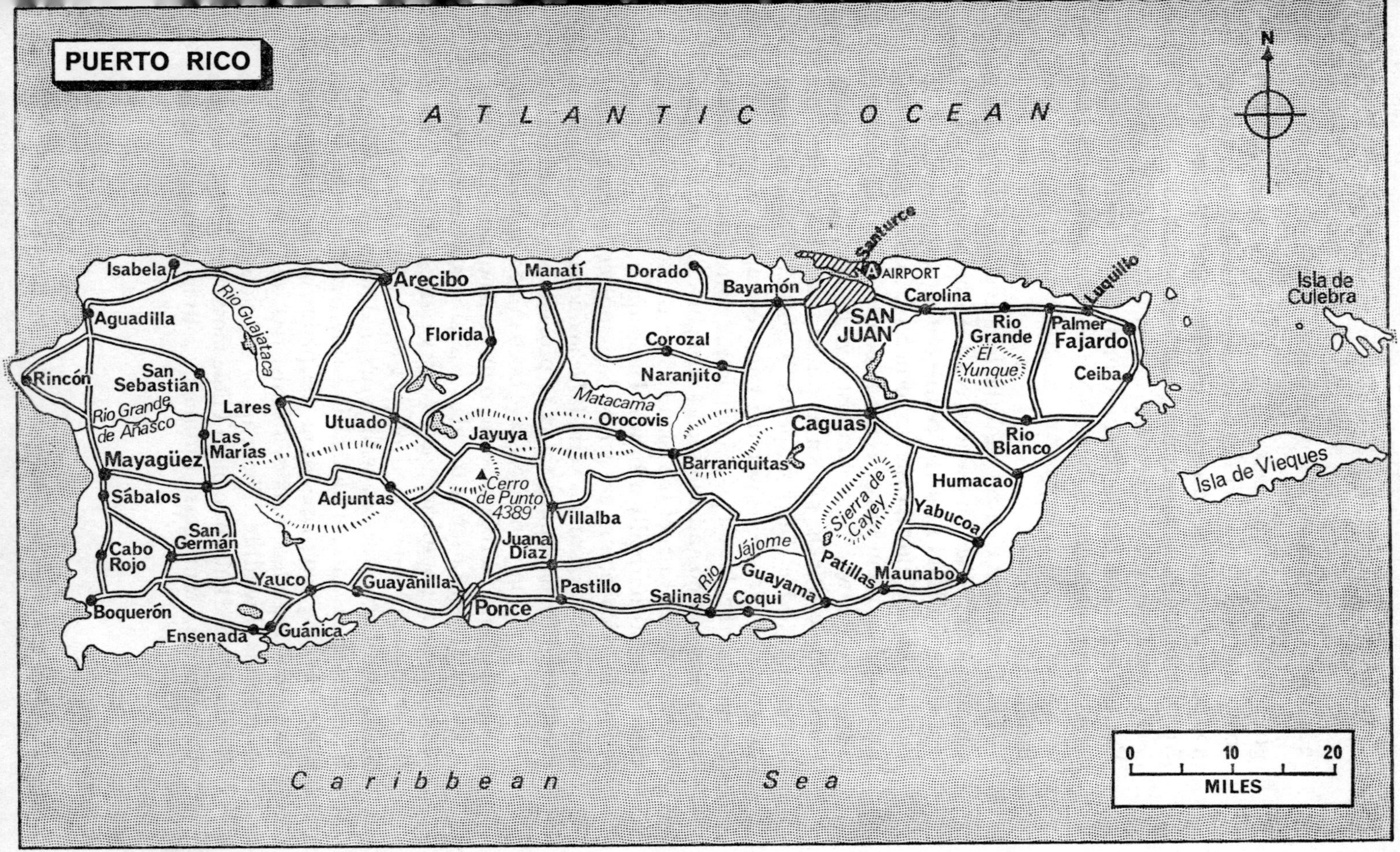
PUERTO RICO
ATLANTIC OCEAN
N
Isabela
Arecibo
Manatí
Dorado
Bayamón
Santurce
AIRPORT
Carolina
Luquillo
Isla de Culebra
Aguadilla
Rio Guajataca
Florida
Corozal
SAN JUAN
Rio Grande
Palmer
Fajardo
El Yunque
Ceiba
Rincón
San Sebastián
Naranjito
Rio Grande de Añasco
Lares
Utuado
Matacama
Orocovis
Caguas
Rio Blanco
Jayuya
Las Marías
Mayagüez
Barranquitas
Isla de Vieques
Cerro de Punto 4389'
Humacao
Sábalos
Adjuntas
Villalba
Sierra de Cayey
Yabucoa
San Germán
Cabo Rojo
Juana Díaz
Jájome
Rio
Guayama
Patillas
Maunabo
Yauco
Guayanilla
Pastillo
Salinas
Coqui
Boquerón
Ponce
Ensenada
Guánica
Caribbean Sea
0
10
20
MILES

given the name of 'haystacks'. The sinkholes average 400 feet across and about 160 feet deep. Inside one sinkhole, which is 300 feet deep and 1,300 feet across, the huge reflector of the Arecibo Ionospheric observatory has been installed.

The Karst country is also full of caves. Camuy Cave along the underground course of the Camuy River on the northwest has been described by the National Speleogical Society as an 'extensive cave system, unique, majestic, and awe inspiring'.

The Cordillera Central runs the length of the island rising almost out of the sea on the west coast. Its highest point, 4,348 feet above sea level near the centre of the island, is Cerro de Punta. On the north-eastern corner of the island on the Luquillo Mountain Range is the 28,000-acre Luquillo Experimental Forest which is administered by the United States Forest Service. It is known popularly as El Yunque, the highest (3,532 feet) of three peaks. Temperatures range from 50° to 90° Fahrenheit over the four vegetation areas of the Cordillera, the lowest of which is the rain forest. Rainfall varies between 80 and 180 inches annually. Rain is abundant in the northern area of the island while the southern is much drier and has normally a brown landscape.

Puerto Rico has rivers which are subject to flash floods after heavy showers and several large artificial lakes have been constructed by damming rivers to provide power and water.

Gold, manganese and iron have been mined in Puerto Rico, and copper and marble exist in commercial quantities. Other resources are silica sands for glass containers, clays and limestone. Enough phosphate for 20 years can be obtained from the guano on Mona Island off Mayaguez. On the island of Mona live bats, iguanas, wild boars and wild goats. Puerto Rico's most distinctive animal is a tiny tree frog, the coqui, whose evening song rises from the plains to the mountains. Occasional harmless snakes, lizards, rats and mongoose are other forms of wildlife. There are nearly 2,000 species of birds of which 89 are known to nest. Those most commonly seen are the thrushes, tannagers, bullfinches, flycatchers, warblers, plovers, terns and sandpipers. Also well known are the 'plain pigeon' and the nearly extinct Puerto Rican parrot.

Excellent sport-fishing may be had two to five miles off the coast, where the fish include yellow fin tuna, the white marlin, sail fish, dolphins (dorados) and wahoos.

Puerto Rico has an annual average surface temperature of 77°. Maximum summertime temperature reaches into the low 90's along the coast, while minimum winter ranges fall to the middle 50's in the high interior. Relative humidity ranges, on average, from high 80's at night to middle 60's during day time, with about 5% variation from winter to summer. Between June and November every year several tropical storms pass close enough to have some effect on the island, but only six major hurricanes have crossed Puerto Rico in the last 60 years.

In 1970 Puerto Rico received over a million visitors, mostly Americans who flock to the Condado strip and Isla Verde near San Juan where luxury hotels facing the Atlantic offer sophisticated comfort and night life. By 1980 Puerto Rico will have more than 40,000 hotel and guest rooms, while a second international airport is to be built on the Caribbean south coast between Ponce and Mayaguez. So highly developed is the tourist industry that air taxis are provided from San Juan for those travelling to Dorado, famous for its palm-lined golf fairways, while a scheduled helicopter service flies from San Juan to El Conquistador, a luxury hotel perched an hour's motor drive from the capital on top of a seaside cliff near Fajardo. From El Conquistador trips can be made by catamaran or native sloop to deserted cays surrounded by coral reefs. An aerial tramway connects the port area to the beach below. Golf, tennis, water sports and baseball are the special recreational activities of Puerto Rico.

In the centre of the island is the government-owned hotel which nestles in green mountains over the town of Barranquitas. Horseback and burro (donkey) riding are popular with those who enjoy tropical landscapes. Horseback riding, fishing and mountain-river swimming are available at the

Hacienda Roses, a guest house on a coffee plantation near Utuado. There the menu includes fresh ground coffee, local fruits and island cooking.

Puerto Rico has several attractive small hotels and inns scattered along the coasts. Villa Parguera and the Copamarina hotel are among the better known on the south-west coast. A string of beach resorts has developed along the western coasts where the 1968 World Surfing Championship was held at Rincon. At Aguadilla the Montemar hotel offers swimming and dining on a terrace high over the sea on the north west. Comfortable guest houses are found on Vieques island, which has an area of 57 square miles and lies 10 miles south-east of Puerto Rico. Puerto Rico's greatest attraction for visitors is the variety of its landscape. There is a choice of low-lying beach-land or lush rainforest with fern trees, orchids, mountain palms, tumbling streams and cascading waterfalls. At El Yunque in the east and Toro Negro in the west there are hiking trails, picnic grounds and places to swim. At El Yunque a mountain-top restaurant offers the refreshment of Spanish and Puerto Rican cooking. The southern half of the island is dry. Scrub and cactus border isolated bays and cliffs on the Caribbean coastline and on Mona a limestone island about 20 square miles in area, lying halfway between Puerto Rico and the Dominican Republic. Mona is distinguished especially for its giant blue iguanas who receive official protection. Hunters are however permitted to shoot the wild boars and goats which are to be found there in relatively large numbers.

Mangrove areas are common in Puerto Rico along the coast east of San Juan, at the north-east tip near Fajardo, in the south-west around La Parguera and elsewhere.

All beaches are public land in Puerto Rico and each coast has at least one public beach equipped with parking facilities, showers, lockers and refreshment stands. The most famous beaches are near the hotel areas in San Juan and at Luquillo, a white, palm-fringed crescent east of the capital. Puerto Rico resembles the American mainland in the excellence of its communications. About 4,000 miles of modern roads run around the rectangular shaped coastlines, and express highways connect the interior to the coastal cities. Mountain roads are steep and winding so cars keep well to the right and sound horns at corners.

Ocean-going ships link Puerto Rican ports to major cities of the Atlantic and Pacific. San Juan is a hub of international air travel with direct flights from New York, Chicago, Miami and other cities.

Spanish at heart, Spanish in speech, modern San Juan yet justifies the sign which greets all air passengers at the airport: 'Welcome to the United States'. As you roll along traffic-filled streets in air-conditioned comfort, gazing up at high-storied apartments or watch the neon signs, you need to pinch yourself and ask, is this Puerto Rico or did the plane land instead at Miami?

GENERAL INFORMATION

Puerto Rico

Religion Catholic, Protestant, Jewish.
Climate Tropical marine, annual average of 77°F. Summertime maximum low 90's. Wintertime minimum middle 50's. Relative humidity from high 80's at night to middle 60's by day.
Clothes Women need slacks, shorts, lightwear dresses, sweater or stole for evenings. Men need lightweight suits, slacks, shirts. In hills medium-weight clothes and topcoat, sports coats.
Communications Modern airport, harbour and highways. Hub of international air travel. Direct flights from major South American and Caribbean cities and from Miami, New York, Boston, Philadelphia, Baltimore and Washington.
To call overseas dial 128 on telephones: to obtain local information dial 123.

Currency, Mail and Measures Money, postal services and measures same as on US mainland, except for road distances which are marked in kilometres (1 kilometre equals .62 mile). Highway signs are also in Spanish.

Documents required No passport or visa from US citizens. All other visitors require documents needed for entry to the United States; passport, visa and international smallpox certificate.

Electrical Current 110 60 cycles and 220 V AC, same as on mainland of USA.

Food and Drink US Food and Drug Administration standards apply to Puerto Rico. San Juan has dozens of first-class restaurants serving European, Puerto Rican, Chinese and American dishes with appropriate drinks. Puerto Rican food is predominantly Spanish. Famous dishes are Arroz con pollo, Asopao (rice soaked with shrimp or chicken), Pastiles (meat wrapped in boiled plantain leaves), Techon Asado (barbecued pig), Jueyes (fresh land crabs) Pastillilos (deep fat fried dough covered meat or cheese). Among many good restaurants La Mallorquina in old San Juan is noted for sea food and Spanish dishes. Also highly recommended in old San Juan is La Fonda del Callejon; Mario's at Isla Verde and Patio Español down town. Whisky, gin, vodka and brandy are much cheaper than in the States. Puerto Rican rum is of high quality.

Holidays Normal US holidays on January 1, February 22, May 30, July 4, 1st Monday in September, November 11, 4th Thursday in November, December 25 plus Puerto Rican holidays January 6 (Three Kings' Day), January 11 (Hosto's Birthday), March 22 (Abolition of Slavery), April 16 (De Diego's Birthday), July 17 (Munoz Rivera's Birthday), July 25 (Commonwealth Day), July 27 (Barbosa's Birthday), November 19 (Discovery of Puerto Rico).

Language Spanish. English is also spoken.

Laundry and Dry Cleaning Good in hotels and San Juan.

Medical Facilities There are 139 modern hospitals throughout the island and 2,738 licensed physicians in all fields of medicine. Most of them are US medical school graduates.

Night Life San Juan has a wide variety of entertainment by night, inclusive of elaborate floorshows and gambling in casinos.

Other Tourist Facilities Art Exhibits, Symphony Orchestra, Piano and other Recitals, Art Films, Fashion Shows, Rum Plant Tours, Guided Tours, Gambling (weekly state lottery, nightly casinos in large hotels, thrice weekly horse races with pari-mutuel). Clubs: Rotary, Lions, Elks, American Legion, Propeller Club, Exchange Club, Knights of Columbus.

Local Customs 'Out on the island' means anywhere outside San Juan and its immediate suburbs.

Sports Gold (Dorado Beach is world famous), Horse riding, skeet and trap shooting, tennis, deep-sea fishing. A 780 pound blue marlin boated off San Juan won the all tackle world record.

Spectator Sports Cockfighting, Saturdays and Sundays (from November 1st till August); horse racing on holidays, Wednesdays, Fridays and Sundays at El Comandante; baseball, tennis tournaments, boxing, wrestling, basketball, bullfighting on Sundays from mid December till April.

Time 1 p.m. Eastern Standard time is noon in Puerto Rico.

Tipping 10% of bill; taxi drivers 15%. Airport porters 25¢ for two bags, then 10¢ for each additional bag. There is no departure tax.

Transportation Taxis, cars, boats, bus services (out of rush hours). Useful buses for visitors are Nos 1, 10 and 17 (to airport). Motor coach services operate between San Juan, Mayaguez and Ponce. Stateside (USA) driving licences honoured for 120 days in Puerto Rico. There are local air and boat services.

Water Safe.

What to See SAN JUAN El Morro, San Geronimo, La Fortaleza, Cathedral of San Juan Bautista, Museum of the Family. Near San Juan: Luquillo Beach, El Yunque rain forest.

MAYAGUEZ Porta Coeli Chapel (1519), Inter American University, Needlework Centre.

NEAR PARGUERA Phosphorescent Bay at night (a short boat ride).
What to Buy Records of Puerto Rican music (*danza plena* and *aguinaldos*), native-made sports wear, needlework, embroidered linens, mahogany bowls, men's linen suits, woven baskets, bamboo products, liquor (note that internal revenue tax is levied on rum). There are no customs duties on articles bought in Puerto Rico and taken into the United States.
Information From Tourist offices in Puerto Rico, New York, Miami, Chicago, Los Angeles, Toronto.

Chapter 13
The Future

Some West Indians believe that their destiny is to come together as a nation. It is possible that some day the descendants of people who were at one time 'British subjects' will be free to move between the islands and mainland territories, which border the Caribbean sea and owe loyalty to one state. It is possible, but few signs are pointing in that direction today.

Jamaica has never been happy about joining a political union with the smaller islands down south; Belize, as British Honduras prefers to be called, is a part of the American continent and has little historical or social reasons for seeking political identity with the islands; Guyana is building a road into Brazil and has a South American destiny. Guyana broke with the centuries-old monarchic tradition of the islands when it became a republic on February 23, 1970. Trinidad and Tobago is also likely to become a Republic and other islands may follow the trend.

Trinidad is near enough to the South American mainland to be considered as a part of that continent; like Barbados and Jamaica it belongs to the Organisation of American States. Trinidad fosters close trading and cultural links with Venezuela and is groomed for the role of mediator between Guyana and Venezuela over the dispute between these countries, which concerns the ownership of the greater part of Guyana. So long as this dispute exists Guyana cannot become a member of the Organisation of American States. If the dispute can be settled there is a strong possibility of Guyana, Trinidad and Venezuela working out a special trading agreement and there might even be a closer union. Anything is possible in a region which has known many trading experiments and where political ties have been loosened many times.

Jamaica's proximity to Cuba, Haiti and San Domingo, Puerto Rico and the Bahamas suggests that in the long term there might be closer association between these territories. At present no signposts point anywhere except in limited directions to Belize. It is important to stress that large trading areas, common markets or other forms of union between the Commonwealth Caribbean territories and the more densely populated countries of Cuba, San Domingo, Puerto Rico, Haiti and Venezuela would put the Commonwealth Caribbean countries at the bottom of a new league. It is unlikely that countries which have displayed so much suspicion of their fellows in the Commonwealth should be content to merge with ex-Spanish territories or to open their markets to more developed trading countries.

The French and Dutch presence in the Windward group complicates problems of an association which geographical location indicates between all the islands that stretch from Barbados up the Antillean arc to the Virgins.

The English Leewards and Windwards already have membership in a Regional Development Agency which could be expanded into an effective administrative and planning unit for all the islands, inclusive of Barbados. Two years experience of the Caribbean Free Trade Agreement has shown the advantages to the area of regional trade, even though the advantages have been heavily slanted in the direction of Trinidad. The formation of a Caribbean Development Bank in 1970, eighteen months after the Trade Agreement became effective will further develop tendencies towards regional co-operation. Indeed the Bank is authorised 'to stimulate and encourage the development of capital markets within the region and to co-operate and assist in regional efforts to promote regional and locally controlled financial institutions and a regional market for credit and savings'. The bank is perhaps going to be most effective because membership is not restricted to the Commonwealth Caribbean, but is 'open to any other non-regional state which is a member of the United Nations or any of its specialised agencies, or of the International Atomic Energy Agency'. It began operations with an equity capital of $50 million (US), of which Canada and Britain have each subscribed $10 million US, as well as $5 million US apiece for the Special Development Fund to which the United States has also contributed.

The Bank's President, St Lucian-born Sir Arthur Lewis, is a happy choice, because he represents the West Indies in association with the world, having achieved eminence in universities of Britain, the United States and the West Indies and an international reputation as an economist. Sir Arthur in an epilogue to Sir John Mordecai's account of the Federal Negotiations expressed the conviction that West Indians will come together as a nation. He went further and stated that federation is needed to preserve political freedom, since independent small islands need a Federal Government to uphold the law, and to protect its citizens from persecution and corruption. The argument might even have been expanded to show that political advancement and maturity requires federation because the mini-legislatures of small islands are too small to permit the roles of backbenchers within parties and the party system is itself endangered by the natural fears prevalent in all small communities of people who are afraid of being called dissidents, or subversive, when they speak their minds.

Even in the University of the West Indies, which is dependent for financial support on the contributions of 14 separate governments, the atmosphere of freedom has not been as clear as many would like it to be. Not everyone would agree today with the claim made by Vice-Chancellor, Sir Philip Sherlock, during the presentation to him of the Freedom of the City of Kingston on 5 February 1964 that the governments of the

West Indies emphasise that 'their University must be free from political control'. The University authorities have no simple task in trying to please 14 separate governments and what is considered normal academic freedom in one island can easily be interpreted as an attack on established government in another.

The word most commonly used about the modern West Indies is fragmentation. People coming from countries where regional association is admitted to be essential for themselves cannot understand why West Indian governments refuse to see the benefits to be gained from emerging out of the chrysalis of parochial administration. They cannot understand why tiny territories with mini-budgets should seek to compete with each other for representation abroad, or why larger territories should be reluctant to co-operate with small when seeking new markets. The creed of a modern West Indian may be described as follows:

'I am a West Indian patriot,
I believe in the West Indies
But I believe that my island
Comes first in the West Indies
Always'.

It is a creed born of the need of political bosses to impress upon the people who vote for them that they alone have their interests at heart. It is a creed that requires repression when people appear to reject their claim; how else can one interpret the attitude of a West Indian leader who, after decades of office, announced that elections might not be held because the people were now showing themselves unfit to exercise the vote?

The problem of the West Indies, and to some degree, the problem of the modern world is concerned with the question of how to divide and rule at the same time. Each territory requires maximum degrees of self government so that each island can enjoy the sense of participation in the social, cultural, economic and spiritual development which is in progress of growth. At the same time the quality of these developments must depend on the calibre of the people who are planning. It ought to be obvious, but it is by no means so, in the Caribbean that such people cannot be found exclusively from within the tiny limits of small islands, even though a surprisingly large number might have been born on any one of them.

Just as happened during the war in the Caribbean, when no less than 148 ships were sunk within three months of the year 1942 and the helpless nature of Caribbean defences against German U-boats was revealed, so today's war against poverty requires the assistance of technologies and methods which are beyond the resources of newly independent Caribbean countries. The French, American, and Dutch countries have entire or partial integration with the highly developed countries which are responsible for their existence. The Commonwealth countries have no integration with parent nations, or amongst themselves. It would seem that their future depends on their ability to achieve something larger than a trading area, however much such an area may help to boost their economic development.

Tips for Tourists

One hundred and forty years ago an Englishman who had spent four years in the West Indies gave ten lengthy suggestions for tourists, summarised as 'Advice to Outgoers'. Among them were the need of summer clothes, preserves, pickles, and a dose of Epsom salts weekly during the long voyage by sea.

Other instructions include a ban on servants ('You will incur great expense and trouble!') and the necessity of obtaining letters of introduction to one or two of the principal inhabitants.

The rest were instructions for a healthy life. You were not to expose yourself too much in the heat of the day, you were to wear flannel ('devilish hot, but very good for the health'), you were to rise at gunfire and, when you could, go to bed at the same sober time, you were to avoid catching cold and finally you had to bear the bites of the mosquitoes and sandflies like a philosopher.

Times have changed and today's visitor to the West Indies is advised by newspaper articles, brochures, travel offices and friends 'who have just come back from the place where you are going'.

Giving advice to outgoers is always a risky business because no two outgoers are alike. Yet those who travel to the West Indies may benefit from the following suggestions:

Before leaving   Make sure that your passport, health certificates and other travel documents are in order.

Weigh your travel bags to avoid excess charges.
Buy liquor, tobacco, perfume in duty free shops at airports, or during flight when possible.
During flight Have pen ready to fill in landing card.
Buy cigarettes on board.
Do not take alcohol with tranquillisers.
On arrival Remember it's hot outside. Take your time walking to the terminal building.
Be patient with the health, immigration and customs authorities.
Ask for taxi rates in island dollars for you and your bags, before you leave airport.
Always pay in dollars of the island.
Health advice Eat simple food and drink the first day.
Watch the sun. Even when skies are grey you can get sunburnt. The best time to be in the sun is up till noon and after three in the afternoon. A good anti-sun lotion is recommended. Wear polaroid sunshades.
Warnings Be prudent with valuables, wherever you are.
Avoid lonely beaches.
Never go beyond your depth when the sea is rough, or smooth.
Remember that sea currents are strong.
Wear shoes when walking over reefs or sharp pointed rocks.
Wet moss is slippery.
Sea egg prickles are painful.
Do not eat strange fruit or berries.
Keep a wary eye out for 'men o'war'.
In rainy months a light umbrella or mac is useful.
Do not lie on 'dead' sand.
General Advice Use banks to exchange money.
Shop early or late unless there is air-conditioning in the store.
Each island has early closing days.
Avoid shopping on 'cruise-ship' days.
For photographers Buy a lens hood for protection against light reflection.
Use ultra-violet filter in bright light, other filters on beaches and for contrast over green areas.

Keep film in refrigerator or air-conditioned room.
Do not leave camera in luggage compartment for longer than 15 minutes.
Use your airline bag for carrying camera accessories.

Dress Islanders judge you by your dress. They dress smartly for town. You are not expected to be as formal, but beachwear is not good manners.

Hotels have their own suggestions as to dress on the premises. If you wear shorts keep out of the sun's reach during the hours from 11.30 a.m. to 4 p.m.

At sea keep a towel handy for protection against sun and wear a floppy hat to protect the back of your neck.

Dining out Always book in advance, two or three days, if possible, and let the catering manager know the type of meal you would like. If it's a place where you just drop in there's no need to order, but it's advisable for most hotel restaurants. A good tip means better service next time, everywhere.

On the Road If you drive yourself be sure you know which side of the road you are supposed to be on, the speed restrictions and areas, where you can park without breaking the law, what petrol to buy, whether you are fully insured, whether your licence is valid.

Hire your car only from reputable dealers.

Note that bicyclists do not ride single-file in the British islands, and that pedestrians walk *in* the roads.

Be prudent with motorcyclists and do not expect all road users to observe the highway code. It is more relaxing to hire a chauffeur-driven car.

Buy island guides and maps to get the maximum value for your tours. Tour operators will keep on the beaten tracks.

In the Air You need all your travel documents if you travel between the islands.

Bibliography

There is a constant stream of books on the West Indies whose history is too inextricably mixed with that of the major European powers over more than 500 years to permit satisfactory general treatment in one volume. J. H. Parry and P. M. Sherlock, *Short History of the West Indies* (London, 1956) is an excellent introduction. Also useful for an understanding of modern West Indian attitudes is A. P. Thornton, *For the File on Empire*. A serious study of the Leeward and Windwards is Dr Carleen O'Loughlin, *Economic and Political Change in the Leeward and Windward Islands* (Yale, 1968). John Y. and Dorothy L. Keur, *Windward Children* (Royal Van Gorcum, 1960) is a penetrating study of the islands of St Maarten, St Eustatius and Saba. Mary Proudfoot, *Britain and the United States in the Caribbean* (London, 1954) is a comparative study in different approaches.

A comprehensive interpretation of nationalism is to be found in Gordon K. Lewis, *The Growth of the Modern West Indies* (London, 1968). The University of Florida Press has published several books on the West Indies of which A. C. Wilgus, *The Caribbean: Its Culture* is helpful to an understanding of a little-known aspect of West Indian development. Eric Williams, *Capitalism and Slavery* (London) and Lowell Ragatz, *The Fall of the Planter Class in the British Caribbean 1763-1833* (New York, 1963) are now generally regarded as essential reading for basic understanding of the West Indian past.

The imperialist viewpoint is presented in James Anthony Froude, *The English in the West Indies* (London, 1888). Richard

Pares, *Yankees and Creoles* (London, 1956) and *War and Trade in the West Indies* (London, 1963) both explain the importance of the triangular trade between England, the West Indies and the American colonies. For the immediate post-war West Indies as seen through the eyes of a talented writer no book is more worth reading than Patrick Leigh Fermor *The Travellers' Tree*. It has little relevance to today's West Indies.

A fascinating description of the West Indies in the early nineteenth century is to be found in John Augustine Waller, *A Voyage to the West Indies* (London, 1820). Thirteen years later Mrs Carmichael, *Domestic Manners and Social Conditions of the White, Coloured and Negro Population* was published in London. It reflects attitudes current at the period, but it is wide-ranging in its observations, and full of human interest.

Coleridge, *Six Months in the West Indies* (London, 1825) is perhaps the most appreciative and nearly poetical description of the islands ever written, unless we include the colourful, *The Alluring Antilles* (New York, 1963) written by the Jamaican yachtsman J. Linton Rigg. For photographs and vivid experiences few books equal Bradley Smith, *Escape to the West Indies* (first edition 1956, New York).

Anthony Trollope, *The West Indies and the Spanish Main* recently reprinted in London reflects a mid-Victorian mentality, but survives no doubt because of its author's gigantic literary reputation. West Indian attitudes to the islands are pronounced in Edgar Mittelholzer, *With a Carib Eye* (London) and V. S. Naipaul, *Middle Passage* (London). Alec Waugh, *A Family of Islands* (London, 1964) is a famous novelist's distillation of what he found most interesting about the islands up to 1945.

For French readers R. P. Labat, *Voyages aux Isles de l'Amerique Antilles* (2 vols, Editions Duchartre, Paris, 1931) is a treasure trove of information about the critical years 1693-1705 and is liberally supplied with illustrations and maps. A London edition translated by John Eaden has been published under the title *The Memoirs of Père Labat, 1693-1705*. An illustrated handy introduction to the French islands is Robert Hollier, *Adorables Antilles* (Paris).

For the Dutch islands S. J. Kruythoff, *The Netherlands Windward Islands* is highly recommended.

The literary minded will find Barbara Howes selections of Caribbean writers published under the title *From the Green Antilles* (London, 1966) representative of a wide spectrum of creative writing in prose.

Those who want to preserve their preconceptions of the Caribbean as the breeding ground of buccaneers and pirates ought to read Arthur Hayward's edition of Captain Charles Johnson, *A General History of the Robberies and Murders of the Most Notorious Pirates* (reprinted London, 1955). Three books published in the United States in 1960 are recommended for Puerto Rico. They are Ruth Gruber, *Island of Promise* (Hill and Wang), Ralph Hancock, *A Success Story* (D. Van Norstrand) and Earl Parker Hanson, *Puerto Rico, Land of Wonders* (Alfred A. Knopf).

Among several books on Dominica Sir Hesketh Bell, *Glimpses of a Governor's Life* (London) and Stephen Haweis, *Mount Joy* are full of personal reminiscences and enthusiasm for the beautiful island.

Very readable on St Lucia and neighbouring islands is George T. Eggleston, *Orchids on the Calabash Tree* (London, 1963). Fr Raymund Devas, *The History of the Island of Grenada* (1964) is a scholarly record of the island between 1650 and 1950.

The first and most fascinating account of Barbados Richard Ligon, *A True and Exact History of the Island of Barbadoes* first written in 1657 has now been republished in the Cass Library of West Indian Studies (London, 1970). A brief and accurate history is Neville Connell, *A Short History of Barbados* (Barbados Museum and Historical Society).

Especially valuable for the study of St Kitts and Nevis is Gordon C. Merrill's account of the historical geography of the islands (University of California). Highly recommended is Robin Bryan, *Trinidad and Tobago. The Isles of the Immortelles* (London, 1967).

Acknowledgments

The contents of this book, apart from the general tourist information which was generously supplied by the tourist organisations of the islands, represent a distillation of thinking about the West Indies over many years and in many places, although the most fruitful period occurred during the years 1953-70 when I was Editor of the Bajan magazine published jointly with my wife; and necessarily my thinking has been influenced by contributors to that magazine, especially Fr Raymund Devas OP.M.C., of Grenada; Fr C. Jesse F.M.I., of St Lucia; Neville Connell M.A., Director of the Barbados Museum; Richard ffrench of Trinidad and Dr John Lewis, Director of the Bellairs Institute, St James, Barbados. To these, my wife Emma who typed the manuscript and to countless islanders, I express my thanks.

G.H.

The Author and Publishers would like to thank the following for photographs appearing in this book: BOAC (14); Anne Bolt (3, 7, 8, 9, 10, 12, 16, 18, 21); J. Allan Cash (13, 17, 20); Feature-pix (22); Stephen Harrison (*frontispiece*); Popperphoto (15); Maurice Yates (2), and to Mary Slater for maps 1 and 4-9; U.S. Travel Service (23, 24).

Index

Abercromby, Sir Ralph, 147, 157, 217
Africa, 42, 53, 66
Agriculture, West Indies Department of, 35
Airlines, 50
Aix-la-Chapelle, Treaty of, 136
Alfred, Prince, 150
American Revolution, 26
Amiens, Treaty of, 85, 143, 175
Anegada, 98, 211
Anguilla, 98, 99, 123
Annandale Falls, 154
Anthony, Michael, 57
Antigua, 21, 26, 33, 44, 49, 54, 59, 60, 61, 98, 110, 111, 113-117, 129-131
Antilia, 11
Antilles, 11
Arawaks, 12, 84
Archaeology, 58
Architecture, 59, 60, 61
Aruba, 99
Asiento, 32
Avon, Earl of, 149

Bahamas, 35, 48, 49, 51, 229
Bajan, The, 58, 190
Barbados, 19, 20, 21, 22, 24, 25, 26, 28, 30, 32, 33, 35, 39, 40, 43, 44, 47, 48, 49, 50, 53, 57, 58, 60, 61, 64, 65, 66, 67, 110, 114, 157, 179-193, 196-201, 206, 207

Barbados Museum, 58
Barbuda, 98, 111-113
Barnard, Cyril, 149
Basse-Terre, 80, 81
Belize, 228
Bell, Sir Hesketh, 66, 139
Bellairs Institute, 151
Bequia, 44, 149
Bermuda, 20, 35, 48, 49, 51
Bibliography, 236-238
BIM, 58
Birds, 47, 177, 178, 221
Blackburne, Sir Kenneth, 114
Bonaire, 100
Botanic Garden, 148
Brandenburg Company, 203
Brathwaite, Edward, 57
Brazil, 70
Bridgetown, 53, 60, 201
Brimstone Hill, 59, 119
Britain, 42
Buccoo Reef, 177
Buck Island, 207
Bustamante, Sir Alexander, 40
Bynoe, Dame Hilda, 157

Caneel Bay Plantation, 207
Caribs, 12, 88, 99, 123, 141, 144, 147, 156, 184
Carlisle, Earl of, 16
Carnival, 63, 86
Calypso, 63
Canada, 58
Cannouan, 151

INDEX

Caribbean Development Bank, 229
Caribbean Free Trade Area, 42, 173, 229
Carriacou, 44, 151, 152
Castries, 59, 144
Castro, Fidel, 220
Cayenne, 25
Caymans, 48
Césaire, Aimé, 57
Chacachare, 174
Chaguaramas, 174
Chamberlain, Joseph, 35, 36
Chance's Mountain, 124
Charles II, 20, 21, 22
Charlestown, 118
Charlotte Amalie, 204
China, 53
Choiseul, 24
Christiansted, 206, 207
Cipriani, 36, 173
Codrington, Christopher, 31, 33, 34, 110
Colbert, 22
Coleridge, Henry Nelson, 114, 115, 124
Coleridge, William Hart, 32
Collymore, Frank, 58
Colonial Development Act, 39
Colonial Development and Welfare Organisation, 39
Colonial Stock Act, 35
Columbus, 11, 12, 15, 78, 80, 87, 94, 100, 110, 141, 144, 156, 174, 175, 202, 216
Columbia University, 31
Commonwealth, 36
Connell, Neville, 58
Cotton, 34
Cromwell, 22, 66
Cuba, 62, 68, 70, 216, 219, 229
Cumberland, Earl of, 217

Curaçao, 51, 100, 105

Dancing, 62, 63, 64
Danish West India Company, 203
De Beauharnais, Eugene, 85
De Bouillé, Marquis, 84, 137, 175
De Cerillac, Comte, 157
De Grasse, 26, 81, 142
De Maintenon, Madame, 85
Demerara, 25, 26
Denmark, 42
De Ruyter, 21, 86
De St Georges, Chevalier, 80
Desirade, 78, 81, 82
D'Esnambuc, 118
Diamond Rock HMS, 87
Disraeli, 34
Dominica, 15, 25, 47, 54, 61, 135, 140, 158-159
Drake, Sir Francis, 15, 217
Drayton, Geoffrey, 57
Dublin, 25
Duchilleau, Marquis, 137
Du Parquet, 156
Dutch Islands, 98-107
Dutch West India Company, 16

Easter, B. H., 58
Eboué, 70
Empire, 35, 36
Empire Marketing Board, 39
European Economic Community, 41, 89

Federation, 40, 69, 71, 72, 135, 184, 185
Fleetwood, Bishop, 31, 33
Food, 90
Folksongs, 64

INDEX

Fomento, 219
Fort de France, 59, 85, 86, 87, 88, 96
France, 41, 42
Franklin, Benjamin, 25, 210
Fredericksted, 206
Freeports, 25
Free Trade, 34, 42
French Islands, 77-97
French West Indian Company, 141
Frigate Bay, 121

Gawsworth, John, 113
Geest Industries, 143
George V, King, 150
Grand Etang, 153, 154
Green Room Theatre, 66
Grenada, 33, 54, 60, 71, 88, 153-157, 167-169
Grenadines, The, 59, 150-153
Grinfield, General, 175
Guadeloupe, 22, 24, 25, 26, 41, 50, 59, 67, 77-81, 88, 89-96
Gustavia, 83
Guyana, 12, 71, 228

Haiti, 62, 64, 68, 88, 216, 218, 219, 220, 229
Hamilton, Alexander, 86, 122, 204
Harris, Henderson, 155
Harrison's Free School, 31
Hawkins, John, 15
Hein, Piet, 16
Hippolite, 62
Hispaniola, 15
Holland, 42
Hood, 175
Hortense, Queen, 85
Hugues, Victor, 77, 137, 142, 147

Hurricane, 25, 32

Imperial Federation League, 35
Imperial Preference, 36
Index, 239-246
India, 42, 53
Issa, Abe, 141

Jamaica, 20, 22, 24, 25, 26, 34, 35, 40, 42, 49, 51, 66, 69, 71, 81, 171, 216, 220, 228
Jefferson, 210
Jesse, Father, 58
Jews, 20
Josephine, 23, 84, 87
Jost Van Dyke, 210

King George V, 150
Kingstown, 148
Knights of Malta, 203

Labat, 12
Lamming, George, 58
Lane, Thomas, 29
Lascelles, Henry, 34
La Soufriere, 80, 81
Laud, Archbishop, 29
Leewards, British, 40, 69, 110, 134
Lettsom, John Coakley, 211
Lewis, Sir Arthur, 230
Lewis, Dr John, 151
Ligon, 28
Little Englanders, 34
Lodge School, 31

Madison, 210
Mahmud II, 85
Manley, 36
Margaret, Princess, 53, 54, 149
Marie Galante, 81, 82

INDEX

Marin, Luis Munoz, 218, 220
Marina Cay, 211
Maroons, 118
Martinique, 22, 24, 25, 41, 48, 53, 57, 62, 67, 68, 84-89, 96-97
Maryland, 20
Maurice, Prince, 211
McLeod, Iain, 184, 185
Miami, 48, 51
Mill Reef, 48, 61, 72, 116
Modyford, Sir Thomas, 28
Molasses Act, 23
Mona, 223
Monckton, General, 142
Mont Pelée, 85, 97
Montague, Duke of, 147
Montego Bay, 40
Montserrat, 21, 44, 123-126, 133, 134
Mount Misery, 117
Moravians, 33
Mordecai, Sir John, 230
Moxley, Rev. Sutton, 45
Music, 62, 63
Mustique, 150

Naipaul, V. S., 57
Napoleon III, 86
Navigation Act, 20, 21
Netherlands, The, 68
Netherlands Antilles, 41, 68, 98-107
Nelson, Admiral, 114, 123
Nelson's Dockyard, 114
Nevis, 98, 110, 114, 118, 119, 121, 122, 123
North, Roger, 15

Organisation of American States, 228
Orinoco, 12
Ottawa Conference, 36

Panama, 70
Paris, Peace of, 136, 157
Pembroke, Earl of, 16
Perse, St John, 57
Petrelluzzi, Mario, 81
Philip, Prince, 53
Philips, Thomas, 30
Philipsburg, 102, 105, 106, 107
Pine, Sir Benjamin, 111
Pitch Lake, 171
Pointe-à-Pitre, 77, 78
Port of Spain, 173
Portsmouth, 137
Portugal, 42, 53
Poyntz, Captain John, 177
Prevost, Sir George, 137
Prince Alfred, 150
Prince William Henry, 122
Privateers, 119
Puerto Rico, 41, 48, 59, 62, 68, 69, 89, 216-227, 229

Queen Elizabeth II, 53

Rain, 47, 48
Redonda, 113
Regional Development Agency, 229
Regional Development Bank, 42
Regional Economic Committee, 39
Rhys, Jean, 136
Riots, 39
Road Town, 98, 208
Rochambeau, 85
Rockefeller, Laurance, 207, 211
Rodney, 25, 26, 81, 104, 142
Roosevelt, Franklin D., 104, 219
Roseau, 137
Royal Humane Society, 211

INDEX

Royal Sea Bathing Hospital, 211

Saba, 98, 103, 107
Saintes, The, 26, 81, 82
Sandy Lane, 48
St Barthelemy, 83, 94, 98
St Christopher, 19, 21, 25, 54, 59, 98, 117-123, 131-133
St Croix, 69, 204, 206
St Eustatius, 16, 19, 25, 98, 104
St John, 69, 207, 208
St John's, 114
St Lucia, 25, 26, 43, 47, 54, 57, 58, 59, 65, 88, 140-144, 159-162
St Martin, 50, 82, 83, 98, 100, 102, 103
St Omer, Garth, 58
St Pierre, 85, 96
St Thomas, 69, 204
St Vincent, 25, 33, 54, 59, 144-149, 162-167
Sam Lord's Castle, 206
San Domingo, 27, 62, 68, 70, 216, 219, 220, 229
San Fernando, 173, 174
San Juan, 51, 59, 218
Scandinavian Airlines, 83
Sea Water Fallacy, 43
Seeley, 35
Seven Years War, 24, 25
Shakespeare, 44
Sherlock, Sir Philip, 230
Shiel, M.P., 113
Shilstone, Eustace Maxwell, 58
Shirley Heights, 59
Slavery, 23, 27, 30, 31, 32, 33, 85, 118
Society for Propagation of Gospel, 31
Sombrero, 98

Spain, 42, 53
Steel Drums, 63
Sugar, 21, 24, 27, 35, 88, 147, 176, 207, 208
Superstition, 65, 66
Surinam, 11, 21, 40
Sweden, 42

Tempest, The, 44
Thornton, Dr William, 210
Tobacco, 15
Tobago, 33, 47, 49, 170, 179, 193-196
Tobago Cays, 151
Tortola, 22, 208
Tortuga, 119
Tourism, 46, 48, 49, 69, 72, 75, 116, 222
Tourist Tips, 233-235
Trinidad, 40, 47, 57, 63, 64, 66, 71, 170-179, 193-196
Tugwell, Rexford, 219

United Nations, 40
United States, 26, 41, 42, 70
University of West Indies, 61, 230
Utrecht, Peace of, 23

Vaval, King, 86
Venezuela, 11, 12, 40, 229
Vergennes, 24
Versailles, Treaty of, 157
Vieux Fort, 144
Virginia, 20, 21
Virgin Islands, 1, 9, 68, 98, 202-215, 212-215

Walcott, Derek, 57
Waller, John Augustine, 32, 33, 80
Ward, Happy, 72

Warner, Sir Thomas, 117
Warner, Thomas, 141
Washington, George, 59, 210
Westerhall Point, 154
Whim's Great House, 206
Wickham's Cay, 98, 211
Wilberforce, 34
Williams, Dr Eric, 170

Willoughby, Lord, 141, 144
Windward Islands, Dutch, 100
Windwards, British, 40, 69, 135, 169
Wooding, Sir Hugh, 99

Young, Sir William, 136